THE WINES OF BULGARIA, ROMANIA AND MOLDOVA

THE WINES OF
BULGARIA, ROMANIA AND MOLDOVA

CAROLINE GILBY MW

infiniteideas

Caroline Gilby MW set out to be a scientist but after a degree in botany and another in horticulture, she changed tracks and joined Augustus Barnett as a trainee wine buyer in 1988, working for them for seven years and becoming a MW in 1992. In 1995 Caroline started her own business as an independent consultant and freelance wine writer. She provides wine consultancy to a range of clients, from major international PLCs to small boutique wineries. Caroline is a member of the Circle of Wine Writers and contributes to magazines including *Decanter, Harpers, Revija Vino* and *Meininger's Wine Business International.* She also writes for *Hugh Johnson's Pocket Wine Book* and has contributed to *The Oxford Companion to Wine, World Atlas of Wine, The Wine Opus, Wine Report* and *Wines of the World.*

Caroline judges regularly at international wine competitions including being appointed Panel Chair for Hungary at Decanter's World Wine Awards in 2011, later adding the rest of Central and Eastern Europe to her responsibilities. She has been President of the Vinistra Wine competition since 2014 and frequently judges in Eastern Europe. Outside wine, she can usually be found in her garden, running long distances to keep the wine trade and its generous hospitality at bay, or out with her horse.

In memory of
Ogy Tzvetanov and Renato Trestini

The right of Caroline Gilby to be identified as the author of this book has been asserted in accordance with the Copyright, Designs and Patents Act 1988.

First published in 2018 by
Infinite Ideas Limited
36 St Giles
Oxford
OX1 3LD
United Kingdom
www.infideas.com

A CIP catalogue record for this book is available from the British Library

ISBN 978–1–906821–87–6

Front cover photo © robertharding / Alamy Stock Photo.

Text photos: page 22 thanks to NVWC; page 135 thanks to Ileana Kripp; page 139 from Dan Muntean; page 297 and plate section page 8 (top) supplied by Cristina Frolov. All other photos by Caroline Gilby.

Maps by Darren Lingard; www.darrenlingard.co.uk

Typeset in India by Suntec

Printed in Britain by 4edge Limited

CONTENTS

ACKNOWLEDGEMENTS

Thanks have to go to Richard Burton and Rebecca Clare at Infinite Ideas for giving me this opportunity to write about three wine countries that are so important to me, and to my family for putting up with endless travelling and writing. Over the years, far too many winemakers to name have opened bottles and shared their stories, and been such welcoming hosts too. Many of them will get a mention later in the text.

The great thing about the wine world is that it is full of people who are generous with their time and happy to share their expertise. Non-winemakers who have gone out of their way to help with information, statistics and answers to my endless questions include:

For Romania: Professor Valeriu V. Cotea, Dr Catalin Zamfir and Dr Cintia Colibaba at the University of Iaşi, Diana Mereanu and colleagues at ONVPV, Arina Antoce, Dan Muntean, Ioan Ştefan at APEV, Szövérdfi Zoltán, José Vouillamoz, Basil Zarnoveanu, Cătălin Păduraru, Cesar Baeza.

For Bulgaria: Kym Anderson, Julia Kostadinova, Emil Koralov, Yana Petkova, Margarita Hristova, Prof. Venelin Roychev, Christo Boevsky, Prof. Dimitar Tsakov, Dimitar Nikolov, Vassil Rachkov, Tanya Koicheva, Yuson Yung, Yassen Zahariev.

For Moldova: Diana Lazar and all the CEED teams, Gheorghe Arpentin (ONVV), Andrian Digolean and team at Wine of Moldova, Lana Melniciuc at Poliproject, Ion Luca, Philip Quick, Beth Willard.

And in general for moral support, advice and proofreading: Angela Muir MW, Elizabeth Gabay MW, Ben Bernheim, Matt Bailey and of course my long-suffering husband, David J. W. Bailey, whose only reward is the leftovers. I should also thank Tom Stevenson for that first opportunity to start writing seriously about Eastern Europe, the mystery person who put my name forward, and Keith Garrard and Peter Carr MW for giving me my first job in wine.

INTRODUCTION: WELCOME TO THE MYSTERIES OF THE EAST

'Whatever happened to Bulgaria?' is a question I'm often asked at wine tastings and this book is an attempt to answer that question, as well as telling the stories of the two other most important wine countries in Eastern Europe. My first faltering steps into the professional world of wine took place around the time that Bulgaria, Romania and Moldova were all taking their own first strides into a new, independent era. We have grown up together, though there have been a few fallings out and squabbles along the way. And with the wonder of hindsight, I realize how privileged I was to witness the beginning of the new era and to see for myself exactly where these three countries have come from in wine terms. It has been a complete revolution from there to here.

My interest in wine really started with the odd glass of my parents' wine at home; my father enjoyed wine though his budget never stretched far. It wasn't until I went to the University of Bath to study for a doctorate in horticulture that I really caught the wine bug. I joined the wine society on the basis that I liked wine and knew nothing about it, apart from being able to tell red from white with my eyes open. My first encounters with Eastern European wine came around this time, planning tastings for fellow students. Bulgaria was particularly exciting in those days (the mid-1980s) – cheerful, fruity wines, at a price to make anyone counting the pennies happy. My real 'road to Damascus' moment actually came in the port region, after I won a competition to visit Quinta do Noval. I was sitting on the terrace with the Douro glittering in the distance,

1

sipping chilled tawny port, when I realized that a life in wine would be more exciting than sitting behind a microscope. I finished my PhD and started applying for wine jobs. After a tough interview with a blind tasting test, I was lucky enough to get a trainee place at a chain of wine shops called Augustus Barnett. I think they liked that I was a scientist as well as enthusiastic about wine and could take over running the quality control programme. I passed my Master of Wine exams in 1992, and that year there were three Bulgarian wines in the red wine tasting paper, hard to imagine now.

Eastern European wine was massive business in the UK in the late 1980s, though it was distinctly the least glamorous part of the wine portfolio. As the most junior member of the buying team, that's where I began. I started in 1988, just as the Iron Curtain began its fall. I've now been tasting, buying and following the wines of Eastern Europe for very nearly three decades, and visited all three countries featured in this book many times. I didn't live through all the changes myself, so can only provide an outsider's perspective. However, I hope that by telling the stories of how I have seen these three countries evolve, I can make readers see why I am so passionate that Eastern Europe is the last undiscovered treasure trove of the wine world. And that now is the time to explore it.

I left buying in 1995 with ambitions of becoming a wine writer, possibly specializing in Italy. Out of the blue renowned wine writer Tom Stevenson (prompted by an anonymous source) offered me the chance to specialize in Central and Eastern Europe for a new book (*The Wine Report*) he was editing, as no one else was really covering it. So I have long been grateful for this opportunity, and far too many people to mention have supported me along the way.

I aim to tell the story of how Bulgaria became one of the world's biggest exporters of wine and a key supplier to thirsty Western markets like the UK and Germany, and how it disappeared again. I will also look at the parallel stories of Romania and Moldova as the other two most important wine producers in Eastern Europe (I consider Hungary to be more Central Europe). Romania followed Bulgaria into the UK (and other countries) on the back of identifying Pinot Noir as a point of difference, but has continued to develop a strong home market that drinks most of its own production. The Republic of Moldova was buried even further behind the Iron Curtain, being part of the Soviet Union itself, and took a different direction, relying on exports to the vast thirsty markets within the union.

I think it is important to set each of the three wine markets in the context of the region's past. History may not seem very relevant to modern wine drinkers, but it has had considerable influence over the shape of the wine industry today, and helps to explain why wine differs so much between these geographically close neighbours. At times, history across these countries has been shared or overlapped, and wine, always important in all three, has ended up shaped differently, with one country (Romania) a major producer and consumer of its own production, and the other two (Bulgaria and Moldova) always relying heavily on exports. Wine styles and grape varieties have also been influenced in part by the politics of the communist era. Arguably only one of these three countries has a historically significant icon wine (Romania's Cotnari). The importance of a flagship like this in creating a reputation for quality wine can be seen by taking a look at Romania's neighbour Hungary. The Hungarian wine industry has made considerable progress in creating a positive message in comparison, using the history and credibility of Tokaji to boost its image and attract investment. Of course, country borders today bear little resemblance to historical ones, but understanding even just a little of the history of the region is important in getting to grips with these ethnic identities.

In the West, we have often been guilty of seeing Eastern Europe's recent past as a single homogeneous mass of grim Eastern Bloc greyness, but the fall of the Iron Curtain meant that all three countries had to face a new reality. Nearly three decades on, it is clear that each country has emerged with a clear and distinctive identity and their wine industries have also evolved in different directions. The change has been a complete revolution from communist, mass-market, wine-based alcoholic beverage, to today's industries where an exciting raft of small producers has added interest and individuality, and pushed quality forward. At the same time, many of the big players have also reinvented themselves.

I firmly believe that Eastern Europe's time has come again after a couple of decades in the backwaters. Drinkers of those cheap and cheerful Bulgarian Cabernets and Romanian Pinot Noirs from the eighties and nineties would barely recognize the diverse and exciting wines on offer in Eastern Europe today. Quality is now as good as from anywhere else in the world, at least in the hands of the best producers, and while the wines are not always cheap (and in some cases prices are rather too ambitious), the value for money can be fantastic. Finally, after I have been a lone voice in the wilderness for so long, the last couple of years have seen Eastern European wines reappearing on shelves and wine-lists in markets such as the UK, Scandinavia and the USA. My theory is that the old-world countries like France, Germany and Spain have been 'done' and are often seen (not necessarily fairly) as boring and traditional. The New World has also been fully explored, and while there are many valid wine styles, they are almost all interpretations of the Old-World originals. The mysterious eastern end of Europe is a landscape with an authentic history, unique grape varieties and something genuinely different and exciting to offer the wine world.

This book aims to explain that authenticity, and the history and geopolitical landscape that have influenced the wine producers of these countries. Wine is a great lens through which to view a country, as it brings together climate, landscape, culture, politics and the people. I will tell the story of challenges overcome, and problems that still lie ahead in today's wine industry. I will also highlight some of the more exciting and commercially relevant producers. I cannot hope to cover everything, because each time I go back there are new producers or significant changes, but I hope the book will give wine drinkers a starting point and encourage exploration of this exciting part of the wine world.

Nazdrave and Noroc!

Note: throughout I will use as far as possible Moldavia to refer to the historic principality, Moldovan Hills to refer to the wine region in Romania and Republic of Moldova or Moldova to refer to today's country.

PART 1
BULGARIA

1
BEGINNINGS IN BULGARIA

Bulgaria is a wine country very close to my heart – exciting and frustrating in equal measure. It was only the second wine country I visited in my professional career, when Eastern Europe was my first buying responsibility as a trainee buyer back in the late 1980s. I've seen this country take its first steps into a new era, just as I did myself. And I like to think that we've matured together, though the relationship has had its rocky moments.

That first trip to Bulgaria was eye-opening, not least because my one and only previous trip had been to Château Lascombes in Margaux. My fellow wine students and I stayed in a grim hotel transformed from the former party headquarters in Sofia, and then in Rousse, where we were duly taken to a nightclub and strip joint because that's what you did with foreign visitors. Memories have stuck fast of grim communist wineries; vast marching rows of vines supported by crumbling concrete; dining in huge, ornate ballrooms empty apart from our group; inevitable cucumber and tomato accompanied by 'tractor fuel' (a.k.a. rakia) at every meal and scrabbling for coins to pay for a few sheets of scratchy toilet paper from a babushka-type with bad hair-dye. I carried on buying Bulgarian wines when I was back in the UK but didn't go back to the country for another dozen years or so.

In 2003 I returned for the first internationally judged wine competition, along with Jancis Robinson and a handful of judges from Norway, Poland and Scandinavia. So much was different; better hotels (with free toilet paper) and much better food (though cucumber and tomato are always standard fare). Usually everything was drowned in a thick fog of Balkan tobacco smoke. A mouthful of food and a puff on a cigarette wasn't uncommon in those days (a habit that only faded with the indoor smoking ban in

2012). Winemaking was evolving, with the first few individual pioneers like Maxxima and Santa Sarah starting to appear, and privatization issues on their way to being resolved. But the larger wineries still seemed to believe that grapes grow in the back of trucks and couldn't understand when we wanted to look at actual grapevines.

For some though, I think the proverbial penny (or *stotinka*) was beginning to drop as they realized that controlling fruit quality was going to be the next step for Bulgaria. Of course, problems of land ownership and vineyard neglect were still huge and have had major implications for Bulgaria.

It was about this time I first met Dr Ognyan 'Ogy' Tzvetanov, my great friend, mentor and guide to Bulgaria and its wines.

A MAVERICK'S TALE

The sudden death of Dr Ognyan Tzvetanov in early 2016 was a huge personal loss. I had known him for at least 15 years, first as a winemaker, academic and consultant to the Bulgarian industry, when he was always happy to answer my endless questions. Gradually this developed into real friendship, and he always took the time to meet me at the airport, to drop off a wine sample, or for a quick coffee, or to squeeze in beer, even if my schedule was tight. Always imported beer at that, as Ogy had no time for what he saw as the lax standards of microbiology in Bulgaria's national breweries. There were often surprises on trips to Bulgaria with Ogy – the ancient Thracian tomb of Dionysius, the stunning golden treasures of Panagyurishte, the Magura cave (where some of Europe's oldest human remains have been found) and a visit to the idyllic mountain town of Koprivshtitsa.

After a conventional start, graduating from the Wine & Spirits Department of Plovdiv University and spending a couple of years as a winemaker, Ogy joined the National Wine Institute, becoming Head of Wine Microbiology and then Senior Research Fellow. He also worked with Californian company Golden State Vintners, looking after winemaking and quality control for their projects in Bulgaria, and with World Cooperage, importing barrels to Bulgaria. This combination of scientific understanding and exposure to international winemaking standards was rare at this time in Bulgaria and gave him unique insights into the potential of a country that was focusing on cheap, high volume production.

Ogy was often opinionated about the rest of the Bulgarian wine industry, but in spite of this he frequently took time to arrange visits for me, so I would understand the bigger picture. He found it frustrating that industry lobbying influenced the division of the country into just two PGI regions. He firmly believed that this was about making life easier for big companies to source wherever they wanted. He felt the old five regions had been based on research and clearly identifiable differences in soil and climate. In the end, it meant he went his own way, feeling unrecognized by the industry and wine press in Bulgaria, and let his wines speak for themselves.

And so they did – quietly gaining listings in the UK at Berry Bros and The Wine Society, among the very few Bulgarian wines to break out of the trap of 'ultra-cheap only fit for supermarket bottom shelf' status. Recognition came in from critics like Jancis Robinson, Robert Parker and others. Just a few months before he died, he got to show his wines at the historic Five Kings House in the heart of London alongside the likes of Bollinger, Château Yquem, Jadot and Schloss Vollrads. He definitely had an air of 'I can't quite believe I'm here', in this company, and in a hall that has been the heart of the wine trade for centuries. Ogy once told me that if his wines were ever sold in Berry Bros he could die a happy man. He achieved that and so much more. I only wish he could have had time to fulfil the rest of his ambitions, but his generous heart let him down in the end.

Like all of Eastern Europe, Bulgarian wine has undergone a complete revolution from those early days of communist-scale, cheap, cheerful Bulgarian Cabernets; the ones I used to drink regularly as a student. I remember waiting with great anticipation for the arrival of Oriahovitza Reserve 1979 in Oddbins in the mid-1980s. There was nowhere else where you could get a wine with this level of maturity for the sort of price that even a student could afford. But the wine industry has undergone a complete revolution since then, through the challenges and problems of privatization, and has emerged as an exciting and dynamic scene, scattered with wines that I would be genuinely happy to recommend to anybody.

There is more to wine than just an enjoyable liquid (though obviously that's important) and the stories behind the wine scene in Bulgaria are fascinating, though it hasn't always been easy to get Bulgarians to genuinely open up and talk about it. And yet on the other hand Bulgarians are outspoken and blunt, and will tell you exactly what they think of you in so many words. Trust is a difficult thing for Bulgarians still, and they always seem to think there's a catch, or a hidden agenda, so getting the wineries to tell me their genuinely personal stories has sometimes been hard. The more Latinized Romanians and even the Soviet-scarred Moldovans seem to have found it easier. And it's a shame, because when you do get through that shell, Bulgarians and their wines are well worth getting to know.

2

BULGARIAN HISTORY

Bulgarians like to tell a tale about the origins of their landscapes. The story goes that God had forgotten all about Bulgaria when he was creating the world and all he could do was shake out what was left in his sack of landscape goodies, leaving Bulgaria with an incredible diversity of mountains, rivers, valleys and lakes. There's no doubt that much of Bulgaria is incredibly beautiful, though equally other areas have been scarred by the industrial farming of communism and rusting concrete factories that appear in the most bizarre places.

PREHISTORY

South-eastern Europe, and especially Bulgaria, lies at the crossroads of Europe and Asia Minor. Humans have been here for a very long time. There are Palaeolithic fossils of Europe's earliest-known, anatomically modern humans from caves in the Balkan Mountains dated to around 43,000 years ago. More recent finds have shown that Bulgaria is the first place where chickens were domesticated, at an early Neolithic settlement located in an area known as Karabilyuk, near Bulgaria's Yabalkovo, in the district of Haskovo. Carbon-dating of fourteen human bones found near this site has revealed that the people buried there died between 6200 and 6100 BC and they had genetic similarities to early Neolithic settlements in Anatolia, in today's Turkey. According to archaeologists from the University of Sofia, these people were agriculturalists; researchers estimate that only 3 per cent of their meat came from hunting. It seems they were picky about their rich diet, consuming mostly young animals and also eating snails, and fishing for large carp in the River Maritsa. They also gathered pistachios, made bread from spelt and probably had wine. Evidence for winemaking specifically has not been reported, but there is evidence of grape harvesting. Grape pips of the wild grapevine *Vitis vinifera* subspecies *sylvestris* have been found at seven different Neolithic sites across Bulgaria (dated to between 6000 and 5650 BC). It's not hard to make the leap to production of wine, as stored grapes will quickly ferment by themselves – humans seem to have been making and consuming alcohol as soon as they moved into agrarian societies, and some researchers believe that making alcohol may even have been a motivation for settling down.

PLOVDIV

Plovdiv is believed to be the world's sixth-oldest continuously occupied city. Its fascinating history begins with a settlement on the ancient hill of Nebet Tepe ('tepe' is the Turkish word for hill), one of the seven historic hills in the city.

The hills, or 'tepeta', are still known today by their Ottoman-Turkish names. Out of all of them, Nebet Tepe has the earliest traces of civilized life, dating back to the sixth millennium BC, which makes Plovdiv 8,000 years old, and allegedly the oldest city in Europe. Around 1200 BC, the prehistoric settlement on Nebet Tepe became the ancient Thracian city of Eumolpia, also known as Pulpudeva, inhabited by the powerful ancient Thracian tribe called Bessi or Bessae.

In 342 BC, Eumolpia/Pulpudeva was conquered by King Philip II of Macedon, who renamed the city Philipopolis. The city developed further as a major urban centre during the Hellenistic period after the collapse of Alexander the Great's Empire. Today the old city is well worth a visit for its stunning hillside amphitheatre, national revival architecture and ancient streets.

THE GOLDEN AGE OF THRACE

The stunning and rich gold artefacts found in the Varna culture have revealed Europe's first known civilization with a sophisticated social hierarchy. These are contemporary with and closely related to Gumelniţa culture in southern Romania. The graves of the Varna necropolis were uncovered in 1972, during excavations for a canning factory. There are 294 graves, found to hold what is probably the oldest set of gold artefacts in the world. One grave contained more gold than was known in the rest of the ancient world; 3,000 gold artefacts were found in total, weighing over 6 kilogrammes. This was a society of rich and well-fed people, although there's no evidence of wine. These finds date back to a relatively brief period around 4600 to 4200 BC. No one knows why the Varna culture disappeared, though researchers speculate that climate change was a factor. It was succeeded by the Bronze Age Ezero culture that occupied much of present-day Bulgaria between 3300 and 2700 BC, and from which evidence of grape-growing reportedly exists.

The Ancient Thracians were an ethno-cultural group of Indo-European tribes inhabiting much of South-east Europe from about the middle of the second millennium BC to about the sixth century AD, in the territories of modern-day Bulgaria, Romania, Moldova, Greece, Turkey, Macedonia and Serbia. The Thracians were the first people to leave lasting traces on the Bulgarian landscape, but they did not leave written records themselves, so information largely comes from archaeological finds and writings from neighbouring countries. Egyptian writer Athanasius considered that Thrace, and its adjacent lands, were a source for sweet wine, while Homer tells us that Agamemnon and his heroes drank Thracian wine every day. Thracian aristocrats had a reputation for loving horses, wars, women and wine and this reputation is supported by archaeological finds of horse trappings, drinking vessels and jewellery. Ancient authors also portrayed Thracians as drinking in an uncivilized way, reporting that they didn't mix wine with water and that women were allowed to drink (unlike in Greece). One story alleges that Thracian kings rewarded soldiers who killed foes in battle with wine, so it is possible that the legend of making wine vessels from skulls of enemies came from this time, not from the later era of Khan Krum. Such tales may be storyteller exaggeration but clearly, wine drinking was well-established.

Wine also had special importance in rites and doctrine from that era and was involved in rituals at every stage of life, from celebrating birth to family weddings and funerals. Ornate drinking vessels from the Thracian period imply that drinking wine was no longer about quenching thirst. Once there are special, ornate drinking vessels, wine has moved on to become a drink of civilization, while primitive cultures drank from wineskins. The oldest *phiale* (which were shallow bowls for drinking wine made from bronze) date to the seventh century BC in Vratsa. Ceremonial cups called *rhytons* are based on the shape of a horn and usually have one opening above and another below. The oldest of these was made from clay and dates to the seventh century BC but perhaps the most dramatic are to be found in the fourth century BC Panagyurishte treasure. This is a stunning collection of nine solid gold vessels weighing over 6 kilogrammes and includes four *rhytons* for ceremonial drinking and three decanters. All are ornately worked and often feature symbols of grapevines and grapes. This treasure was uncovered in 1949 by three brothers digging clay for bricks. Bulgaria has numerous other rich treasures, often linked to wine and drinking, showing that it is something that has been important in these lands for a very long time.

WINE AND RITUAL

It appears that the entire ancient world was convinced that the god Dionysus was of Thracian origin, and Herodotus includes him among the three names of the Thracian Pantheon. The theory is that, like other Indo-European people, the Thracians worshipped a deity (possibly Sabazios) linked with a sacred plant and drink. Greek writers then connected this with their own Dionysus, a wanderer from outside Greece connected to wine. Part of the Thracian culture lives on in folk customs, rituals and local legends in Bulgaria, as winemaking has survived here uninterrupted for many millennia. In fact, the Thracian word for wine, ('Zela' or 'Zelas') is one of the few ancient Thracian words which survives today, perhaps a reflection of wine's importance.

The cult of Dionysus disappeared with rise of Christianity, although some rituals seem to have been adopted – such as wine at the centre of Christian rites. One tradition that appears to be strongly rooted in folklore around Dionysus is the feast of St Trifon Zarezan (meaning Trifon the pruner). There are confused stories as to who St Trifon (or Tryphon) actually was – he may have been a brother of the Virgin Mary who insulted her because he had a bad hangover and then cut his nose while pruning vines, or alternatively he was a Roman martyr. Either way, celebrations on 14 February involve rituals around blessing the vines with wine, feasting, dancing and drinking.

MACEDONIANS, CELTS AND OTHERS

It seems that Bulgaria's location at the crossroad between East and West meant that waves of settlers from both Europe and Asia turned the plains of Thrace, Moesia, Macedonia and the Balkan Mountains into scenes of fierce clashes. Philip of Macedon conquered much of this landscape (around 341 BC), which had previously been occupied by the powerful Odrysian Thracian tribe. The Odrysian Kingdom was a union of Thracian tribes that existed between the fifth and third centuries BC, and has left significant remains in the shape of a fortress and tombs near Starosel in central Bulgaria. Later, new Thracian states under various tribes including Bessae, Astae, Getae and Dacia emerged from the fourth to the first century BC. The ongoing scuffles allowed for an invasion from Rome.

The year 298 BC also saw the arrival of Celtic tribes in today's Bulgaria, establishing a short-lived kingdom called Tylis. By 212 BC this had fallen, but a Celtic tribe called Serdi survived in western Bulgaria giving its name to Serdica, later Sofia.

ROMAN INROADS

The first military clashes between the Romans and the Thracian tribes are believed to have occurred as early as the first half of the second century BC. All of Ancient Thrace south of the Lower Danube was eventually conquered by the Roman Empire in 46 AD. The most famous Thracian in human history is Spartacus, the man who led a rebellion of gladiators against Rome in 73–71 BC. The Thracian (Geto-Dacian) regions north of the Lower Danube were conquered by the Romans under Emperor Trajan in 106 AD. Within the Roman Empire, Thrace was structured into provinces called Moesia (along the south bank of the Danube) and Thrace. Agriculture and cattle breeding were important, and the Thracians became fully fledged citizens. It was during Roman rule that the first ever vineyard law in history was issued by Emperor Antonius Pius (138–161 AD). The Decree for Preservation of Vineyards in Lower Moesia (now central and northern Bulgaria) stated that nobody was allowed to destroy a wine-producing grapevine. However, in the third century

AD, this settled life was swept away in waves of barbarian invasions. The Romans tried to fight back and divided the empire, with Constantinople becoming the capital of the Eastern Roman Empire with today's Bulgaria as its hinterland.

While the Thracians had had a mighty civilization, by the seventh century AD, they had been subjugated or subsumed by Philip of Macedon, Alexander the Great, the Romans, Byzantium and various tribes of Goths, Celts and finally Slavs. Little is known about the origins of the Slavic tribes who came to exist in the lower Danube and north-western Black Sea in the fifth to sixth centuries AD, but it appears their civilization was based on small family groups and tribes, possibly with Byzantium as their nominal masters. By the time the Bulgarian tribes arrived in the seventh century, traces of Thrace had largely disappeared.

BULGARIAN ORIGINS

The original homeland of the Bulgarian people is still speculative, but some scholars believe that they may have come from an area of northern Afghanistan called Balkhara, part of Bactria. This area came under Alexander the Great's rule in the fourth century BC and many Macedonians settled there. Some of these tribes drifted back towards Europe, settling north of the Black Sea in the second century AD, in due course becoming a state called Old or Great Bulgaria with its capital at Phanagoria. The other view is that the ancestors of present-day Bulgarians came from Mongolia. However, evidence from graves shows that they were tall and slender Indo-Europeans reaching a height of 1.75 metres at a time when the average European was 1.6 metres tall. They almost certainly had a rich diet from their highly productive cattle herds, so the Bactrian origin theory seems a better fit.

The first Bulgarian kingdom that overlaps with Bulgaria's current geographical location dates from 681 AD. Khan Kubrat, who ruled Old Great Bulgaria north of the Black Sea and based around the capital Phanagoria, was a Christian. He had been baptized in Constantinople and educated there until the age of 22. In 632 AD he declared himself an independent ruler, uniting all the Bulgarian tribes into this state. He died in either 651 or 665 AD. There is speculation that the rich tomb found in Pereshchepina in Ukraine marked the border of this kingdom and its battles against the Khazar people (a Turkic people who dominated the zone from the Volga–Don steppes to the Crimea and Caucasus). There is a legend that on his deathbed, he asked his five sons to break a bundle of grapevine stems, which they were not strong enough to do. The dying man then separated the bundle and broke each stem one by one, to demonstrate the importance of cooperation. However, his sons seem to have ignored this and headed off in different directions after disintegration of the state under Khazar attacks in 668 AD.

One son, Khan Asparukh found his people in an inhospitable part of Old Great Bulgaria. He therefore sought out new territories in Moesia, an area occupied by a group of seven Slavic tribes from the mid-seventh century. Details are unclear, but the Slavs and Bulgarians seem to have formed an alliance. After various wars against Byzantium, a peace treaty in 681 AD recognized the Bulgarian state on at least part of its current territory, headed by Khan Asparukh. It appears that Slavs and Bulgars formed a society on equal footing, though the Slavs seem to have been numerous enough to dominate linguistically. The Slavic language came to dominate, however recent genetic analysis links today's Bulgarian population to the Old Bulgarians and not to the Slavs.

KHAN KRUM THE HORRIBLE

The early ninth century Khan Krum is regarded as a ruler who did much to establish Bulgaria as a strong, independent nation. He probably took the throne in 803 or 804, helping the country gain independence from the Eastern Roman Empire. A programme of war-like expansion followed, conquering Serdica (today's Sofia) in 809 and the Pirin, Rhodope and Rila mountains, which have remained part of the country ever since. In one battle, Krum defeated the Byzantine emperor Nicephorus and, according to legend, ordered his skull to be turned into a cup for wine-drinking. He died in 814, but during his rule he had established written laws and a centralized state. Drunkenness had been a problem and he is credited with issuing a law for pulling out vineyards, though this is probably a legend as there is no evidence that any vineyards were destroyed. There's a folk tale that the name of Mavrud came from a brave young man who saved a city from being terrorized by a lion. Krum sent for the man's mother to find the cause of his bravery, and the mother admitted that she had saved a vine in secret, and wine from this vine had given her son courage. Krum's successors turned the state into a European superpower. By 852, this included Pannonia (Hungary), Transylvania, Wallachia, Moldova and Thrace. The First Bulgarian Kingdom would last for another 200 years, finally dissolving in 1018. Bulgaria then lost its independence and remained a Byzantine subject until 1185, when the Second Bulgarian Empire was created.

THE CYRILLIC ALPHABET

During the ninth century, the Bulgarian nation emerged under a centralized monarchy speaking a Slavic language, with only an estimated 20 per cent of the original ancient Bulgar language remaining. In 852, Boris I declared Christianity the official religion and opted to follow the Eastern Orthodox Church. However, he was concerned about religious services all being held in Greek, so decided to invent a script based on the vernacular Bulgarian language to be used for church and state administration. This was a very important step in the political and cultural history of the country. Two monks, Constantine Cyril and his brother Methodius, invented the earliest Bulgarian alphabet and translated key books into it. Eventually this was adapted by Cyril's disciples, and named Cyrillic in his honour. By 893, this became the official language of church and state, as well as becoming the fourth language of the Christian church. This was hugely significant for literacy in Bulgaria as the teachings of the church were given in the language of the people (whereas in other countries Latin, Greek and Hebrew were the languages of religious teaching).

CHRISTIANITY AND THE MEDIEVAL PERIOD

Christianity is always closely connected to wine and this gave viticulture an impetus from the ninth to fourteenth centuries, where we find wine mentioned many times as a sign of prosperity. Yassen Borislavov's 2004 book on Bulgarian wine history mentions eleventh-century writings describing life in the Bachkovo Monastery, where monks were supposed to drink four cups of wine per day and were allowed up to eight cups for certain religious celebrations. Archaeological studies on pottery from that time indicate that a cup held around 180 to 230 millilitres, suggesting a daily ration of up to a litre of wine per day. As well as its religious connection, wine is frequently mentioned in early medieval writings, including the diaries of French crusader Gofrois de Villardouaine who found excellent wine in Asenovgrad in 1205, while an Italian document from 1366 notes that Count Amadeus of Savoy purchased fine wine from Anchialo (Pomorie).

OTTOMAN RULES

In 1352 the Ottoman Turks started to make moves into Europe, which Bulgaria, weakened through internal struggles, failed to resist effectively. By 1387, Bulgaria had to accept political alliance with the Turks and by 1396 the country was totally in the hands of the Ottomans. Being under Ottoman rule separated Bulgaria from progressive trends in Europe such as the Renaissance and Enlightenment. The country lost its leaders and any self-organization or state and religious structures. Peasants were deprived of land and only allowed a limited number of plots for growing crops. This was a period of burdensome taxes while conscription and genocide were used to force people to convert and to take Islamic names. Many people fled to neighbouring countries.

Ottoman rule was largely disastrous for wine in Bulgaria, as Islam did not encourage winemaking or drinking, and the Bulgarian nobility was virtually wiped out. But wine hung on in the Christian community, as it was an important ethnic marker. Mentions of wine during this period are largely from Western travellers and there are several records that mention wine in this region as variously 'poor and sour' or 'extremely sweet and strong'. The mid-eighteenth century saw an upturn in winemaking, possibly due a resurgent affluent class among the Christian population. Production seems to have soared so much that wine could be exported. Shipments were made to Russia and

Poland according to French diplomat Charles de Peysonnel, writing in the 1760s.

In 1706, a French doctor Paul Lucas visited Stanimaka (Asenovgrad) and was impressed by 'the local wine which is splendid', while the Melnik region had a lively trade with Central Asia and Austro-Hungary in the seventeenth and eighteenth centuries. In the nineteenth century, even more encouraging assessments of Bulgarian wine started to appear. Frenchman P. Seiget travelled across Bulgaria in 1829, finding that wine was 'quite good' around Malko Turnovo (near Bourgas); around Lozengrad there was 'good quality red, like Petit Bourgogne' with 'fine red' near Topolovgrad but 'bad local wine' in Bourgas itself. Sliven wines were praised by a Hungarian ethnologist called Felix Kanitz who travelled in Bulgaria in the 1870s, writing that 'Sliven wines are to Bulgaria what Tokay [sic] wine is to the Hungarians', while in 1877 Englishman James Baker wrote that 'Sliven wines are excellent and similar to red burgundy.'

NATIONAL REVIVAL

The Bulgarian National Revival was a period from the late eighteenth century when Bulgarians started to recreate their own identity and seek liberation from the Ottomans. A new middle class emerged, making money through trade and encouraging literacy, education and culture. Several of the movement's activists wrote about local wine. Historian Borislavov writes about an 1859 book called *Introduction* by Georgi Rakovski. Rakovski described local vine growing and winemaking in minute detail, from the choice of suitable canes and places for planting, to the technique of winemaking and distilling *rakia*. He also listed 18 black and white grape varieties including Gamza, Red Misket and Pamid, though others mentioned have disappeared. Perhaps his most famous statement was that, 'In Bulgaria, it is rare for Bulgarians not to have vineyards. This is their favourite occupation. A peasant considers himself unhappy and feels ashamed if he does not have a vineyard.' Borislavov goes on to explain that Rakovski, as an ideologue of the Bulgarian National Revival, obviously believed that a nation that could make good wine deserved national independence and would gain it eventually by a moral revolution and force of arms.

The first Bulgarian cookbook was published in 1870 by another character in the National Revival, Petko Rachov Slaveykov, who included detailed information and recipes for making mead, beer, fruit wines and *rakia*. He devoted a chapter to good wine, offering advice on how to make wine, when to rack it and how to prevent souring. Some of the basics it covered included picking the grapes when they are perfectly ripe, working in clean rooms with clean vessels and separating ripe and unripe grapes. The first Bulgarian manual of winemaking was published in 1873 in Vienna by Grigor Nachovich. He apparently saw modern knowledge of winemaking as an important facet of an independent nation and so compiled a manual from French and German sources. It was advanced for its day and included detailed instructions on choosing the location of a vineyard, planting and fertilizers as well as technical advice on separating grape skins and stems, the role of oxygen, temperature and yeast. He also offered the first classification of Bulgarian wines: as 'wine for dinner and wine for after dinner'.

LIBERATION AND THE MARCH OF PHYLLOXERA

During the wars of 1876 and 1877, land was redistributed to Bulgarian peasants. Despite this division, and a lack of capital for improving farming, by the time of liberation from the Ottoman Empire in 1878, Bulgaria's vineyards were still in surprisingly good condition. This pattern of small private landowners marked Bulgarian agriculture and viticulture until 1944. In 1878, it is believed there were nearly 50,000 hectares of vines in Bulgaria and the next few years saw a rapid increase in area to over 100,000 hectares.

The first legislation introduced in 1879 in the newly liberated Bulgarian kingdom, even before the country's constitution, was a 'temporary statute for excise duties on drinks'. The implication is that grape and wine production was sufficiently developed for the government to see this as a source of revenue.

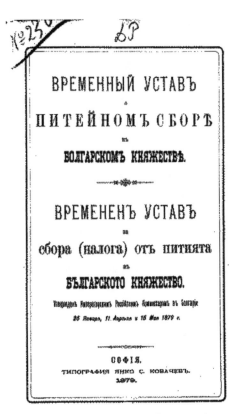

Image of 1879 temporary statute for excise duty on drinks

Unfortunately, just as Bulgaria's viticulture was on the path to recovery, phylloxera appeared, being identified first near Vidin in the north-west. George Gale in 'Dying on the Vine' suggests it was spotted in 1881 but Borislavov says it was 1883. By the turn of the twentieth century one-third of the country was infested. At first, there was a lack of serious state organization and it was left to regional consortia or individuals to fight the louse. It wasn't until 1896 that there was an official plant protection agency and by this stage the Bulgarian Ministry of Agriculture was learning from the destruction across Europe. French expert Pierre Viala, from Montpellier, was invited to Bulgaria to advise on the problem. He suggested the American solution, involving trials of American vine species as rootstocks. He also suggested the development of nurseries, teaching the skills of grafting, and recommended the establishment of a research institute. This resulted in the founding of the Pleven Institute in 1902, only the fourth such institute in Europe.

A report to the Ministry of Trade and Agriculture by Stefan T. Gudev on the state of Bulgarian winemaking in 1896 indicated that Bulgaria's vineyards were divided between 366,000 owners, meaning an average size of around a quarter of a hectare. There were just 223 owners who held more than 0.4 hectares. This definitely limited the spread of modern winemaking technology as well as renewal of vineyards. By 1919, the vineyard area had dropped to just 45,000 hectares and production was targeted at the domestic population; it was reckoned 55 per cent of households made their own wine.

A report in the publication *Geography* from the London Geographical Association published in 1938 included a statement that, '*Phylloxera* is defeated, it is destroying only the last remnants of old vineyards in the Struma Valley region of south-western Bulgaria'. This report also pointed out that certain damp and sandy soils in Bulgaria allowed old vines to resist for a long time, so poor growers were persisting with their old vines (this is perhaps why old varieties hung on in the sandy soils of the Melnik region).

Today it's a rare Bulgarian who does not still claim a patrimony and heritage of winemaking from this time.

GRAPE VARIETIES AFTER PHYLLOXERA

Dimitar Dimov (winemaker at Vinarna Yalovo) has a deep interest in the history of viticulture. He says,

> There's an ampelographic book from 1922 describing the varieties typical for Veliko Tarnovo region. It is written by the manager of the State Vine Nursery in Gorna Oryahovitza – Georgi Sirakov. This is just into the post-phylloxera period. Sirakov describes the visit of the French professor Pierre Viala who was invited by the state to help solve the phylloxera crisis. During this visit Viala suggests the establishment of a viticulture research centre, founded in Pleven in 1902 and a grapevine collection (still in existence today). Sirakov notes that Professor Viala tasted some of the popular Bulgarian wines from some of the best wineries at that time. He appreciated Gamza and Kokorko from Pleven; Mavrud, Cherven (Red) Misket and Pamid from Sadovo; and Dimyat from Varna. The varieties that Sirakov describes are: for red wines: Gamza, Zarchin (Serbia's Prokupac), Sifta (Turkey's Papaskarasi, still found

> *in a part of Turkey called Strandzha that was previously part of Bulgaria). For rosé wines: Pamid, Muscat de Hamburg (introduced 15–20 years before). For white wines: Dimiat, Vinenka, Cherven Misket, Zlatanka (Croatia's Vugava) and an unknown variety called Prisednitsa, apparently an astringent white variety.*

According to Dimov, Georgi Sirakov made some very interesting and accurate comments about the viticultural and oenological aptitude of these varieties. He noted that to produce good wine, yield must be controlled, and described the varieties that easily overcrop and thus produce low quality wine (Gamza, Dimiat, Vinenka). He noticed a problem of grafting with Sifta, a grape that had been widely planted before phylloxera, which may explain why it fell out of cultivation in Bulgaria. Furthermore, he mentioned the ripeness and the acidity of these varieties, so for instance Vinenka achieved 19 to 22 degrees Brix (a measurement of the sugar level at harvest) and 6 to 6.5 grammes per litre total acidity, with 75 to 77 per cent juice. He described Vinenka as having very thin skin (and existing as two clones, pink and yellow) so often the wines were watery. However, when Sirakov was working at a winery in Sliven, he was macerating the grapes until the beginning of the fermentation and then draining the juice. This was done to make the wines more full-bodied and balanced with a yellowish colour, rather like the way orange wines are made today. These observations were based on the old style of viticulture practised at the time – gobelet system (bush vines), with spur pruning and 7,000–10,000 vines per hectare.

BETWEEN THE WARS

The 1920s and 1930s saw the introduction of wine and vine cooperatives in Bulgaria as an attempt to overcome the established problems of fragmented holdings. Gamza at Suhindol was the first of these in 1909, followed by Lovech, Melnik, Chirpan, Pleven, Sliven and others. And in fact, 60 of these wine and vine cooperatives had been founded by 1939. There was French influence in the development of the wine industry during this period as wealthier people from wine regions sent their sons in France to study grape growing and winemaking.

COLLECTIVIZATION

By 1944, there were 143,103 hectares of vineyards producing around 2 million hectolitres of wine. The new government after the Second World War recognized that if wine was to become a competitive product for Bulgaria, it was vital to undertake a major reorganization programme. Over the next 15 years, more than 3,000 state cooperative farms were established, with 93 per cent of all arable land going into these collective farms. In 1948, the government formed Vinprom, to take charge of all wine production and marketing. Then in 1952 came decree number 1058 of the Council of Ministers, on the promotion of viticulture and winemaking in Bulgaria, which was a significant turning point for Bulgaria. This encouraged the development of wine science and led to the establishment of the Institute for the Wine Industry in Sofia, followed by the Higher Institute of Food and Beverage Industry in Plovdiv, and other institutions. Publication of specialist viticulture and oenology journals was encouraged, including *Lozarstvo and Vinarstvo*, which continues today. In 1955, decree number 273 established a commission of 35 scientists under the chairmanship of Professor Kunyu Stoev, and up until 1959 they conducted a detailed investigation across about 3,000 settlements. The result was that four viticultural regions – north, east, south and south-west were outlined and established. The French-educated Professor Nedelchev suggested that a fifth region, the sub-Balkan region should be separately identified, but this was never made law. A further decree (number 162) in 1960 divided each region into three sub-regions and described which grape varieties (both wine and table) should be grown where. In the 1950s, a team of researchers started work on the five-volume *Bulgarian Ampelography*, which was eventually completed in 1989 and covered over 1,350 grape varieties grown in Bulgaria. In the 1970s, Margarita Hristova was working in the library of the Research Institute in Sofia. She says, 'In the scientific information department we subscribed to nearly all the specialist vine and wine journals in the world – more than 80, from France, Germany, Italy, Spain, America, Australia, and more. We issued lots of information for oenologists at the wineries to keep them up-to-date. Sadly we cannot afford to maintain such a library nowadays and it was all destroyed when the institute was pulled down.' She adds, 'It's not true that we were shut off from Western science, and especially in the 1980s, a lot of Bulgarian vine and wine scientists travelled in Western wine countries to exchange experience. People today forget that we have a long tradition of making quality wines, it did not just start recently.'

The Bulgarian wine industry had a major role to play in the planned economy of the Soviet Bloc, which started with a programme of modernization and developments in the 1950s. It was this planned role that led to the extensive planting of international varieties: Rkatsiteli, Cabernet Sauvignon, Merlot, Chardonnay, Muscat Ottonel, Sauvignon Blanc, Aligoté and others. Vineyards were enlarged and moved from difficult landscapes on the hills to the fertile plains, to focus on higher yield and allow mechanization, as hand labour was not feasible on this scale. Vineyard density dropped to between 2,500 and 3,500 vines per hectare to suit growing conditions, which also allowed use of large Soviet tractors, though Bulgarians did invent their own Bolgar tractor to fit between narrow vine rows. Being on the plains rather than the slopes almost certainly made these international varieties more at risk of frost damage, so higher training systems were required, typically the Lenz Moser system with taller vine trunks. Instead of spur pruning, in order to achieve quantity, they changed to mixed pruning with both canes and spurs on the cordon. Most of the historic varieties are not suited to this system and so were replaced. Dimov explains, 'In the literature from the 1960s, Vinenka's potential Brix was 16 to 18 per cent and very high acidity! You can understand why Vinenka and Dimiat were replaced.' Rkatsiteli became particularly popular at this time, accounting for 40 per cent of white grapes by the 1960s.

By 1956, Russia was importing 26 million litres of Bulgarian wines, marking the start of a golden period for Bulgarian producers and exporters. Another important step was the development of a plant for processing, filtering and stabilizing bottled wine. Vinzavod Sofia was constructed from 1962 to 1963, followed by another six factories with bottling capability. These plants had strict microbiological control using French, German and Italian equipment and allowed the blending of large, consistent volumes of wine in batches as large as 400,000 litres. These plants helped to contribute to Bulgaria's bottled wine export business and, at its peak, the country was one of the global top ten wine exporters and the fourth biggest exporter of bottled wines worldwide.

EXPORT PEAK

By the 1970s, there were 150,000 hectares of wine grapes in Bulgaria. Christo Boevsky (retired head of department for Controlled Origin wines) explains: 'The Vinprom State Economic Union functioned as a holding with its main influences for technology and equipment from Germany, France and Italy, and the Soviet Union and Comecon countries as markets, and also a large share on the Japanese market. The Americans came later.' International wine expertise then arrived from California, in connection with deals by PepsiCo. PepsiCo was keen to sell its cola brand into communist countries (Pepsi was the first US brand in the Soviet Union in 1972). They couldn't sell their brand directly for currency so set up a series of barter deals for goods they could turn back into dollars, including wine in Bulgaria's case. PepsiCo employed Professor Amerine of the University of California, Davis for advice, which influenced the style of winemaking in Bulgaria. And Cezar Baeza who was PepsiCo's travelling winemaker explained, 'I met a group of very capable winemakers, young and ambitious. We usually communicated in French because many of them had trained there. But there wasn't much Chardonnay, so we planted some, and developed it in the style of California Chardonnay with heavy malolactic fermentation and lots of American oak. We also had a great Trakia Merlot that won a grand prix in New York'. Winemaker Ogynan Tzvetanov pointed out, 'I became a happy owner of the copy of Amerine's book *Modern Winemaking* which he left to Vinprom. Later, it was given to me as a gift by the deputy director and head of the Production Department.' Boevsky explains how strict the control systems were: 'The wine year started in August, when the Production Department of Vinprom gave the harvest goals to every winery. During the harvest, the guys from the Production Department were monitoring everything. In December a large wine-tasting commission decided which batch of wine was to go where (German Democratic Republic, Soviet Union, Japan, etc.) and then supervised the bottling.'

Another turning point in the development of Bulgarian viticulture was the establishment of the Wine Act of 1978 and especially the 'Ordinance on Wines with Controlled Appellation of Origin'. Professor Dimitar Tsakov explained that after potential areas and grapes were identified, the research institute at Pleven was commissioned to do research into soils and climate, while the institute in Sofia developed the technical standards for wine processing and bottling. The director-general of Vinprom, Stoyan Kinderkov established working groups of scientists to carry out the detailed research, which took 3 to 4 years and included strict mapping of the vineyards and the establishment of techniques for producing quality grapes. Vineyards were visited at least three times per year, according to strict protocols, to keep Vinprom informed. The date and quality of harvest were decided by a joint commission with representatives from Vinprom, the grape producers and a state quality inspector. There was strict control over fermentation and ageing, and records kept to track each wine. Wines were monitored through analysis and tasting, including special tastings held for the controlled origin wines. Only if the wine complied did it get the Ministry of Agriculture and Food order of approval. Twenty-three controlled origin wines were approved between 1982 and 1986 including Gamza from Suhindol, Gamza from Pavlikeni, Rosé from the South Coast (the first rosé wine in Bulgaria), Misket from Sungurlare, Mavrud from Asenovgrad, Merlot from Sakar, Chardonnay from Novi Pazar, Old Red from Oriahovitsa, Merlot from Stambolovo, Aligoté from Lyaskovets, Cabernet Sauvignon from Yantra Valley, Cabernet Sauvignon from Svishtov and several more (see Appendix I). The name Controliran was often used for this category of wines, from the Bulgarian 'Vino s kontrolirano naimonovanie za proizhod' (literally, 'wine with a controlled name of origin'). This level of research and control over quality gives context to Bulgaria's ability to offer such consistent large volumes of wines to Western export markets in the 1980s. Boevsky explains, 'This was the turning point, when the Bulgarian wine industry started to change from production of quantity to production of quality. I visited Spain to get to know the Spanish AOC system, the head of the wine institute in Sofia visited France about the same time, so we had enough knowledge how to manage the things in this field.'

This law was in place until the wine act of 1999. From the 2000 vintage onwards, Bulgaria started to align its laws with the EU. Wines could have one of two quality categories. The first was table wines with the option of adding a regional indication (subject to certain restrictions such as variety and origin of grapes). The other category was 'quality wines produced from a specified region' subject to rules on grape variety, yield, production method and region of production. Within this category there were either wines of 'controlled designation of origin' or for certain wines identified as having an established reputation, 'controlled and guaranteed designation of origin'. This was then superseded in 2006 by Bulgaria's full compliance with the latest EU law in time for accession in 2007.

EXPORTS TO THE WEST

Throughout the 1970s, Bulgaria was still supplying wine largely to the Soviet Union and Comecon countries. The industry structure was set up so that 70 per cent of all grapes were grown by the state-sponsored cooperative farms known as Agro-Industrial Complexes (AICs). Another 20 per cent came from vineyards owned directly by Vinprom (the state wine production monopoly) and the remaining 10 per cent came from privately owned vineyards (individuals in rural populations were allowed to own 0.1 to 0.2 hectares). Vinprom's winemaking facilities were subdivided into groups, each with a central winery and two or three satellite wineries, which often performed only part of the vinification or maturation process. Eighty per cent of wine was produced by the 29 Vinzavod, or state-run processing plants under the Vinprom umbrella, one of which was for bottling only. The other 20 per cent was produced in Perushtitsa, Targovishte and Septemvri, which were set up as a new form of experimental economic organization or 'vine and wine complex'. They had their own vineyards and winemaking facilities, but still functioned under the direction of Vinprom. Boevsky explains, 'Implementing some new technology or equipment was always according to the wish of Vinprom Production Department, so if there was something new on the market we bought one, the Wine Institute in Sofia tested it in some of these wineries and then decided to buy it or not.'

All exports went through the state monopoly Vinimpex. When it decided to expand its export markets to the West, such as in the key market of the UK, it worked initially through an agent (Halewood International, in the 1970s) then, in 1980, Vinimpex set up a subsidiary in London called the Bulgarian Vintners Company. This turned out to be perfect timing, because demand from the vast Soviet market started to decline. This accelerated in the mid-1980s with President

Gorbachev's campaign against alcoholism in USSR. This meant that thousands of hectares of Bulgarian vines were uprooted or abandoned, and few were treated to any systematic training or pruning. Dead, dying or diseased vines were not replaced. Some of these were poor quality sites, but better locations were also abandoned. Grape prices were fixed every year, irrespective of quality, which encouraged the state farms to turn their attention away from vines to other crops. Schmitz et al. report that Bulgaria lost 15 per cent of its vines between 1980 and 1990, and that the Soviet Union market demand fell from 1.4 million hectolitres to 0.8 million hectolitres by 1989 approximately (15 to 9 million standard 12-bottle cases). Comecon countries were still taking 84 per cent of Bulgaria's exports in 1985, with the Soviet Union taking nearly two-thirds of this volume, but as this fell, focus on hard currency markets in Western Europe became increasingly important for Bulgaria.

BULGARIA IN THE UNITED KINGDOM

The UK started with 95,000 standard cases (8,550 hectolitres) of Bulgarian Cabernet Sauvignon in 1982 and Bulgarian wines quickly built up a reputation for being a good source of cheap, cheerful and easy-to-understand wines. Volumes increased rapidly, reaching 193,000 hectolitres (more than 2 million cases) by 1990, according to Schmitz et al. Bulgaria became the fourth largest red wine supplier to the UK market after France, Italy and Spain, and the UK was by this time one of Bulgaria's most important export markets.

Bulgaria was the first country to market its wines under their varietal names, long before the New World jumped on this bandwagon. There was a rumour that at one time Sainsbury's own-label Bulgarian Cabernet Sauvignon was its single biggest selling wine. Former head of Beers, Wines and Spirits at Sainsbury's, Allan Cheesman, can't confirm this, but does remember in the mid-1980s selling 100,000 cases of Cabernet Sauvignon in just a fortnight on promotion at £1.99. His colleague Howard Wynn, recalls placing an order one Christmas for a million cases of Bulgarian Cabernet Sauvignon, their biggest ever order at that time.

PEERING BEHIND THE IRON CURTAIN

An early customer for Bulgarian wine was Tony Laithwaite (Direct Wines/ Laithwaites). Here he recalls his first flight into the unknown East:

We were travelling in a Balkan Airways slightly-converted bomber; it still had the perspex blisters where the guns had been. Their wine was pretty rich too, and safer than tea from the steaming iron kettle brought round by muscular communist attendants.

The wine wasn't going to be too hard to locate as Bulgarian wine was a state monopoly so there was only one sales office. I sat in reception at 19 Lavele Street (an address permanently engraved on my brain) for days until the Commissaire for Wines – or whatever – at Vinimpex agreed to see me. And say 'Niet'.

Rather a useless trip, I thought. Until somehow, shortly after, word of my interest got round and a man from a well-known brand of cola asked to meet me in London. It seems he had just sold a lot of his cola to Bulgaria and, as was the tradition in those days, been paid by barter. He now owned rather a lot of Bulgarian Cabernet Sauvignon and didn't know what to do with it. So, I took it off his hands at an excellent price. We shipped a full container – about a thousand cases – of 'Balkan Vine' Cabernet Sauvignon. It took a while to arrive, as the ship's steering jammed and our wine spent several days going around in circles in the Black Sea.

However, it was a great success. And more containers followed. Then more. Then masses. The quality, amazingly, held up. I went back to see how they did it. The wine came from what to me looked like a cooperative in a place called Suhindol. It had been built on co-op lines by the French. They had also planted mile after mile of Cabernet vineyard in suitable gravelly soil. I had seen nothing like wine production on this scale in Europe – only in California – and I started referring to Bulgaria as Europe's California. In Europe – and this is still true – if you want to make a big mass-market wine you have to buy many bits and pieces of wine from wherever you can and stick them together as best you can. Here was just one huge vineyard and one huge winery so it was not so surprising that they could do a proper, good solid job.

> *The guys in the winery were wine people just like wine people anywhere.*
> *They took pride in their work and loved opening their special bottles –*
> *secreted away from their bosses in Sofia – when we visited. We discovered*
> *more such wineries and expanded the range to include Chardonnay,*
> *Riesling, Merlot and great Bulgarian varietals like Mavrud.*

By 1994, 3.3 million standard cases of Bulgarian wine were shipped annually to the UK, while Germany and the Benelux countries also became important customers. I was also buying significant quantities of Bulgarian wine in this period and a buying file from 1994 shows that I was purchasing a range of 6 different Bulgarian wines. These included a Riesling at a cost price per dozen bottles of £9.00, Cabernet from Sliven at £11.50 and a Cabernet Reserve at £15.20.

At this time, there were also rumours that embargoed South African wine was making its way to Bulgaria to be relabelled. This seems hard to believe for several reasons: one is that Bulgaria had a scientifically advanced industry with high technical standards and knowhow developed in the 1970s and 1980s; second South African red wines then were very different to the style of wine that Bulgaria was producing, and that could be tasted directly at wineries. At that time, there was a high level of virus infection in South African red grapevines, resulting in wines that were pale, thin and harsh. Third, during visits to Bulgaria at the beginning of the 1990s it was easy to see vineyards that, though large-scale and collectivized, were well-managed and clearly capable of producing substantial volumes of wine. Allan Cheesman confirms, 'I visited just once in 1996 – an interesting visit just 6 years after the "wall" came down! Very backward facilities though very good base quality wines.' Indeed, it is clear that Bulgaria's climate is more than suitable for producing the kind of soft fruity reds that made it famous. Historical import/export data from this period is limited but Kym Anderson at the University of Adelaide confirms that there were no shipments recorded from South Africa to Bulgaria in the period from 1988 to 1990.

3

LAND REFORM AND THE MODERN ERA

LAND RESTITUTION

The year 1989 saw the beginning of a new era for Bulgaria with the end of one of the Eastern Bloc's most staunch, hard-line communist regimes.

Land reform was critical in shaping the future direction of the wine industry. This started with a 1991 law for agricultural land ownership and use. It aimed to return land to the original owners prior to 1947. Agricultural cooperatives were liquidated, and their assets distributed or sold. One winemaker reported that to make this process easier vines, animals and other assets were often destroyed, or stolen to sell for cash, because few people had money to pay for these assets. In 1989 vineyards covered 3.7 per cent of Bulgaria's cultivated land or about 170,000 hectares. Because of the right to a small patch of family land under the previous regime, individuals actually held 37 per cent of the country's total vineyard, though most of this was for home consumption and fell outside official statistics. This has had far-reaching consequences for the significance of home-made wine in the Bulgarian market.

The details of land restitution laws changed up to twenty times in the first ten years after independence. Land had to be restituted in the same amount and location, and according to old boundaries where possible, and where evidence was available (such as land deeds, photographs, village registers). Poor evidence was often a problem as families had become divided, and in many cases family members had moved abroad.

For a very short period at the start of the 1990s land could be returned in consolidated plots, but this did not last long and most land was returned in very small parcels.

Later, the government assigned local committees for land distribution to the previous owners and these worked for many years to assign unique pieces of land to each, (i.e. exactly those which had been given as in-kind contributions to the cooperatives some 50 years previously). Private companies were commissioned to reorganize the land register (often called a *cadastre*) and to enter each individual land plot onto the digital map of the area and country. Often people got land of the same size and quality as their original holding but in a different location, while one winery owner explained that land commissions sometimes acted for personal benefits or for the benefit of their friends and associates.

IMPACT ON VINEYARDS

Officially the land restitution process ended in 2000, having taken up to 5 years to complete for individual owners, though in reality it is still not completed in full nor entered onto the digital map and cadastre of the country. There were many legal appeals because of poor evidence and this halted any market reallocation of land. In 1999, the government adopted a short-term scheme allowing land transfers based on temporary documents. This was intended to address a problem with co-ownership. Where there were multiple owners (such as descendants of the original owner), documents did not specify ownership shares and this created conflicts. This turned out to be serious in the wine sector where it was estimated that around 40 per cent of the land was held in co-ownership. Small plot sizes and the fact that land had been reallocated to often absentee owners was a problem for viticulture. Such people usually had no interest in wine because they had other careers, so this meant that land fell into disrepair. The small size of plots meant that any sort of professional viticulture was also impossible, so even where vines were managed, it was an occasional evening or weekend hobby. A lack of information in *cadastre* offices about ownership made it difficult to track them down for anyone interested in buying land.

Another problem was that while land ownership was being disputed, there was no incentive for any investments into permanent crops like grapevines. Vineyards are expensive, and no one would risk long-term investments like vines, posts, wires and so on, if they are not certain who actually owns the land. By the year 2000, national statistics showed that 72 per cent of vineyards were older than 21 years, indicating that very little had been replanted during this period. In 1999, data showed that yields had also decreased to 3.1 tonnes per hectare, indicating lack of professional viticulture.

Winery owner Nikola Zikatanov summed it up: 'The results were tragic – for many years the land was in transition and nobody knew who was the owner of any specific land plot. Investments stopped, nobody was taking care of orchards and vineyards, on the contrary – in many cases vineyards were burnt, supporting systems were taken out and sold abroad.'

WINERY PRIVATIZATION

In 1990, the wine sector was suddenly liberalized, and Vinprom itself was disbanded in 1991 as part of the free-market reforms introduced in the wake of the fall of communism. The wineries themselves were privatized in two stages. First, winery groups were established as separate organizations, each with a foreign currency account, managed separately but still state-owned. Second came privatization, mainly to worker-manager teams, similar in principle to western management buyouts, though as one source points out there was 'only nominal participation of workers and usually one, or two political "paratroopers" as managers. For years, the goal of the leading persons in these teams was milking the companies while making no investments or development.'

Privatization of the wineries was slow but by the end of the 1990s, all major wineries were in private ownership and Vinimpex was sold to the French-based Belvedere group in 2003. The main disadvantages were lack of funds and the ban (since rescinded with EU membership) on foreign investment in land and buildings. This was a marked contrast with the position in Hungary, which benefited greatly from foreign investment in developing its wine industry. As much of the industry was privatized through management buyouts, with little or no external capital, grape purchases were frequently funded using bank loans (at high interest rates). This meant that many wineries found themselves in serious financial trouble and were not able to invest in up-to-date equipment or vineyards.

Bulgarian wine was also hit by the twin scourges of economic problems, with the loss of spending power in the domestic market, and the collapse of export markets in the former Soviet Union. Wine exports fell by 71 per cent between 1985 and 1991 but wine production only decreased by 20 per cent, leaving a considerable amount of unsold stock in a saturated market. This meant that demand for grapes also fell, leaving growers struggling for income and lacking money for plant protection products and fertilizers. The separation of grape-growing and wine production continued very largely unchanged until the early 2000s when statistics show that there were 23,000 growers and 130 wine processors. Vineyards remained the main permanent crop and in 2004 still accounted for 4 per cent of total cultivated land.

The separation of grape production and winemaking under communism left a legacy of poor understanding by winemakers of the issues of fruit quality and control of their raw materials. By 2002, only 4.6 per cent of grapes came from wineries' own production. Even worse, most of the grapes were sourced through intermediaries, so there was very little contact between wineries and growers. In 2005 winemaker Dimitar Panov commented that, 'The gulf of understanding was so huge, growers and wineries hated each other.'

Even in the mid-2000s, very few wineries actually owned vineyards, and winemakers rarely got involved in managing any viticultural issues, believing that their role began when grapes arrived in trucks. Grape growers tended to be focused on harvesting and getting paid as quickly as possible, before bad autumn weather – or indeed theft, of which there was a high risk – lost them their harvest. At the same time, a continuing lack of professional viticulture or vineyard management meant already low yields declined further.

The position was not helped by a series of low-volume vintages and by the end of the 1990s, the Bulgarian wine industry was suffering from a serious shortage of fruit. This led to wineries competing for supplies and they often would take fruit early to secure grapes and pay a premium to do so, and in many cases, growers wouldn't release grapes until they were paid. This led directly to much thinner, under-ripe wines with higher costs at a time when the West had got used to ripe, fruity New

World styles, and Bulgaria rapidly lost export market share. This was exacerbated by the arrival of New World countries like Australia, which was not only making varietal wines better, fruiter and more consistently than Bulgaria was now able to achieve, but was also creating much more effective marketing to a fellow English-speaking market – the UK – which had been so important to Bulgaria's export success.

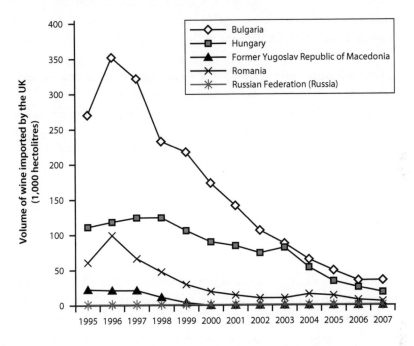

Falling sales in the UK (cited with permission from Panzone, L. 2011)

THE NEXT MILLENNIUM

In the 2000s, many wineries found themselves in trading difficulties, due to falling sales, reliance on bank loans, and lack of investment. A further round of secondary privatization and takeovers then followed, with investment largely from foreign sources or, if Bulgarian, from outside the wine industry (banks, lawyers, industrialists, magazine publishers, vegetable growers and more).

From around 2000 onwards, Bulgaria's state fund for agriculture supported over one hundred projects aimed at creating 2,200 hectares of new vineyards in preparation for accession to the European Union. Undoubtedly, the EU's pre-accession funding programmes such as SAPARD (Special Accession Program for Agricultural and Rural Development) were significant. Subsidies of up to 50 per cent for both winery and vineyard investments brought in substantial foreign investment, described by one high profile investor as a 'massive scale [vine] BOGOF' ('buy one, get one free'). It also enabled the rise of small individual projects and wine estates, which were a novelty in Bulgaria at that time. By the time of EU accession in 2007, the industry had benefited from an estimated €115 million.

The realization that wine quality could only be regained through control of fruit sourcing meant that many wineries took on the huge bureaucratic burden of putting together consolidated landholdings. EU funds were tempting enough to make it worth the legal paperchase of tracking down multiple tiny landowners to put together the sizeable vineyard plots that the industry so desperately needed. Nikola Zikatanov (owner Villa Melnik) summed up: 'In theory, by the year 2000, almost any single piece of land had its owner, boundaries, known neighbours, etc. identified. The problem was that the title was in the name of the owner from 50 years ago, who had most likely died and his heirs were 5 to 10 people, or even 50 individuals, living all around the globe. For a legitimate land sale transaction, it was a requirement to have all of the heirs appear in front of the Notary Public to declare and confirm a sale. But at least by this point, once a land parcel was purchased, it was very clear where is this land and it was possible to start working on it.'

Stephan von Neipperg of Château Canon La Gaffelière (St-Emilion) and German partner Karl Hauptmann invested in one of the first new private wine estates. This project, the Bessa Valley winery at Pazardijk near Plovdiv, reported dealing with 600 landowners to assemble its 200-hectare plot. The team at the new Castra Rubra investment took 3 years buy its land in the Harmanli area and had to negotiate with over 1,000 people, some of whom were abroad. Other wineries such as Katarzyna Estate chose to buy up land in the unplanted no man's land border zone to avoid dealing with such paper trails.

One downside of the EU SAPARD programme was that producers had to be able to fund the project upfront and then claim back subsidies later. They also had to be debt-free, which was a problem in an industry where bank loans to fund grape purchases were common, and this limited the possibility of raising further funds against a future SAPARD project. The bureaucratic burden was also huge, requiring hundreds of documents, and a real headache for small producers who simply did not have the skills or people to write funding applications. Additional complications came when Bulgaria was accused of mismanaging funds by the EU, putting a temporary halt on the process. This created an additional delay and headache for wineries who had secured loans which needed to be repaid within a tight timescale and had started projects using these funds. Despite the bureaucracy and political challenges to be overcome, there's no doubt that EU money made a huge difference in kick-starting a new era for Bulgarian wine.

4

INTO THE EU FUTURE

VINEYARDS

The landscape of the Bulgarian wine industry has changed dramatically since the fall of the Iron Curtain and even more so since the completion of privatization. Accession to the EU in 2007 accelerated the pace of change, bringing with it reformed laws on winemaking as well as significant investment.

As part of the EU membership negotiations, Bulgaria agreed a vineyard area of 153,000 hectares, and official data for 2006 showed an area under vine of 135,760 hectares. However, this was never a realistic reflection of the area of viable productive vineyards and was most likely a political decision to give the industry maximum possible planting rights (which were extremely limited within the EU, basically requiring like for like replacement). Vineyard area continued to fall and the Ministry of Agriculture's Annual Agrarian Report stated there were just 46,145 hectares in production in 2011, which fell further, to 36,551 hectares, by 2016.

Nearly half of Bulgaria's vines are more than thirty years old, but in the last five years 6,000 to 8,000 hectares have been renovated each year. This almost certainly reflects purchase of land and planting or replanting of vineyards by large wineries, as well as the emergence of small and medium-sized new wineries with quality aspirations. Today, the majority of wineries have their own vineyards supplying all or part of their needs, and where they don't own vines, longer term contracts specifying fruit quality and vine management are typically in place.

Vineyard development is likely to continue. Bulgaria had established a government-funded wine sector programme, worth nearly €70 million from 2014 to 2018, to support further conversion and restructuring of vineyards, plus investments in wine cellars and green measures. The change in attitude from technology towards the land shows the major mental switch that the industry has undergone. However, there is still a need to get to grips with the next step, which is to understand what the right locations for specific varieties are, and not just plant vines wherever a winery has been able to buy a plot of land. Look at France for examples of where the link from people to land has been uninterrupted for centuries (unlike Bulgaria where the link between land and individual people was largely destroyed over the years of communism). There are long established reasons why Pinot and Chardonnay grow in continental Burgundy while Cabernet and Sauvignon Blanc reign in the Atlantic climates of Bordeaux and the Loire, and Syrah and Viognier suit the baking heat of the Rhone. It's worth noting how little varietal overlap there is too, unlike in Bulgaria where many of these grapes are found together in the same vineyard. The alternative way of looking at this is that Bulgaria is experimenting with freedom from prescriptive laws about what to plant where.

There are two aspects to quality: the first is freedom from faults and off flavours, while the second relates to the individuality and complexity derived from a location that imparts its unique character. Bulgaria needs to learn from the mistakes of her New World competitors. Frequently vines have been planted without considering the suitability of the variety for each site, with winemakers putting their faith in the power of technology and modern winemaking to overcome any disadvantages, such as the wrong soil or excess heat, and ending up with uniform and even boring wines. In the early years of the new era, it was such a challenge to put together enough land in Bulgaria for a commercial vineyard that owners may have rushed into planting without thinking through what grapes might work best. Terroir may determine character and complexity, but the human factor determines quality level.

New vineyards have their place, and young vines do get older and better balanced in time, which is starting to happen now in Bulgaria with the first wave of new era vines. The earliest investments from the early to mid-2000s are now getting over this problem, and the wines are better for it, showing ripeness at lower and better balanced alcohol levels. Just as an example Bessa Valley Reserva 2006 was 15.7% abv and the latest release is a more harmonious 14.3% abv. But the industry should not forget the old vines – especially gnarly ancient things planted decades ago. Such vines are often naturally in balance with roots reaching deep into the soil, but importantly, they are not the modern clones that are increasingly widespread, which suggests they have survived because they suited Bulgaria's conditions. I would love to see someone taking cuttings before this potential treasure trove disappears in a sea of French or Italian clones. And the myth that old vines are automatically better is often disproved by the reality here. Older vineyards from communist times were planted for quantity, on vigorous rootstocks and fertile soils. Just getting old will never completely solve that problem, and in many older vineyards there are missing and sick vines, as well as a few that are overcropping, so giving very inconsistent results.

To explore the idea of terroir a bit further, three factors need to come together. First is the place itself – the soil, climate, microclimate, aspect, rainfall, wind, sun, altitude and nearby water – and of course vine varieties that suit all these factors. Second is competent winemaking, which allows what the place gives to shine through. It mustn't dominate, either with faults, or through being too technical and manipulative. Third and arguably most important is the human factor – the passion to aim for high quality and to experiment. And yes, this may mean winemakers being prepared to put their reputations on the line and admit they got it wrong sometimes (and I know this is not something that comes easy to proud Bulgarians). There also needs to be a dose of realism, as there must be a market place to sell these wines into. Recent years have seen several Bulgarian producers embracing 'terroir' in a move to be recognized for fine wines. As Yuson Jung points out in her 2014 paper: 'Terroir is a compelling narrative to legitimize the premium quality of their wines and enter the ranks of fine wine in the global wine hierarchy,' adding that, 'wine is not simply an alcoholic drink but a cultural commodity and a symbol of identity'.

TALES OF TERROIR

While it seems that there are plenty of vineyards in Bulgaria planted where it was possible to buy land and take advantage of EU subsidies, and planted with varieties driven by perceived market demand, there are also definite signs that producers are now getting to grips with the idea of terroir.

In the early 2000s, projects like Bessa Valley and Miroglio carried out pages and pages worth of soil assessments and made plans to match varieties to soil and microclimate. At Bessa Valley, the similarities to St Emilion led to a focus on Merlot with Cabernet Sauvignon, Syrah and Petit Verdot in supporting roles, but no Cabernet Franc because the soils weren't right. Miroglio's plans included planting Pinot Noir on cooler north-facing slopes with a selection of clones and rootstocks. Then there's been the development of single vineyard wines that highlight a particular location such as Domaine Boyar's Solitaire Merlot from Elenovo. This was a pioneering concept, at least for a large winery, when it was first released. Borovitza's wines too are in effect a series of single vineyard wines from individual batches of fruit. Back in the 2000s, Bulgarian viticulture was still largely about high yields from vines grown in fertile soils, but Ivana and Iulian Yamantiev had started to take every possible opportunity to travel in order to learn what to do better. After a trip to Rioja in Spain in 2005, Iulian says, 'I was gobsmacked to see the hard work that was going on in the vineyards and then realized how little we really knew. The same year we planted 25 hectares on marble, some of them directly in the rock.'

And at Burgozone near the Danube, Biliana Marinova (daughter of the founders) explains that they called in Professor Marin Penkov, one of Bulgaria's leading experts on soil and grapevines to help them decide exactly where they should plant. She says:

Our proposed vineyards were a special place for him. When he started his career as agronomist more than 40 years ago, he carried out his first soil studies in our vineyards. One day he was so busy digging down to the roots of a vine that he did not notice that everyone had left. He found himself trapped in a deep hole and could not get out. In this era before mobile phones, he was stuck overnight in the hole until the first winegrowers arrived in the morning. Despite his overnight stay, he was very happy as

> he had reached the end of this vine's roots at 7 metres deep. He concluded that in these vineyards we should never worry about the vine's access to minerals and water. Based on this experience and his extensive studies of our soils, Professor Penkov was categorical that this is one of the best terroirs in Bulgaria and that we should plant there.

HOME-MADE WINE AND BULGARIA'S HOME MARKET

Today many Bulgarians still see home-made wine as their cultural heritage and by 2016 there were still over 12,000 hectares of small back-garden plots. This is something they've always done, as did parents and grandparents, albeit on the tiny plots of land they were still allowed to own under communism (0.1 hectares in most of Bulgaria). Such people truly believe that this home-made wine is the most genuine and from-the-heart product, and free from 'chemicals', unlike the industrial wines from commercial wineries. Anyone who is brave enough to taste it will almost certainly find a horrible, faulty liquid that bears little resemblance to wine as most people understand it.

WINE FROM THE HEART

One of the most valuable tastings I ever did was with Ogy Tzvetanov and Adriana Srebrinova on our way to see the derelict winery they had just bought in north-west Bulgaria in 2007. En route, we stopped to do a tasting in a rather boarded-up hotel, so we sneaked in via the kitchen – as ever, Ogy had a friend there. The tasting that greeted me was a line-up of odd-looking liquids in a random selection of reused water and soft drink bottles. These had been bought from roadside stalls and the local market. I can't say it was the most fun tasting I ever did as the 'wines' showed every wine fault you have ever heard of, plus some weird aromas from use of hybrid grapes too. But the point was well made and has stuck with me ever since. Ogy wanted to show me what local people firmly believe to be the most genuine wines. He wanted to highlight the huge gulf of understanding that had to be bridged when trying to persuade them what would be required to make quality wine as we might understand it in the West.

It's hard for producers making wines like these to understand ideas like reducing yield and green harvest (which they see as throwing away perfectly good grapes). Basic understanding of hygiene and preserving wines from the damaging effects of oxygen or stray microbes also seem to be missing. Wines like this are also served in local restaurants and bars, even in the heart of Sofia and certainly in tourist spots like Melnik. Such wines tend to be offered with hearty local food which is often very tasty and fresh but could rarely be described as a fine cuisine. Even in 2017, wines like this appear regularly and the men (usually) or women who have made them will take offence if you prefer to drink commercial wine out of a bottle.

Unfortunately, it seems this type of home-made wine still accounts for as much as half of wine consumption within Bulgaria, though it is impossible to track accurately. However, there are encouraging signs that commercial wine is increasing its share at the expense of such home brews. The US GAIN report for 2016 expected total wine consumption to reach over 1.15 million hectolitres in Bulgaria by 2017 and for commercial wine to reach 550,000 hectolitres. The domestic market appears to have outperformed this prediction, with the NVWC reporting sales of 700,000 hectolitres of domestic commercial wine and a further 50,000 hectolitres of imported wine for 2016. The home wine market is incredibly important to the success of Bulgarian wine, particularly as it's reckoned that over 90 per cent of mid-to high-end local wine is consumed here (where the average price is 7 leva, just over €3.50), while exports are still predominantly in the 'value-for-money' sector.

There are positive signs of wine education and a food and wine culture developing. Divino.bg is the country's leading on-line magazine and wine website, produced under the watchful eyes of the dynamic editor-in-chief Julia Kostadinova and publisher Emil Koralov. It has now been going for 14 years, and the team has also created the country's best consumer wine event in Divino-Taste. Run every November it is a must-visit for anyone who wants to get the latest picture on Bulgarian wines. The only Wine and Spirit Education Trust provider is the Bulgarian Wine And Spirit Academy, run by Dimitar Nikolov and Edward Kourian, and the Bulgarian Sommeliers' Association now claims 100 members. Still, smaller producers and distributors complain that they don't have a fair playing field, especially in the restaurant sector where the big producers can fund extras (like coolers, fridges and glasses, or even commissions per cork) to gain listings and sales. At the same time a better food culture is developing, at least in the cities, with more subtle flavours based on traditional ingredients. Wine that will enhance, rather than dominate, the food will also become important. Restaurants will need to learn how to offer a better customer experience, which is potentially more profitable too, by thinking about matching wines to food rather than selling the wines they have – in effect – been bribed to list. In the wine regions themselves it would be good to see restaurants featuring their local wines.

BEER, *RAKIA* AND TOBACCO

Bulgaria may be a wine producing nation, but still Bulgarians are not really wine consumers. World Health Organization data for 2017 show Bulgarians drinking 11.4 litres of pure alcohol equivalent per year. Looking at the NVWC figure for domestic market sales volume and adult population (6,066,309), it seems that a fairly realistic figure for wine consumption is 12.4 litres per head, and this is also confirmed by Statistica.com for 2016. Statistica.com also shows that Bulgarians are heavy spirits drinkers, ranked seventh in the world at 12.8 litres per capita, and a significant part of this is grape spirits like brandy and *rakia* (see Glossary). Bulgarians famously love their *rakia* and inevitably every meal begins with a glass to accompany the salad. '*Rakia* is part of everyday life in Bulgaria – it's a must have drink,' said one source. There are variations on the *rakia* theme across the Balkans and it can be made from all sorts of fruit. In Bulgaria, grapes are typical (and aromatic grapes like Misket or Muscat are preferred), or often grape skins left over from winemaking, so strictly it is more like *grappa* or *marc* than brandy.

Recent archaeological discoveries suggest that distillation has been part of Bulgarian life for a long time. Two distillation vessel fragments dated to the eleventh century have been found at the medieval fortress of Lyutitsa near Ivaylovgrad and another found in the medieval fortress of Drastar, which is in the town of Silistra, also dated to the same period.

There have been strict laws around distillation in place since Bulgaria joined the EU. Around 1,500 pot stills are registered for production, though grey market production still appears to be widespread. Since accession, each family is now limited to 30 litres, at half the standard tax of 3.30 leva (€1.70) per 75 cl bottle. If this volume is exceeded, then full excise tax is due on the whole quantity. At the time, this was widely regarded as an attack on family traditions and accompanied by widespread protests. *Rakia* must have a minimum strength of 37.5% abv or 40% abv if it is made from grapes. And here lies a problem for the wine industry, as it is hard for a subtle wine to follow such a 'palate-killer'.

Tobacco used to be huge crop in Bulgaria (in 1918 it made up 80 per cent of Bulgaria's exports and was nicknamed 'Bulgarian gold') and by the 1960s, Bulgaria was the world's largest exporter of cigarettes. Until very recently, all Bulgarian food was accompanied by a thick fog of tobacco as Bulgarians believed it was their absolute right to smoke. It is still a common habit in Bulgaria, though thankfully it has been banned indoors since 2012. Just about every restaurant has an outdoor smoking area, thick with smoke, and in rural areas the law is often ignored. I can't help my suspicion that the combination of *rakia* and tobacco has influenced Bulgarian tastes in favour of strong, heavily-extracted, tannic and oaky red wines.

THE INDUSTRY STRUCTURE TODAY

There are 263 registered wineries today. Bulgaria was the twenty-first largest wine producer in the world in 2015 making 0.67 per cent of the world's wines and ranking thirty-first in wine consumption. In 2016 it produced 1,207,785 hectolitres, of which 608,285 hectolitres were white wine, while red and rosé combined accounted for 599,501 hectolitres. Non-industrial wine accounted for a further 126,196 hectolitres. Wine remains a significant economic factor and it is claimed that Bulgaria has the highest proportion of exported wine of any EU country (Moldova, which is outside the EU, exports a higher proportion).

Bulgaria continues to be a very significant wine exporter, though in 2016 wine exports fell 25 per cent from the previous year to 288,210 hectolitres. Eighty-two per cent of exports go to the European Union, of which Poland is by far the most significant importer, taking close to half of all export volume. Sweden comes second, taking most of its

Bulgarian wine as bulk, almost certainly largely destined for bag-in-box sales, which dominate the Swedish market. The UK comes next, taking 15,197 hectolitres of wine in 2016, all bottled in Bulgaria, though bulk business has increased in 2017 for UK bottling. This is followed by the Czech Republic (see Appendix I). In some years, Russia has been an important export customer, but this is a very fickle market. For instance, Russia took 113,210 hectolitres of bottled wine in 2014 but only 36,070 hectolitres the following year, dropping further to 14,149 hectolitres in 2016.

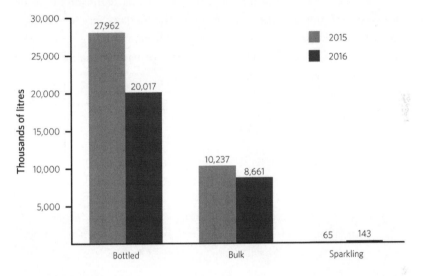

Bulgarian wine exports in 2015 and 2016. Source: NSI, Preliminary Data for 2016

As for where Bulgarian consumers buy their wine, unsurprisingly the off-trade accounted for 80 per cent by volume of wine sold in Bulgaria (and 58 per cent by value in 2015). The most significant sector is still table wines with no geographical indication, which tend to be in the lowest price segment, often sold in bulk or bag-in-box packaging and these take about 68 per cent of the domestic market. Bag-in-box has a 35 per cent share by volume. Quality wines with PGI or PDO have about a 9 per cent market share. Imports account for 7 per cent of commercial wine sales and most of these seem to fit into two categories: very cheap wine to undercut local producers and more expensive wine from classic regions in countries like France, Italy and Spain. Certain New World wines of styles that can't be produced locally such as New Zealand Sauvignon Blanc are also strong. Sparkling wine imports in 2015 were dominated by Italy at 1,417 hectolitres and France at 889 hectolitres, almost certainly the increasingly trendy Prosecco and champagne, as the average import price was €8.23 per litre. Rosé is the fastest-growing category in the local market, showing an increase of 5 per cent a year, and the trend here seems to be super pale wines with a dry palate profile.

This represents a challenge and an opportunity for wine producers. The top 10 producers account for over 55 per cent of the market. But this leaves 250 wineries or more fighting for market share and many are not able to compete in the volume end of the market. Very few of these smaller wineries are yet self-supporting, with many relying on external funding either from the EU or in the form of bank loans, or support from an owner's other business interests.

THE ROAD AHEAD

The first challenge in Bulgaria is to switch drinkers from home-made to commercial wines. This does mean that every time a consumer picks up a bottle or indeed a glass of Bulgarian wine, it must be of sound technical quality, honestly made and pleasant to drink whatever the price level. And this is not always the case. There also needs to be education to switch consumers from believing that home-made wines (with all their faults) are the most authentic style towards understanding that wine should taste nice and be free from faults. Then once in the commercial wine category, the next step is to move them into the more premium segments, such as wines with geographical indications, and premium quality and pricing. Developing a sense of patriotism for good local products is important, while for exports establishing a Bulgarian identity for wine will also be important – education and communication are vital tools in this.

THE RISE OF THE ICON WINE

It is easier in many ways for small individual producers to push the boundaries and take risks. Bulgaria's first high-quality icon wine was launched in 2000 by a tiny producer called Maxxima with a Reserve

Cabernet and Merlot 1999. Owner Adriana Srebrinova was inspired by tasting E&E Black Pepper Shiraz at Vinexpo saying, 'I am dreaming of the day when Bulgaria makes wines like this.' However, instead of just dreaming, she cut short her trip, bought some new oak barrels and went in search of grapes of the right quality to match.

Former Vinprom winery, the privatized Damianitza, followed suit not long after with ReDark, made by Frenchman Marc Dworkin. This trend has continued with new boutique wine estates launching every year and most of the large producers also investing in premium 'boutique' brands. It is possible for a large winery to make a successful icon wine – witness Grange from Penfold's in Australia. However, it is generally more difficult for a large winery to produce a convincing icon wine that is more than simply marketing, packaging and price. There is a notable tendency to establish a premium product for the local market through pricing, along with very heavy glass and ornate packaging. Some of these bottles can end up weighing more than 1.2 kilogrammes for the glass alone, and this is really frustrating and wasteful to Western minds – all that energy wasted on transporting and recycling such heavy glass. However, in Bulgaria it is important that a premium wine is a visible status symbol so that people can see that you are 'splashing the cash' in a restaurant.

I am convinced that making good and even excellent wines in Bulgaria is possible and is happening. It's always a good test in the wine world to ask people what they spend their own money on to drink rather than taste, and there are now several Bulgarian wines that I am very happy to pay for with my own money. However, the question for export markets is a wider one about how the country will establish a place in the wine world outside its borders and traditional markets. And if Bulgarian producers want to export, then an outside perspective may be at least worth listening to.

Realistically, exports are a necessity, given that more wine is being produced than can be drunk in the domestic market and there are some high price levels that are out of reach of economically disadvantaged Bulgarian consumers. Then there's the question of whether wine styles will suit global tastes. Bulgaria in the new era, like so many of its neighbours, followed a typical path of aiming for concentrated, intense wines made with generous amounts of new oak – all about establishing a clearly different and premium style. And there's nothing wrong with wines like this if consumers want them (after all, the first duty of wine is to be sold, and ideally purchased again). But it is worth keeping an eye on global trends because Bulgarian consumers will eventually follow this and globally there is a move towards lower alcohol, less oak, and more freshness.

Bulgaria might have a long history in wine, but what it doesn't have is a flagship like Hungary's Tokaji, and it still needs to develop its national identity. It also needs to seize the opportunity of its domestic market, especially as young people seem to be more interested in commercial wine and are moving away from the home-made wines and rough *rakia* of their parents and grandparents. Communication and education for these customers, and the trade that is selling to them, is going to be critical to support all the recent investments in the Bulgarian wine industry. It is important for the domestic market consumers to develop a sense of pride in their country's own products. If drinkers opt for these, rather than seeking out classic international wines, this is going to be an easier way forward than trying to develop a niche for Bulgarian wines in the global wine world. If a country cannot be proud of its own wines, it has a problem (and in this regard it is perhaps worth comparing Bulgaria with countries like Hungary and Romania that consume so much more of their own wine).

OTHER CONTEMPORARY ISSUES

Biodynamic, natural and orange wines

At the time of writing, it is impossible to ignore the topic of environmental impact which is creating a lot of buzz in the wine world. Few Bulgarian producers are yet moving in this direction, but given that wine is a luxury, not a necessity, it will inevitably come. Whatever one's views (and I have written elsewhere on this topic several times) about the science, or otherwise, behind biodynamics, some highly reputed names in wine are pursuing this philosophy, creating a definite halo effect. Biodynamics adds a layer of mysticism, marketing, and pseudoscience to the more widespread organic approach to winemaking and grape growing. There is no guarantee that being biodynamic will make wines any better, but it does provide a belief system for producers to help them put in the extra effort and attention that is required. Bulgaria still has a lot of unspoilt landscape and it makes sense to protect the local flora and fauna by minimizing as far as possible the use of harmful synthetic agrochemicals.

So far Swiss-owned Eolis has announced that it plans to develop a biodynamic approach, while Damianitza is also using a biodynamic and holistic approach with some of its vineyards where this is feasible. Unfortunately, as owner Philip Harmandjiev points out, this is not possible in small, scattered plots where neighbours take a more conventional approach with liberal agrochemical use. There are a few certified organic producers in Bulgaria including Zagreus, Neragora, Terra Tangra and Orbelus, while producers such as Miroglio and Castra Rubra claim organic approaches. Bulgaria's Ministry of Agriculture reports that there were 5,390 hectares certified by the end of 2016.

Orange wines (sometimes called amber wines) are made from white grapes using skin contact in a similar way to vinifying reds. Grapes are usually destemmed and macerated during fermentation for anything from a few days to several months, and often barrel-aged. When made well, orange wines can be complex, textured and very good food wines. There's growing interest in Bulgaria in this niche category, particularly as a way of adding value and character to local grape varieties. This applies especially to Dimiat and Misket Cherven which have reputations for producing often uninteresting and short-lived wines. Bulgaria's first orange wine producer was Rossidi, which used Chardonnay, before subsequently moving on to a very good Gewürztraminer version. Villa Melnik makes a highly regarded orange Sauvignon Blanc with a little Keratsuda, while several producers are making orange versions of Dimiat and Misket Cherven. Notable examples include Gulbanis and Via Vinera Karabunar under the Bulgarian Heritage label.

Natural wine is the term used for the nebulous (and not legally defined) idea of low intervention winemaking. Typically, use of sulphites will be minimal with no other winemaking additives, and spontaneous fermentations are normal. Bratanov and Rossidi are two producers known to take this approach, while Orbelus makes a no-added-sulphite wine.

Local or international – does Bulgaria need a flagship variety?

For the international market, local grape varieties are a good way of gaining interest and starting conversations, though selling a grape no one has heard of from a country with little reputation for quality wine can be a big ask. If a grape only comes from Bulgaria, it is – by definition – a wine of its place, and such local varieties can also be used to add Bulgarian character to blends. In some cases, the fact is that local grape varieties have remained local because they only suit specific local conditions or because they are too ethnic or rustic to gain wider attention. Shiroka Melnishka Loza for instance, only really suits the Struma Valley and its wines can be challenging to drink without modern winemaking. Grapes like Pamid appear totally unsuitable for producing quality wine that will appeal to modern drinkers.

In other cases, with a more knowledgeable approach to viticulture and winemaking there could well be some gems to discover. At the moment, Mavrud seems to be leading the way as Bulgaria's red flagship, and today it is the most widely planted of the quality native grapes. By no means does everyone agree that this is the only choice, with supporters for Rubin, Melnik 55 and even Gamza. However, as Radoslav Radev (head of NVWC) pointed out to me, the situation is the opposite in the domestic market, where young people often associate local grape varieties with what their parents and grandparents drank. International grapes are the ones with glamour for new drinkers rebelling against their parents.

Finding the balance point between these conflicting demands is a challenge. There is also a valid argument that showing the world what Bulgaria can do with well-known grape varieties helps buyers understand what quality the country can offer. Adriana Srebrinova (owner of Maxxima and Borovitza) explains, 'I think we will have a better chance of showing the unique qualities of Bulgarian wines through the place where we grow our grapes, because wine lovers in the world know how a Cabernet Sauvignon from Napa or a Bordeaux tastes, it is easy for them to discern the difference in a Bulgarian Cabernet.'

BULGARIAN FOOD

Bulgarian food is a mosaic of different influences at the crossroads of Europe. From the Thracians came cabbages, garlic, onions, lettuce and carrots, and they were also believed to be the first to sour milk. The Slavs brought rice, wheat, rye, green peas and lentils. From the proto-Bulgarians, a nomadic people with a meat and milk diet, came various preserved meats and sausages. From connections with Greece came olives (though on the whole Bulgarian winters are too cold for olives to grow here), lemons, aubergines and bay leaves. Turkish cuisine brought the use of spices like pepper and paprika. And herbs like summer savory (used for a condiment called *sharena sol*), parsley and mint are typical.

Cheese appears at just about every meal, or to accompany wine tasting, and comes in two forms – yellow cheese called *kashkaval* and white, brined cheese called *sirene* or simply cheese. This is similar to feta, but firmer and can be made from cow or sheep milk, or a mixture. Yoghurt is also hugely popular, appearing for breakfast, with starters or in soups and stews. In 1905, a young Bulgarian researcher called Stamen Grigov working in Geneva (with some pots of yoghurt from his village) identified the bacteria that were causing the fermentation as *Bacillus bulgaricus*, now more properly called *Lactobacillus delbrueckii subsp. bulgaricus*. Bulgarians reckon that they've been eating yoghurt for a very long time and that its name may even mean 'thick milk' in the ancient Thracian language.

A typical meal will always start with a salad, and traditionally a glass of *rakia*. Brandies are made too and can be amazing (one winemaker friend used to have a secret source for 'party special' brandies with up to 40 years of ageing in barrel). Most typical is the iconic *shopska* salad made with cucumbers, tomatoes and peppers and covered with grated white cheese. But other salads will be offered depending on what's in season. In winter, a salad of pickled vegetables called *turshiya* appears and includes cauliflower, peppers, carrot and cabbage. Pickled wild mushrooms are another seasonal treat.

Banitza appears for breakfast and as a snack or appetizer. The pie is made with very thin dough (similar to filo) and stuffed with white cheese before being rolled up and baked. Sometimes leeks or spinach are added to the stuffing. Other typical starters include: *lyutenitsa* (a puree of roast peppers and tomato); *kyopulu* (roast aubergines and peppers mashed together with garlic and herbs); *tirosalata* (a dip made from crumbled white cheese); *katak* (a very thick concentrated yoghurt, sometimes mixed with pepper); *snezhanka* (literally 'snow-white'), a mix of yoghurt, cucumber (pickled in winter) and dill; all accompanied by bread. Bulgarians like their cured meats too, such as *lukanka*, *sujuk*, *pastarma* and *elenski but*. A soup or *chorba* comes next – tripe is popular but vegetarian options include lentils or beans (*chorba bob*), or cold soup called *tarator* made from yoghurt, garlic and cucumber.

Main courses tend to be meaty, with pork or chicken and lamb in season, or meatballs like *kyufte* or *kebapche*. *Kavarma* is a slow-cooked meat stew, while *sarma* is stuffed leaves (either sour cabbage or vine leaves), filled with chopped meat or rice and herbs. *Gyuvech* is an earthenware vessel that gives its name to the stews cooked in it – vegetable or meat. A mixed grill called *meshaw skara* is also common. Bulgaria's version of moussaka is popular and in summer a dish called *mish-mash* with tomatoes, peppers, cheese and eggs is eaten. For non-meat eaters, fish is typically trout, unless you are close to the Black Sea, and grilled vegetables, especially courgettes, are always available. Stuffed peppers and aubergines appear too.

At Christmas, Bulgarians prepare a special meat dish in a clay pot. Called *kapama*, it consists of chopped sour cabbage with rice, wine and at least 3 different types of meat (usually fresh pork sausage, beef chops and chicken) and is cooked for 5 to 6 hours. For Easter and on 6 May (St George's Day, a national holiday) a roast lamb dish called *drob sarma* is typical (the lamb is baked for 5 to 6 hours with mint and usually stuffed with rice and chopped lamb's liver).

Bread is served at every meal. Special breads like *pogacha* are made from white flour and yeast; usually round, they are offered at ceremonies with salt and honey, while around Easter an egg-enriched bread called *kozunak* is baked.

Desserts include *baklava*, pumpkin stewed in sugar syrup and rosewater, and baked fruits such as apple or quince.

5

LOOKING AHEAD

Bulgarian wine in its current form is still a young industry, and while it has made considerable progress in recent years, there are still quite a few issues to address if it wants to regain status on the world market and to improve sales at home. There continues to be a huge gulf in Bulgaria between big and small producers, and this has become extremely political. It wasn't until after land restitution that the idea of a wine estate with vineyard and winery (as is the standard model in Western Europe) became possible, so it took time to develop. Today's industry includes giants like Power Brands and SIS industries which crush up to 40,000 tonnes of grapes alongside small wineries making just a few tens of tonnes (a tonne of grapes gives very roughly around 800 bottles of wine depending on winemaking and style). It is only once wineries have their own vineyards in a fixed location that it becomes in their interest to add value by communicating a sense of place in their wines. It also means stories about history and tradition become important so almost every winery tells tales of its links to Thracian culture and early days of wine in this territory.

UNITED FRONT

Another issue that is significant in Bulgarian wine is that of communication and cooperation. It takes time, and possibly a change of generation to shift attitudes from production-led to market-led. Biliana Marinova (Burgozone) points out: 'One of the specific problems we have to overcome is the intergenerational difference in approach concerning the role of the social media. For our parents, social media are not important nor worth investment as their impact is not easily measurable. For me and my sister however … they are key to the success of any middle sized winery and constitute the cheapest and most efficient means of communication'.

The wine world (and indeed the Bulgarian market) is already saturated, so communication is critical in creating a space for Bulgarian wine. In the past, producers have tended to rely on the government or the EU to fund wine promotions, but it would be better for them to commit to their own promotional activities. As Matt Kramer (*Wine Spectator*) said in December 2017, 'Ultimately it's the producers' responsibility. If you don't bang your own drum, then you can hardly expect others to do it for you.'

It is intellectually understandable that in a culture where people were forced to be collectivized they might want to go their own independent ways, and indeed see other wine producers as competition. As one winemaker, who prefers to stay anonymous, explained: 'The biggest problem we had at the time was our mentality, shaped in the communist era. That was a time which did not promote individuality and carried an all-encompassing envy of the success of others. This was a battle that we had to win ourselves and we still see it as a problem in society three decades later. There is a deficiency of good will in Bulgaria, people do not take on responsibility and never answer for their actions to anyone.' In export markets, competition is not the winery down the road, but producers in other countries, and Bulgaria could usefully learn from Australia, Austria and even Moldova, about presenting some sort of united front. Unfortunately, there is a huge gulf between the large wineries and the small ones, and neither side sees the other as playing fair. This is the area where government intervention could be useful in ensuring that everybody complies with the law, and that there is no fraudulent wine or unfair business practice going on in the industry.

There are signs that groups of like-minded wineries are starting to come together to benefit their own regions. The Bulgarian Association of Independent Wineries has brought some of these smaller wineries together in various events for export markets. And there are informal groups in places such as South Sakar. Tanya Avramova (Bratanov Winery) explains: 'We haven't yet established any official organization (in any case, it will be a non-profit association) though we have intentions. Otherwise we cooperate by presenting this micro-region together at exhibitions, festivals, in wine tourism brochures, etc. Being officially recognized will take probably years but we would like at least to create awareness of the region, its terroir and wines.'

The Plovdiv region recently produced Bulgaria's first wine route map, led by Krassimira Kodukova (Villa Yustina winery) who explains:

> As a relatively young wine cellar we are always looking for opportunities to develop wine tourism not only in our winery but as well as in the whole region. That is why in 2015 we decided to go straight to the Tourist Department of Plovdiv Municipality. This gave birth to the idea of creating a wine tourist map. It was not hard to convince the owners and managers of the wineries that if we want to achieve something, we have to work together. There were some wine cellars which refused to participate, but later they wanted to be included in the second edition of the map. We all know that if we collaborate, we will be more successful in every field.

Perhaps the most effective of all these regional programmes has been in the Melnik region.

THE MELNIK WINE ROUTES INITIATIVE

This is an exciting example of how Bulgarian producers can work together and use modern technology for greater impact. A map is available from the tourist office and some tour companies, and a Facebook page details all the producers in the region who are open for visits and wine tastings. It also shows the location of key tourist destinations such as the dramatic Melnik sand pyramids, the Kordopulov house (the largest Renaissance house in Bulgaria, with a lavish interior and an ancient wine cellar dug underneath it), the town of Melnik itself and historic sites at Sandanski and Heraclea-Sintica that offer something to tourists who want more than just wine. The region also is organizing joint events such as open cellars around the feast of St Trifon Zarezan, working with social media and tourism agencies to bring visitors.

Militza Zikatanova (organizer of the Melnik wine route map initiative) explains that the region is working hard on developing a PDO, which is likely to be called Melnik River. Producers here believe that the region's current PDO is not fit for purpose, but a new one will actually be useful as it will be based on research into soil and grape varieties. She comments, 'The process is quite long – we are almost done preparing the application. Once we submit the application, it will take three years of control by the EU and the state agency, until it eventually gets approved by EU regulators. The PDO will be defined by the location of the vineyards along the shores of the Melnik River and also by usage of indigenous grapes in the wines.' She adds that, 'we have agreed with the local Sandanski Professional Agricultural High School to include the education of professionals in topics related to winegrowing in the government-funded curriculum – vine growing, wine production, maintenance and operation of machines, etc. So if this gets approved, students in their last two years will be spending half their time working at the wineries and half taking related classes.'

So why is all this possible in the Melnik region? It's a compact and geographically distinct region with a long history and culture of winemaking and now has a respectable number of wineries that are geographically close together and, importantly, similar in outlook. The businessmen who have come back into wine in this region typically have fond memories of wine from their youth but have also travelled and become open-minded. The new modern wineries in the region are of comparable size and with similar market orientation: high quality wines with focus on indigenous grapes. They sell locally and strive for more exports. For the most part, the owners themselves are involved and therefore decision-making is quicker than in wineries where owners are absent working in other businesses as is the case in much of Bulgaria. This is a region that has gone from one winery 17 years ago, to 18 wineries today, of which seven are normally open to visitors. Food and wine culture in the region is improving, and it has gained Bulgaria's first Relais & Château hotel and restaurant at Zornitza.

BOTTOM SHELF BLUES

It is important to mention pricing here as many wineries are quite ambitious, but in a poor country the amount of spare cash that consumers have to spend on premium wine is limited. Bulgaria has the EU's lowest minimum wage at approximately €260 per month. However, quality costs no matter where in the world it is produced. While labour and land costs may be lower in Bulgaria, the cost of equipment such as barrels and winemaking technology is as high as anywhere in Europe. There are certain wines that have been priced to make a statement (retailing at the equivalent of €75–100), which then encourages other producers to also make expensive wines without stopping to think about who will buy them, how big the pool of potential consumers is, and how the market will react to them. It seems rare for producers to think beyond the vines and winery towards investing in marketing and PR. In global terms, Bulgaria needs to identify what its opportunities might be.

Looking to the future, Bulgaria is an increasingly popular tourist destination, and handled well these visitors can become ambassadors when they go home. Young people (really anyone under 40) don't remember the old days of Bulgarian wine as cheap glugging stuff. They see Eastern Europe as exotic, and ripe to be explored.

For me, having followed Bulgaria for around a quarter of a century, the country has come a long way from my earliest visits to that grim and rundown country still reeling from communism, complete with wine that was cheap and cheerful at best. Today, while there are still issues to overcome, this is a modern, dynamic and even exciting wine industry, at best making wines that can take their place on any shelf with pride.

6

GRAPE VARIETIES IN BULGARIA

Bulgarian vineyards are a fascinating mosaic of local and international varieties, with international varieties coming to dominate in the 1960s as part of the planned economy and Bulgaria's role as supplier of wine to Comecon. State policy was to raise Bulgaria to global world level, hence a preference for international grape varieties. This was strengthened in the 1980s by the pursuit of Western markets for whom buying wine labelled with a grape variety was a relative novelty, and an appealing way of demystifying wine.

It is often claimed that several of Bulgaria's local grape varieties like Pamid, Mavrud, Red Misket and Shiroka Melnishka Loza date back to the very early days of Bulgarian viticulture in Bulgaria's first kingdom (681–1018) or even back to the days of ancient Thrace. Unfortunately, there is little written evidence to support or refute this. However, it does appear that immediately after the phylloxera outbreak, local grapes were still dominant. In the 1930s, the magazine *Vine Review* claimed that Bulgaria was planted with Pamid at 46 per cent, Gamza 15 per cent, Misket 6.3 per cent, Cinsaut 2.5 per cent, Mavrud 0.5 per cent, Melnik 1 per cent and others 28.7 per cent.

Data on grape variety plantings in Bulgaria are not robust. What is available from the Executive Agency of Vine and Wine is based on EU returns from 2013 (see Appendix I). Merlot leads the way with 10,550 hectares, then Cabernet Sauvignon at 10,191 hectares. Pamid accounts for 6,029 hectares, followed by Rkatsiteli on 5,409 hectares. Red Misket covers 7 per cent of vineyards at 4,388 hectares, followed by

Muscat Ottonel with 4,136 hectares. Chardonnay appears next in the list at 3,416 hectares, then Dimiat with 2,869 hectares. Local Mavrud is grown on 1,362 hectares, followed by Syrah at 966 hectares, Shiroka Melnishka Loza on 957 hectares, Sauvignon Blanc on 954 hectares and Gamza with 855 hectares. Traminer is grown on 822 hectares while Ugni Blanc covers 699 hectares. Other whites make up 2,795 hectares and other reds 3,901 hectares, giving a total of 60,299 hectares.

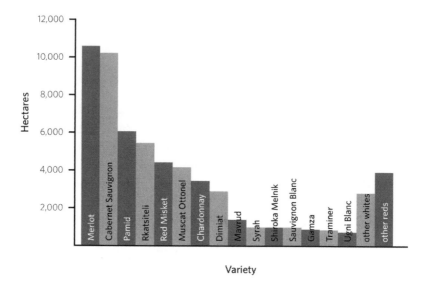

Bulgaria, grape varieties by area. Source 2013 EU Returns

There is a problem with these data though. While the total area is not too far out of line with the total vineyard area of 62,916 hectares declared by the Ministry of Agriculture Agrarian Report for 2016, the volume of vineyards actually harvested in 2016 was 36,551 hectares. It is therefore hard to work out from these statistics whether any of these grape varieties have been disproportionately abandoned.

LOCAL RED GRAPES

Bouquet/Buket

Described by Ogy Tzvetanov as a combination of 'beauty and the beast', this is a crossing of Pinot Noir and Mavrud, produced at the Pleven Institute in

1951. A cold-resistant variety ripening in the middle of September, it does not cope well with drought so is potentially more suited to the north and cooler zones in Bulgaria. It can produce well-coloured wines, with good tannins and acidity and a hint of black cherry. There are very few people making this commercially though Roychev claims there are around 197 hectares in the country and that its potential for quality means it should gain more attention.

Producers worth trying: Borovitza, Miroglio.

Evmolpia

A crossing of Mavrud and Merlot, this was not officially registered until 1991 and is grown on 57 hectares. It ripens about 30 days earlier than Mavrud and appears to tolerate lower winter temperatures too, meaning it may have potential in areas that are too cold for its parent. It can produce soft, juicy wines which are ready to drink early, and appears to benefit from a little blending to give it structure.

Producers worth trying: Borovitza

Mavrud

This ancient grape variety has long been known in Bulgaria's vineyards. It is late ripening and needs an area with a long growing season, requiring 176 days from bud burst to cropping. It is not very cold tolerant, and is susceptible to mildew, but is resistant to grey rot. It appears to be difficult to graft onto rootstocks that were common in the communist era which may have limited its spread, though modern viticulture appears to have solved this problem. The berries have thick skins, giving good colour and extract, and it also usefully retains high acidity. It can produce wines with good quality potential and ageability. However, it is a very fertile vine and easy to over-crop, so good vineyard management and limited yields are vital. It also accumulates sugar quickly in very warm regions, ahead of flavour ripeness (also limiting where it can be grown well) and potentially leading to unbalanced wines.

It can be very versatile in winemaking, making white, pink and red wines, with or without oak. Traditionally the grapes have been dried before vinification to concentrate flavours, a technique which has been revived by Zagreus winery. In a previous era, Mavrud was used for making sparkling wines. As Ognyan Tzvetanov explained:

Little do people today know that while the state-owned 'Sparkling Wine Factory' in Chirpan was in operation (until the early 90s), Mavrud was used primarily for the production of base wine for the (white) sparklers (sometimes up to 40 per cent of the blend). The then general manager of Vinprom (Stoyan Kinderkov, an iconic person in Bulgarian wine) and the production manager (Hristo Dermendjiev, the most intelligent person in the Bulgarian wine industry) knew the potential of Mavrud, at least Mavrud grown in the conditions then. The grapes were whole-bunch pressed and they never had a pinking problem to decolourize!

Adriana Srebrinova also mentions that when she worked for Perushtitsa, they used to produce about 1.5 million bottles per year of red sparkling from 100 per cent Mavrud. Today Mavrud is most often seen as a dry and full-bodied red wine, though there are also some successful blends and rosés.

Producers worth trying: Bratanov, Dragomir, Katarzyna, Maxxima, Medi Valley, Miroglio, Neragora, Rumelia, Terra Tangra, Villa Melnik, Zagreus.

Melnik 55

This is also known as the early vine of Melnik, Ranna Melnishka Loza or Early Melnik. Bulgarian grapevine researchers in the communist era were enthusiastic crossers of vines, usually combining a local variety with an international one. Here Shiroka Melnishka Loza was crossed with a mixture of pollen from three different grape varieties, Durif, Jurançon and Valdiguié, but DNA analysis has subsequently shown that the second parent was in fact just Valdiguié. In 1977, it was approved as a new grape variety, and it was first vinified as a commercial wine at Damianitza by Stoycho Stoev. It ripens earlier than its parent by about 15 days and is a very fruitful variety with good yield.

It has increased in popularity and is now being grown on 254 hectares. It suffers from mildew but is resistant to grey rot and can tolerate low winter temperatures, so it may have possibilities in other parts of the country. While there have been some trial plantings there has been no commercial success so far. It gives richer, juicier fruit flavours and deeper colour than its parent Shiroka Melnik and offers earlier drinkability along with slightly softer tannins and acidity. There is also a Melnik 82 produced in 1963 by a similar cross and also identified as offspring of Valdiguié, now planted on 40 hectares, but not commercialized.

Producers worth trying: Logodaj, Medi Valley, Orbelia, Rupel, Villa Melnik, Zlaten Rozhen.

Melnik 1300

Also known as Melnik Jubilee. It was created in 1963 but renamed in 1981 for the 1,300-year celebration of Bulgaria as a nation. Shiroka Melnishka Loza is one parent and the Georgian variety Saperavi is the other. It's relatively rare (just 8 hectares) but looks promising for production of quality wines.

Producer worth trying: Villa Melnik.

Melnishki Rubin

This is another rare offspring of Shiroka Melnishka Loza. The official story is that it was created as a cross with Cabernet Sauvignon, though inconveniently, genetic analysis does not uphold this theory, and the other real parent remains unknown. It's not related to the other Rubin. There are around 14 hectares planted and it's regarded as having quality potential in warmer areas.

Producers worth trying: Zlaten Rozhen (in a blend with Melnik 55).

Pamid

This appears to be a genuinely local and historic grape variety as there are at least five biotypes to be found in Bulgaria. In Professor Roychev's 2012 Ampelography, he says that it is believed to date back to ancient Thracian times. It is widely grown but rarely seen in wines with aspirations for quality and Roychev describes it as only suitable for table wines for mass consumption. It is cold tolerant, high yielding and quite resistant to grey rot. However, it is pale in colour, gives low levels of extract and has low acidity, making pale red wines that need to be drunk quickly. It is most useful for making young drinking rosé. It is also found in Romania under the name Roșioară.

Rubin

This is the more widespread grape called Rubin (grown on just over 200 hectares according to Roychev's Ampelography). Unusually for Bulgaria, where grapevine breeding typically crossed a local grape variety with an international one, this is a cross of two European grapes, neither of which was present in Bulgaria at the time. There is a speculative rumour that one of the researchers had an Italian girlfriend who was the inspiration. It was created in 1944 at the Pleven Research Institute by crossing Nebbiolo and Syrah and was approved in 1961. Opinions vary about this grape variety; Logodaj and Dragomir believe that it has the best potential to be a flagship red variety for Bulgaria, while others maintain that its ageability is unproven. For Konstantin Stoev at Dragomir, between Mavrud and Rubin the latter is the better grape, 'You have to work much harder with Mavrud to get the same quality as Rubin,' he explains. It ripens mid-season, producing very dark and often quite tannic red wines. It contains 50 per cent more anthocyanins than Cabernet Sauvignon and accumulates high sugar levels as well as having moderate acidity. It's not very cold or disease tolerant, limiting its growing range.

Producers worth trying: Bendida, Dragomir, Logodaj, Medi Valley, Rossidi, Santa Sarah, Terra Tangra, Yalovo.

Ruen

Another rare variety, only grown on approximately 12 hectares in the whole country, all in the Struma Valley. It's a cross of Cabernet Sauvignon with Shiroka Melnishka Loza produced in 1951 and registered in 1964. It produces strongly flavoured and slightly rustic deep reds in the Melnik region, and sometimes appears in blends.

Producers worth trying: Damianitza, Villa Melnik.

Shevka

An old local variety with a famous name among Bulgarian grapes – Shevka was also the name of one of the state Vinprom wineries, which subsequently became Vini Sliven. Although not grown for commercial winemaking today, Roychev reckons there are 266 hectares of it, confined to small, private vineyards mainly around Sliven. It is particularly tolerant of dry and barren soils so may be useful if drought becomes a regular threat in Bulgarian conditions.

Shiroka Melnishka Loza

Often called Shiroka Melnik or Melnik for short, its name means 'broad-leafed vine of Melnik'. This is another ancient grape variety that is – more or less – restricted to the Struma Valley. There are records of wine merchants from Dubrovnik buying this grape and exporting it to Venice in the Middle Ages. It was also rumoured to be a great favourite of Winston Churchill, who is supposed to have ordered 500 litres for his personal cellar. It is a late ripening grape, needing 175 days from bud burst to harvest, usually in mid-October. It only grows in the Struma region and no-one is quite sure why. It certainly seems to need the summer heat in what is Bulgaria's warmest region (active heat summation here is over 4,000°C) and it doesn't ripen adequately in other regions. Winters are relatively mild here as the valley opens to the Aegean Sea, 100 kilometres to the south, which may also be a factor as this vine does not tolerate winter cold.

This grape variety ripens to high potential alcohol while retaining good acidity. The skins are rich in extract, and red wines made from this grape can be high quality, typically full-bodied and tannic, with brick-red colouring and good ageing potential. There is something Nebbiolo-like in the style of Shiroka Melnik: as young wines they can be quite hard work to enjoy. Perhaps this characteristic does not appeal to today's wine drinker, so many wineries in the region are experimenting with different winemaking approaches and blends. It also makes successful rosés and is even being used to make both white and pink bottle-fermented wines, notably at Logodaj. There is also a tradition of drying the grapes to make sweet wines and fortified port-style wines.

Producers worth trying: Damianitza, Logodaj, Orbelia, Orbelus, Villa Melnik.

Storgozia
This rarely seen cross of Bouquet and Villard Blanc was bred in a programme to develop strong fungal resistance.

INTERNATIONAL RED GRAPES

Cabernet Franc
As in southern Hungary, Cabernet Franc is starting to prove its mettle in Bulgaria. It is more resistant to over-ripeness than Merlot and keeps more moderate alcohol levels and fresher acidity. It is appearing both in Bordeaux blends and as a single varietal wine.

Producers worth trying: Angel's Estate, Bratanov, Eolis, Damianitza, Gulbanis, Korten, Midalidare, Minkov, Miroglio, Salla Estate, Villa Yustina, Zlaten Rozhen.

Cabernet Sauvignon

Bulgaria's second most planted red grape is the grape that made the country's name in Western markets, starting in the 1980s, when Bulgaria was one of the world's biggest producers of Cabernet Sauvignon. Undoubtedly the grape produces good results in Bulgaria's growing conditions, though currently very few of the quality-conscious producers are offering varietal Cabernet Sauvignon, preferring to focus on its role in blends.

Producers worth trying: Angel's Estate, Domaine Boyar, Miroglio, Rousse Wine House, Santa Sarah, Svishtov, Villa Melnik

Gamza

Also known as Kadarka in Hungary and Cadarcă in Romania, according to current knowledge this grape probably originated around Lake Ska-dar in Montenegro, though a possible parent–offspring relationship with Papaskarasi has recently been identified. It's practically a local grape in Bulgaria as there is more grown here than anywhere else in the world. Local producers insist that the variants grown in Bulgaria are distinct from those of other countries so researchers such as Stanimir Stoyanov (head of the Oenologist's Union) have been working with a nursery in Greece to try and identify the best Bulgarian clones. And at Burgozone, they have selected material from the Pleven institute and sent it to Germany to be multiplied, before planting. In the communist era, it was often grafted onto the vigorous, late ripening rootstock SO4, which is not helpful with an already late variety like Gamza.

The name Gamza is apparently Arabic in origin and means 'a capricious woman', which gives a clue to its nature. It can yield very generously but has thin and fragile skins and is prone to grey rot, so needs an airy, hilly location and swift picking once autumn rains arrive. Its wines are often quite delicate, producing pale, raspberry-scented and sometimes spicy wines with light tannins. It's generally viewed as a wine to be vinified for simple fruit and early consumption. However, with low yields and the right handling and judicious use of oak (not new) it can produce serious and elegant wines in the mould of Pinot Noir, and is at least as tricky to handle as this variety. It is perhaps overdue for a new focus (as is happening in Hungary).

Producers worth trying: Borovitza, Lovico.

GAMZA TALES

At Borovitza winery, there are several versions of Gamza. One day Ogy told the tale of the intriguingly named Borovitza Gamza 'Black Pack':

It comes from a vineyard aged between 27 and 45 years, which we liked very much because of the quality of the grapes. When we first made this wine, we had to decide quickly if we would buy the grapes or not. There was no time to truck plastic cases from Borovitza so we bought plastic bags from the local shop. These bags turned out to be only black like garbage bags and when we asked for a 'normal, transparent' bags, the locals with beer in hand laughed at us. We were curious and asked what was wrong with the normal bags and one of them said, 'No one in his right mind here will offer transparent bags, you can see what is in the bag!' We agreed but it was a compromise, the grapes were so beautiful. Gamza is typically drunk young, as the people in the past needed their vats empty before the next harvest. But this one deserved more, and we put it in American and Bulgarian oak barrels for ageing. The intention was to obtain a wine which could eventually age well, contrary to the general wisdom in the region.

Merlot

Merlot is well-known and popular within Bulgaria, both as a varietal wine and in blends, though it can suffer from over-ripeness.

Producers worth trying: Angel's Estate, Bratanov, Katarzyna, Korten, Logodaj, Medi Valley, Rumelia, Stratsin, Santa Sarah, Svishtov, Villa Yambol Kabile.

Pinot Noir

Bulgaria's domestic market still largely associates quality in red wines with deep, intense colour, robust tannins, structure and generous oak. This means paler, more Burgundian styles of Pinot Noir are relatively hard to sell. Wines that do well domestically tend to have deep colour and spicy, jammy fruit, with more tannins and extract than would be typical in cooler climates. Lighter, more elegant red Pinot Noirs can be found though, particularly from the cooler north of the country close to the Danube. Pinot Noir is also becoming popular for rosé wines and for the growing market in 'traditional method' bottle-fermented sparkling wines.

Producers worth trying: Better Half, Borovitza, Burgozone, Miroglio, Rossidi, Rousse Wine House, Salla Estate, Tsarev Brod, Varna Winery, Villa Yustina, Zelanos Winery.

Syrah

A recent arrival in Bulgaria, this variety seems to suit the relatively warm growing conditions particularly found in the south of the country. Wines are usually labelled Syrah rather than Shiraz, though both options are seen.

Producers worth trying: Bessa Valley, Bratanov, Eolis, Katarzyna, Korten, Logodaj, Medi Valley, Midalidare, Rossidi, Villa Melnik, Yamantiev's Villa Armira, Zagreus, Villa Yambol Kabile.

The rest of the reds

The list of other international grape varieties in Bulgaria today is quite long. Grapes in commercial production include: Sangiovese, Nebbiolo, Malbec, Petit Verdot, Saperavi, Carménère, Gamay, Caladoc, Marselan, Mourvèdre, Regent, Dornfelder, Grenache, Alicante Bouschet, Tempranillo and almost certainly others.

LOCAL WHITE GRAPES

While white varieties account for less than 40 per cent of Bulgaria's vineyard plantings, market demand appears to be growing, so many producers are seeking out quality local white grapes or trying to add value to the better-known varieties. Bulgaria still lacks a native white grape with the credibility and quality potential of its native reds. In 2016, 11,631 hectares of white varieties were harvested compared to 22,911 hectares of red grapes.

Dimiat/Dimyat

This is also known in Serbia as Smederevka. The parentage of this grape variety has recently been discovered and it turns out to be a cross of

Coarnă Albă, a Moldovan table grape that was widespread in the Balkans, with Heunisch Weiss (synonym Gouais Blanc) making it a half sibling of famous grapes like Chardonnay, Furmint and Gamay among others. No one knows when it first appeared, though it is likely to have been at around the same time as its more famous relatives, in other words some-time in the Middle Ages, after Heunisch Weiss appeared. This would mean tales of its origins dating back to Thracian times are unlikely, nor does it seem likely that it came from Egypt with the Greeks as some writ-ers have claimed. It was the predominant variety in Bulgaria until the 1960s and is in character a fairly neutral grape that retains good acidity. High yielding, it is grown widely but is particularly typical for the Black Sea coast around Varna and Bourgas, and the sub-Balkan region. It is late-ripening, but susceptible to winter cold, so is not usually grown in the far north. It is usually used for the production of dry wines but can also be used for sparkling wines and *rakia*, and has been popular in the past for making brandy. Some producers are working to improve both quality and common perceptions, either using it in blends, experimenting with oak ageing, or using extended skin maceration to make orange wines.

Producers worth trying: Dragomir Sarva (with Chardonnay), Maryan, Yalovo, Via Vinera Karabunar.

Gergana

Produced relatively recently, in 1972, not much is yet known about the viticultural characteristics of this cross of Muscat Ottonel and Dimiat. It is produced commercially by only one winery, Tsarev Brod, and grown in very small areas around Varna. It can also be used for fresh grapes or distillation. The winemaker reports that it has big bunches and large grapes and the challenge is to make it not too aromatic. It has good weight and texture, rose petal aromas and fresh acidity.

Producers worth trying: Tsarev Brod.

Keratsuda

This rare white grape is apparently native to the Struma Valley, where there are around 81 hectares. It possibly fell out of favour in the communist era as it needs to be bush-trained. It also doesn't ripen easily, and when it does, it has unusually low acidity and is prone to oxidation, making it difficult to vinify. As a unique local variety, a few wineries are experimenting with it, such as Nikola Zikatanov of Villa Melnik, though efforts have been frustrated by the unreliability of Bulgarian vine nurseries (a batch he planted turned out to be only 25 per cent Keratsuda). He believes that orange wine with extended skin maceration may be the best way to handle this grape, to give structure to compensate for its lack of acidity.

Misket Cherven

Also known as Red Misket. Other synonyms include Karlovski Misket and Sungurlarski Misket. Confusingly there is another grape called Misket Sungurlarski, created by the crossing of Misket Cherven x Sauvignon Blanc in 1966 and grown on 126 hectares around Sungurlare. Misket Cherven is believed to be a very old Bulgarian variety and the name 'cherven' (meaning red) is due to its pink-coloured skin. It's very rare in any other country and there are no known foreign synonyms. Genetic analysis has found a parent-offspring relationship with an obscure Hungarian variety called Beregi Rozsa, but nothing else is known about its origins. It is found all over the country but predominantly around Bourgas, Plovdiv, Varna, Schumen and Stara Zagora. It is late ripening but appears to resist frost damage well and only produces high quality fruit if yields are restricted. Used to produce delicately grapey white wines, it doesn't accumulate high sugar and has balanced acidity at best. It is prone to oxidation and because of the relatively low acid level some producers blend it with grape varieties with better acidity. It doesn't suit vinification in oak, and wines are generally consumed young. A few producers are trying to make a more serious style with this grape by vinifying it as an orange wine with extended skin contact.

Producers worth trying: Château Copsa, Vinex Slavyantsi, Via Vinera Karabunar, Yalovo, Zelanos.

Misket Kailashki

This 1976 crossing of Muscat Hamburg and Villard Blanc was an attempt to make a fungal-disease resistant white grape. Produced under the brand 'Flowerface' by Gulbanis winery, it has grassy and citrusy characters, green fruit flavours and fresh acidity even at ripeness levels of 14% abv.

Producer worth trying: Gulbanis

Sandanski Misket

A cross produced in 1963 from Shiroka Melnishka Loza and Tamjanka (also known as Muscat à Petit Grains). There are around 67 hectares in the Struma Valley, but it is growing in popularity. It ripens mid-season needing 159 days from bud burst to harvest, and accumulates up to 25 grammes per litre of sugar, while keeping balanced acidity. It produces appealing, grapey aromatic wines but the moderate acidity suggests that it should be drunk young.

Producers worth trying: Orbelia, Orbelus, Via Verde, Zlaten Rozhen.

Varnenski Misket

This is a Bulgarian grape variety produced by crossing Dimiat and Riesling in 1951, registered in 1971 and planted on around 371 hectares. It is a late-ripening, fertile and vigorous vine variety, particularly associated with the Black Sea region around Varna. It has understated varietal aromas, but fine, crisp acidity, and does best in cooler areas. In warm zones, it reaches high sugar levels, making it better for liqueur wines or distillates.

Producers worth trying: Stara Oryahovo, Varna Winery

Vinenka

A historic local variety not in commercial production, it is grown on just 17.4 hectares in the north and north-east of the country, according to Roychev's Ampelography. It is reported to be late ripening and susceptible to both winter cold and fungal diseases. Arguably the real reason it has virtually disappeared is that it only achieves very low sugar levels and retains very high acidity. Roychev suggests that it could be useful in sparkling wine base or in blends with Misket Cherven to compensate for that variety's low acidity.

Vrachanski Misket

Misket is a common name among Bulgarian grapes though most are not related to each other. This is claimed to be an old Bulgarian variety typical of the north-west around Vidin, Vratsa and Montana. However, DNA analysis has revealed that it is synonymous with a Hungarian variety called Pecsi Szagos which turns out to be a cross of Coarnă Albă x Muscat à Petit Grains (so a half-sibling of Dimiat too). It's typical of this region of

Bulgaria and produces floral, grapey and quite low-acid white wines for drinking young.

Producers worth trying: Magura, Rousse Wine House, Salla Estate, Stara Oryahovo.

INTERNATIONAL WHITE GRAPES

Chardonnay

A grape that really needs no further description is possibly Bulgaria's best white hope for quality wines, at least today. It grows widely and there are examples of good and even fine Chardonnay from all over the country, made both with and without oak (though the local market appears to prefer more obvious oak than is the global trend).

Producers worth trying: Angel's Estate, Better Half, Borovitza, Bratanov, Domaine Boyar, Dragomir, Logodaj, Miroglio Elenovo, Preslav Rubaiyat, Medi Valley, Rossidi, Rousse Wine House, Svishtov, Varbanov, Villa Melnik, Yamantiev's, Zelanos.

Muscat Ottonel

This is the most popular Muscat in Bulgaria, a French-made cross of Chasselas and Ingram's Muscat. It copes with colder winter temperatures than Muscat à Petit Grains and makes grapey but more textured wines. Very popular in the domestic market.

Producers worth trying: Château Copsa (Stradivarius blend), Miroglio.

Rkatsiteli

A Georgian grape, this became hugely popular in the communist era for its high yields and ability to cope with the high-cordon trellising introduced during that period. It also retains high acidity which made it useful for distillation. It spread rapidly after 1953 and by 1981 was reported in Roychev's Ampelography as covering 47 per cent of all Bulgaria's vineyards, falling back to 9 per cent today. It is late ripening (168 days from budburst to harvest) and has good tolerance of winter cold, but not drought. It has typically high acid levels (especially malic acid) and generally neutral flavours, especially at high yields, and is susceptible to oxidation. Today it is rarely vinified by quality wine producers though occasionally appears in blends for acidity. An exception is Borovitza's Cuvée Bella Rada produced from 50-year-old vines and vinified in barrel.

Producer worth trying: Borovitza.

Sauvignon Blanc

Sauvignon Blanc is incredibly trendy all over the world, and Bulgaria is no exception. It is produced here in two styles. The first is aromatic and crisp in an attempt to mimic New Zealand Sauvignon Blanc, though this is difficult to achieve in much of Bulgaria because the climate is simply too warm. Because of this, many producers focus on a more tropical, more textured, less aromatic style.

Producers worth trying: Burgozone, Better Half, Maryan, Midalidare, Santa Sarah, Stratsin, Svishtov, Terra Tangra, Tohun, Varna Winery, Zelanos Winery.

Tamjanka/Tamianka

Although once thought to be a truly local Muscat relative, DNA analysis shows that this is actually Muscat à Petit Grains. It produces finer Muscat wines than its Ottonel cousin but is less tolerant of winter cold. South Sakar appears to suit it.

Producers worth trying: Bratanov, Gulbanis (Moscato), Ruppel.

Traminer/Gewürztraminer

Usually simply labelled Traminer, but better known internationally as Gewürztraminer, this is popular in the domestic market as a dry to off-dry white, and particularly famous from LVK Targovishte. Boutique producer Rossidi produced an impressive orange Gewürztraminer in 2016 and 2017 with 30 days on skins.

Producers worth trying: Bononia, Medi Valley, Miroglio, Rossidi, Villa Yustina.

The rest of the whites

There are good examples of Riesling (Better Half, Vinex Preslav, Salla Estate, Minkov Brothers, Tsarev Brod, Varna), Pinot Gris (Zelanos, Varna

Winery), Vermentino (Alexandra Estate, Better Half), Viognier (Burgozone, Damianitza, Medi Valley, Yamantiev's), Marsanne, Roussanne (Borovitza MRV) and almost certainly others that don't appear in available statistics.

THE BLEND STORY

Bulgarians are most proud of their red wines, and the wines that receive the highest praise are often blends. In style, they are usually concentrated, with generous use of oak, though it's encouraging to see more focus in recent years on less extreme alcohol levels, with better balanced acidity and more judicious use of oak. For instance, wineries are switching to fermentation in oak barrels on rollers, using a lower proportion of new oak and working with larger-sized barrels. While many of these wines will benefit from several years of ageing before opening the bottle, the resulting wines still have better drinkability than some of the earlier versions from the mid-2000s.

There are several contributing factors to this change. The first is that the young vine problem of the early to mid-2000s is now solving itself, with a closer match between sugar ripeness and physiological or flavour ripeness. The second is that today's producers also have better understanding of their vineyards. This means they are starting to rein back on sheer power and look for elegance and finesse, which also means better harmony. Third is the question of oak use. It appears that the local market enjoys the specific flavour of new oak, but all over the world the trend is towards reducing these flavours and using oak as a polish and seasoning rather than as a dominant ingredient. Bulgarian oak cooperage is still not up to the standards of the best French barrels, so the latter dominate with quality producers.

There is also now a track record of ageability, as some of Bulgaria's more iconic wine labels have been made for long enough to show that they can age with grace. More mature wines from producers like Bessa Valley, Borovitza, Santa Sarah, Domaine Boyar, Vinex Preslav and Miroglio all show that some of Bulgaria's leading wines can keep well for at least a decade. This is a crucial step in demonstrating that this is a country that can produce fine wine rather than just good wine.

At the time of writing, many of Bulgaria's best and most ambitious wines are blends (mostly variations on a theme of Bordeaux blends), but this is also a dynamic industry that is still free from onerous restrictions. Many producers are experimenting freely, with what appear to be distinctly non-traditional choices that often work surprisingly well. Producers listed have a track record over more than one vintage, while other names are not yet established enough to highlight, though some will be bright stars for the future.

Blends worth trying (alphabetical order by producer): Bessa Valley Grande Cuvée (previously BV), Bessa Valley Reserva, Better Half Zmeevo (Cabernet Franc, Cabernet Sauvignon, Syrah), Borovitza Dux, Borovitza Sensum, Castra Rubra Butterfly's Rock, Damianitza Kometa, Damianitza ReDark, Domaine Boyar Suprême Grande Cuvée, Dragomir Reserva, Dragomir Pitos, Katarzyna Reserve, Korten Grand Vintage, Maryan Reserve, Medi Valley Incanto Black, Midalidare Mogilovo Village, Minkov Brothers Oak Tree, Miroglio Soli Invicto, Preslav Rubaiyat Red, Rumelia Erelia, Santa Sarah Privat, Terra Tangra Roto, Villa Melnik Hailstorm, Villa Yustina Special Reserve, Yamantiev's Marble Land Red.

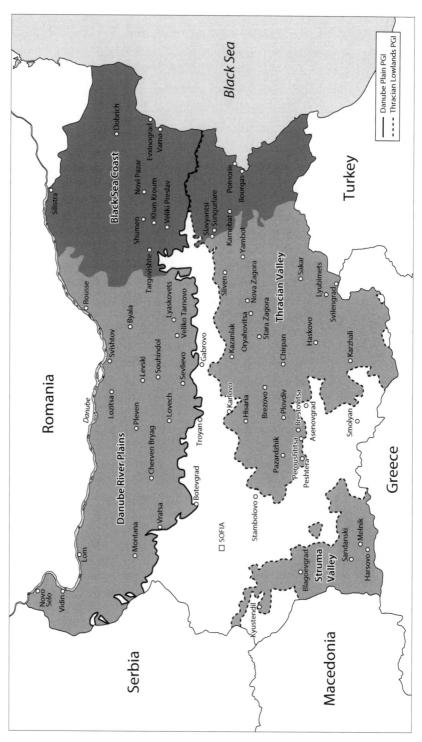

Bulgaria's main wine regions and PGIs (information courtesy of NWC)

7

BULGARIAN WINE REGIONS

GEOGRAPHY AND CLIMATE

Bulgaria is a small country, just 450 kilometres/280 miles from the western border to the Black Sea and 300 kilometres/200 miles from Romania in the north to Greece and Turkey in the south. With the exception of the Stara Planina mountain range, which runs from east to west, and the environs of the capital Sofia, vines are planted all over the country. The modern wine industry has been based largely on rolling fertile flatlands, with rather few steep locations, and vineyards lie mainly between 100 and 300 metres in altitude, although some south-western vineyards are as high as 600 metres.

The climate tends to be dramatically continental, with hot summers reaching temperatures of up to 40°C, while the temperature can fall to −25°C in winter (which means risk of freezing damage, and even killing vines, so protective measures like earthing up are required). The Black Sea has a moderating effect on the eastern side of the country, while the Aegean Sea has the same effect on the south-west.

The most common viticultural hazards are fungal diseases caused by humidity. In non-drought years rainfall and warm temperatures combine to promote rot and both sorts of mildew. The *Phytoplasma* disease, grapevine yellows, has occasionally been mentioned as a concern in recent years, but does not appear to be causing an economic impact yet. Irrigation has so far not been generally necessary, though increasingly water shortages mean that new vineyards are being planned with access to irrigation, including construction of ponds or dams to store water.

VINEYARD STATISTICS

Ministry of Agriculture, Food and Forestry (MAFF) data show that total vineyard area in Bulgaria has declined significantly in the past ten years. In 2006, total vineyard area was 128,857 hectares, of which 43,537 had been abandoned leaving 85,320 hectares in production. In 2016, a decade later, total vineyard area was 62,916 hectares with 12,024 hectares abandoned and 50,892 hectares in agricultural holdings. Of these, 36,551 hectares were harvested in 2016. Unharvested areas include 791 hectares of young vines as well as fragmented and neglected plots.

White grape varieties account for about 32 per cent of the vineyards, table grapes are approximately 6 per cent and black varieties account for 62 per cent. White varieties only dominate in the north-eastern Black Sea region. Average yields for the whole country in 2016 were 5.8 tonnes per hectare, a fall of 14 per cent compared to 2015. Yields for white grapes are significantly higher than for red, given that total production of white wine is slightly higher at 608,285 hectolitres than red and rosé at 599,500 hectolitres.

REGIONAL DESIGNATIONS

Explaining Bulgaria's wine regions is not simple. Two protected geographical indications (PGI) and 52 protected designations of origin (PDO) are recognized by the European Union. Only Spain, Italy and France have more PDOs, though they also have considerably bigger wine industries than Bulgaria. The introduction of just two PGIs remains controversial. The decision was taken at a general meeting of the National Vine and Wine Chamber, where some large producers were even lobbying for a single PGI for the whole country. It appears to have been driven by the needs of large wineries who were used to sourcing their grapes from all over the country and it certainly did not have a basis in any scientific research. From the mid-nineties onwards, the viticultural chaos that was created by the process of land restitution meant that wineries were often struggling to source enough grapes. For large wineries that did not own vineyards, the ability to continue to source fruit wherever they could get it was important so they lobbied hard for these very large PGIs. Today PGI wines account for 30 per cent of production but each region is so big as to be virtually meaningless in indicating any specific regional characteristics. The northern PGI called the Danube Plain stretches from the far north-west of Bulgaria on the Serbian border around Vidin all the way to the Black Sea coast. Similarly, the southern PGI called Thracian Lowlands encompasses regions as diverse as the Struma Valley in the south-west all the way across the country to the southern Black Sea coast.

Of the 52 PDOs (See Appendix I), many are not used at all; it is rare to see a PDO on a wine label. One source reckons that only 5 or 6 are in use, so it seems clear that the current legislation is not fit for purpose. The point of a PDO system is to protect products with a specific geographical origin, and thus implied quality, that gives them additional value and therefore premium status. In Bulgaria, it is still the case that the brand name of the producer has the most value today. Looking to the future, Bulgaria really needs to invest in research into specific microzones for higher quality, PDO wines. Indeed, in the early 1990s there was a project under Professor Kiril Popov, jointly funded by the EU, that conducted trials into microzones, but there was no further funding after the pilot stage.

To illustrate how insignificant PDO wine is in Bulgaria, statistics for the 2016 harvest show that 2,212 hectolitres of white wine (0.4 per cent of whites) and 7,299 hectolitres of red wine (1.2 per cent of reds) were being produced with a PDO declaration, less than 1 per cent overall. The total harvest for that vintage was 1,207,785 hectolitres produced by commercial companies. Within that, PGI wines amounted to 135,344 hectolitres of white wine and 225,640 hectolitres of red and rosé wines, so table wines account for close to 70 per cent of production. Data from MAFF also show a further 26,765 tonnes of grapes destined for non-commercial wine production outside so-called 'industrial facilities'. This is a category that would include home-made wine and wine sold in bulk at rural restaurants and bars.

The old regions renewed?

Prior to the introduction of the current PGIs and PDOs to comply with EU regulations ahead of accession in 2007, Bulgaria was divided into four regions, with one notable sub-region, the Sub-Balkan region or Valley of the Roses. Today, most producers and writers still refer to these old regions because they reflect clearly recognizable differences. The divisions were the result of detailed assessments carried out in the 1950s and 1960s, based on climatic and geographical differences. There is talk within the wine industry bureaucracy and among producers about returning to a more divided system, but as ever the wheels of law-making turn slowly and no one is quite sure when this might happen. The latest map and information from the National Vine and Wine Chamber (NVWC), which is Bulgaria's competent body for the wine industry, divides the country into four viticulture and winemaking regions. These are close to the old regions which were written into law in 1978 but not exactly the same. These regions also do not exactly reflect the split of Bulgaria into just two PGI regions as part of the eastern (Black Sea region) would fall into the Danube Plain PGI and part would fall into the Thracian Lowlands PGI.

Just to confuse matters further, from an administrative point of view there are six wine regions used in the statistics produced by the Executive Agency for Vine and Wine. These administrative regions are north-west, north central, north-east, south-east, south-west, and south central.

Over recent years, Bulgarian wine has lost its once strong position in many key export markets and, if the country wants to be recognized on the global wine stage again, she needs to be producing wines that have something unique about them, supported by formal classifications that recognize and support this. In other words, something that makes them stand out and justify their place – a unique signature of Bulgaria if you like, or even a sense of 'terroir'. Otherwise the wines will just be copies and buyers may as well seek out the originals.

Northern viticultural region

This region is located on the Danube plain, lying between the Balkan Mountains to the south and west, and the Danube River to the north. The climate is continental, with high summer temperatures, frequent drought and relatively cold winters, occasionally seeing extremely low temperatures with risk of frost damage to vines.

Climatic parameters of the northern viticultural region

Active heat summation	3,500–3,980°C
Vegetative period	200–210 days
Frost-free period	82–213 days

Spring frost frequency	5–20 per cent
Growing season start	5–15 April
Growing season end	15–25 October
Lowest winter temperature	-18 to -25°C (approx. 1 year out of 5)
Annual rainfall	530–350 millimetres

Soils in the region are chalky/limestone to chernozem (fertile black soil, rich in humus). There are loess soils (silt-based sediments) in the valleys and hills along the Danube River, and grey soils at the foot of the mountains. Grapevine roots can grow deep and have good nutrition, water availability and air movement. In winter, the inflow of frigid air masses from the north can lead to a risk of frost damage across all grape varieties.

Eastern viticultural region

This is located along the Black Sea coast. To the north, it reaches the border with Romania and to the south, the border with Turkey. In the northern part, the Black Sea strongly influences around 100 to 120 kilometres of the coastline. Its influence in the southern part of the region is partly limited by the low mountain ranges of Sakar and Strandzha. However, the Black Sea is the key climatic influence in the region, making the winters mild and moderating summer temperature. The effect is lower summer temperatures with higher atmospheric humidity compared to regions further inland.

Climatic parameters of the eastern viticultural region

Active heat summation	3,500–4,000° C
Vegetative period	200–218 days
Frost-free period	198–250 days
Bud burst	around 20 April
End of vegetation	mid-September
Spring frost frequency	very rare
Lowest winter temperature	-12 to -16°C
Annual rainfall	469–633 millimetres

The soils in the region include black soils and brown forest soils, with a deep rootzone, good water supply and good nutrient availability. This is the only region dominated by white grape varieties though there are sub-regions that are suitable for red grapes.

Southern viticultural region

This region encompasses both the Thracian Plain and the Sub-Balkan zone. This is also known as the Valley of the Roses – a spectacular site when the rose fields are in flower. Bulgaria produces up to 85 per cent of the world's rose oil. It covers land between the Balkan Mountains to the north and the Rhodope mountains to the west and south-west, with the Strandzha mountains to the east. The climate here is continental, with very hot and dry summers and relatively mild winters. Key climatic indicators are shown in the table below. The soils are typically brown forest soils, however in the mountains there are also limestone and alluvial soils. The rootzone is moderately deep, with good nutrition and water availability. This region is best known for the production of red wines, though the Sub-Balkan zone close to the mountains is known particularly for white grape varieties.

Climatic parameters of the southern viticultural region

Active heat summation	3,500–4,000°C
Vegetative period	180– 200 days
Frost-free period	202–220 days
Bud burst	around 5 April
End of vegetation	around 4 November
Spring frost frequency	once every 5–10 years
Lowest winter temperature	-14 to -16°C
Annual rainfall	534–653 millimetres

South-western viticultural region

This region covers land along the valleys of the Struma and Mesta rivers. The climate is temperate Mediterranean and quite distinct from the rest of Bulgaria. The river valleys of this region open towards the Aegean Sea, allowing warm air masses to penetrate, which means long warm autumns followed by a relatively mild winter.

Climatic parameters of the south-western viticultural region

Active heat summation	> 4,000°C
Vegetative period	over 220 days
Frost-free period	230 days
Bud burst	1–5 April
Spring frosts frequency	rare
Average winter temperature	2.5°C
Lowest winter temperature	-15° C
Annual rainfall	500–550 millimetres

The main soil types in the region are brown forest and alluvial soils, with sand in some areas. The rootzone is quite shallow, and vines can suffer from poor availability of nutrients and water.

8

BULGARIAN PRODUCER PROFILES

The wine scene in Bulgaria continues to evolve rapidly. There were 263 wineries in 2017, with more launching every year. Many of the historic former Vinprom wineries have reinvented themselves as private companies with greater or lesser degrees of success. Wineries featured here have demonstrated some consistency over several years, have established a notable presence and reputation in either the domestic market or export sector, or have impressed by pushing forward the boundaries of quality. Some of the newest wineries simply don't have the track record yet to be featured, but names to keep an eye on are listed in brief. Here they have produced at least one wine that shows promise so far.

THE BIG PLAYERS

Black Sea Gold
Pomorie, Bourgas 8200
Tel +359 5963 5701
www.bsgold.bg

The original winery was founded in 1932 and then developed into a conglomerate in the 1950s to supply volume to the East. By the 1970s, it had an astonishing 12,000 barrels. The company invested in top-notch pot stills in 1994 to improve its spirits sector. The period from 2007 to 2013 saw investments in new winery equipment and more handcrafted wines, plus 700 hectares of vines. Today it ranks tenth in Bulgarian wine, crushing 14,000 tonnes of grapes in 2016. Wines are bright and modern (particularly the whites) and labels include Pentagram for single varieties, Villa Ponte for blends, Villa Marvella for less common international grapes using a micro-vinification approach, Salty Hills for premium blends and Golden Rhythm for oak-aged versions. The winery is also very proud of its super-premium *rakia* and brandy.

Domaine Boyar

Sliven Industrial Zone, Starozagorshko shose
Tel.: +359 4461 9101
www.domaineboyar.com

The first private wine company in Bulgaria after the fall of communism, this was founded in 1991. It was ranked the third biggest wine producer in Bulgaria according to leading online newspaper Capital.bg in 2017. After a somewhat difficult history with various failed investment projects, it currently seems more settled. It has two production sites: the large Australian-designed Sinite Skali (Blue Ridge) winery for most of its wines and the boutique cellar of Korten, acquired in 2003 and used for its more premium ranges. Both are close to the town of Sliven. It does not own any vineyards and selects grapes from across the country, mostly from the Thracian region.

The company has 67 grape suppliers on contract; grape production is surveyed and monitored, and the winemakers work together to decide on treatments and picking time. It crushes around 10,000 tonnes a year and has a team of four oenologists led by the highly respected team of Kapka Georgieva and Dimitar Panov. This is a winery that has courted controversy at various times in its history, perhaps most famously for marketing its wines in 1990s with the slogan 'Does it matter where it comes from?' to de-emphasize its Bulgarian origins. Labels today include Elements, Quantum, Deer Point and Domaine Boyar, with wines that are usually competent and modern. Better wines come from the boutique Korten winery. Korten Natura is a range that focuses on local grape varieties including a Melnik rosé and a Mavrud and Rubin blend. At the premium end there are impressive wines in the iconic Solitaire, Suprême Grand Cuvée and Grands Cepages ranges.

Castra Rubra/Telish

Castra Rubra Winery 6460 Kolarovo
Haskovo +359 2963 1773
www.telish.bg

Telish has long been established as a reliable supplier of good value reds, but in 2006 owner Jair Agopian added another major project, Castra Rubra, intended to take Bulgarian winemaking to another level. Persuading the renowned Michel Rolland to become his exclusive consultant was quite a feather in Agopian's (and for that matter Bulgaria's) cap. The name means 'Red Fortress' and the winery is close to the site of a legendary Byzantine fortress, in the foothills of the Sakar mountains near Kolarovo in the country's south-east. Rolland was involved in planning vineyards (which are managed organically) and the smart stone-built winery was equipped with oak fermenters and an immaculate barrel cellar. Releases so far have impressed, under labels such as Via Diagonalis, Motley Cock, Castra Rubra itself and top label Butterfly's Rock.

Katarzyna Estate

Svilengrad, Haskovo District POB 58
Tel.: +359 2491 1732
www.katarzyna.bg

Katarzyna Estates is ranked fifth in Bulgaria in 2016, after showing strong growth of around 25 per cent in its main domestic market in 2016. It's now owned by a Swiss-registered entity called Balkan Estates, which in turn is owned by one of its founders Krysztof Trylinski and linked to the smaller Concerto and Belitza wineries. In 2005, this was a huge investment by the French-based Belvedere group with an initial 365 hectares in the red soils of the abandoned no man's land border zone that neighbours Greece. Today, it has 550 hectares and a state-of-the-art winery decorated with images of the Thracian wine god Dionysus. There's a swooping line of 132 tanks and around 2,000 barrels, and all the toys any winemaker could want. Wines produced here reflect their sunny origin; ripe and soft in style. Labels include Mezzek (named for a nearby medieval fortress), Contemplations, 10 Harvest, Halla, Encore, La Vie en Rose, Twins, Voyage and many more, plus a new Bio range. Flagship Katarzyna Reserve is a blend of weighty Cabernet and velvety Merlot that is extravagantly priced to make a statement.

Lovico Suhindol

156 Rositsa Street Suhindol, Veliko Tarnovo 5240
Tel.: +359 6136 2411
www.lovico.eu

This is the successor to the first wine growing cooperative Gamza founded in 1909, which went on to become a leading wine producer in the 1920s and 1930s before being taken over by the state, and becoming world-famous for Suhindol Cabernet Sauvignon. Privatized in 1991, today it manages 300 hectares though they are still very geographically fragmented. The story goes that if you placed all its rows of vines end to end they would cover the distance between Suhindol and Venice. The winery has always had a focus on Gamza, one of the few that still does.

Domain Menada

'H.D.Asenov' 16000 Stara Zagora
Tel.: +359 4260 4191
www.domainmenada.com

Named for the Maenads depicted on Thracian pottery found near to Stara Zagora, this large industrial winery was originally founded as the Loza cooperative, and winemaking has gone on here for over a century. Today it is part of French-based Marie Brizard Wines & Spirits Group and is one of Bulgaria's biggest wine producers (number 7 in 2016) with a grape-crushing capacity of 8,000 tonnes. It has 428 hectares, planted in 2006 and 2009, which supply 80 per cent of the company's needs. The emblematic Tcherga label, themed on the typical Bulgarian bright, handwoven rugs, is its most famous range; a premium version, Tcherga 10 has recently been added to celebrate a decade of the brand. Exports are a strong sector here.

Power Brands

Yambol 8600, kv industrialna zona
Tel.: +359 4666 1612
www.villayambol.com / www.newbloomwinery.com

Formerly Vinprom Peshtera, today this is a strongly spirits-focused group whose products include Bulgaria's bestselling *rakia* – at least half of the 40,000 tonnes it crushes goes into the national spirit. The group would be Bulgaria's second biggest wine producer if both of its wineries, New Bloom Winery at Saedinenaie and Villa Yambol, which operate separately, were considered together. Villa Yambol owns or controls 1,000 hectares of vineyards in Bourgas and Yambol, while the huge industrial-looking New Bloom winery has 700 hectares close to the winery, with varieties including the unusual Dornfelder (40 hectares) and Regent (80 hectares), both more typically grown in very cool climates, but undoubtedly offering a point of difference in the F2F range. Both wineries also have micro-vinification sites and have focused on making their wines more modern and consumer driven. Yambol labels include a good commercial range, Villa Yambol, and the more premium well-made Kabile (named after a nearby historical site) with good fruit-driven reds from Merlot, Syrah and Mavrud–Cabernet Sauvignon, plus an appealing Syrah rosé and a Chardonnay–Sauvignon Blanc blend. New Bloom wines sell as Pixels, Verano Azur ('Blue Summer') and F2F.

Vinex Preslav

Veliki Preslav 9850 Industrial Zone
Tel.: +359 5384 2015
www.vinex.bg

This winery was founded in 1948, taking its name from the town of Great Preslav, the second capital of Bulgaria in the ninth century. It produces wines (Preslav, Golden Age, Rubaiyat) from the micro-regions of Preslav, Novi Pazar and Khan Krum and is one of the few producers marketing wines with PDO status, especially Novi Pazar Riesling – Riesling was planted as state policy in the communist era but turns out very good results here. Rubaiyat is the winery's top label, with a Chardonnay that regularly features among the country's best whites and an increasingly assured red blend. The recent departure of the longstanding winemaker and 'face' of the winery may change things. Khan Krum winery, dating from 1939, is under the same ownership and most famous for its whites, especially Chardonnay and Traminer.

Vinex Slavyantsi

Slavyantsi, 8460
Tel.: +359 5571 4500
www.vinexbg.com

The second biggest wine producer in Bulgaria has four winery plants and 700 hectares of vines (one of the first big wineries to understand the need for control over its fruit sourcing, especially for red grapes), producing wines, vermouth and brandies. The main site is in Sungurlare in the Valley of the Roses region, noted for its wide valley and Black Sea breezes. Its most recognizable export brand, notably popular in Scandinavia, is Leva, always fruity, clean and reliable, especially the whites, based on Red Misket and Traminer. The winery impresses particularly for its social responsibility programme. The Leva Foundation was set up in 2008 with the help of the winery's Swedish importer and is funded by sales of Leva wines. It was certified 'Fair for Life' (the first in Bulgaria and Europe) in 2014. Recognizing its heavy dependence on workers from the local ethnic-minority Roma population, the winery provides legal aid, healthcare and educational opportunities such as scholarships and heavily subsidized nursery places as well as language lessons, so children can learn Bulgarian.

Vinprom Karnobat/Minkov Brothers

8473 Venec, Karnobat
Tel.: +359 882 151500
www.minkovbrothers.bg

The umbrella holding company is SIS Industries, the biggest wine company in Bulgaria, which improved its domestic sales by 200 per cent in 2016 (according to Capital.bg's wine sector report). The group, which renovated its production in 2003, claims a 50-year history in winemaking. It sells competent wines under the Château Karnobat and Ethno (blends with local varieties) labels. Minkov Brothers is the boutique arm, based on a winemaking tradition dating back to 1875, when three pioneering brothers returned to Bulgaria to make wine, eventually winning Bulgaria's first ever international gold medal in 1894. The group owns 2,000 hectares of vineyards 65 kilometres from the Black Sea in five villages. Minkov Brothers owns 400 hectares and has a barrel cellar with a mere 7,000 barrels. Minkov's labels include Cycle, From The Cellar, Déjà Vu, Jamais Vu and Le Photographie (one of original brothers was a photographer), which provides snapshots of less common grape varieties such as Cabernet Franc and Riesling. Oak Tree is the flagship Bordeaux-style blend. Minkov Brothers is open to tourists.

THE STRUMA VALLEY REGION

Damianitza

2813 Damianitza, Sandanski District
Tel.: +359 7463 0090
www.Damianitza.bg

An old winery in the Struma Valley, this was founded in 1940, nationalized in 1947 and then privatized in 1997. When I first visited, it was still a concrete Vinprom complete with an abandoned distillery, and it was hard to imagine anything good could come out of it, but eventually it did. Owner (and former newspaper publisher) Philip Harmandjiev says he ended up there in 1998 by accident. He had been asked by a banker friend to help sort out a troubled old state winery on the basis that he liked wine and had travelled. He says, 'My first day at Damianitza was shocking, to say the least. Concrete tanks, huge capacity, mediocre wines … It was not my wine. I was asked to stay and help for three months. These were the longest three months in my life. Now, I cannot imagine life without wines, vineyards and grapes.' Eventually, he bought the winery, sold all his publishing interests and overhauled the business, switching from bulk wine to premium wine and producing one of the country's earliest icon wines, ReDark. Today the winery has undergone another conversion towards organic, biodynamic and holistic production, with the company's own farm animals providing compost for the vines, and vine clippings going to feed them. Not all the vines are certified though – as Philip points out, his oldest vines tend to be in scattered plots which are hard to manage organically, but these also give some of the highest quality fruit, for instance to produce the flagship Kometa. 'Younger vines just can't match this quality as their roots don't go so deep,' he says. Another key brand is No Man's Land, focusing on local grapes grown in the narrow strip of land that used to keep the worlds of socialism and capitalism apart.

Logodaj Winery

Village of Logodaj 2700
Tel.: +359 7388 2906
www.logodajwinery.com

Logodaj is located in the beautiful Struma River valley, Bulgaria's warmest and sunniest region. It was founded in 1993 by Peter Drosanski and a couple of friends, initially just to produce high-strength spirits. Fierce competition in the spirits sector and passion for wine brought a change of heart in 2003, the first year of the wine business. The three partners are very much rooted in the region and Peter had studied Italian at school, so he was inspired by visits to Tuscany to try and do something similar in Bulgaria. His dream was to offer fantastic quality at affordable prices from local grapes, and the goal was to produce Bulgaria's Tignanello.

Winemaker Stoycho Stoev was a key figure at the beginning, helping to establish an identity for local grapes and winning Logodaj's first awards. When he moved on, Peter's Italian inspiration led him to bring on board renowned Italian consultant Riccardo Cotarella, also a believer in saving ancient grape varieties. As Peter explained, 'The problem with Broad-leafed Melnik is that due to its very late ripening, we were finding it difficult to source the highest quality fruit. We were working closely with Murad Ouada (of Cotarella's team) who suggested that we pioneer the first sparkling Melnik. It turned out that sparkling wines were his PhD thesis.'

Peter is a relentlessly driven but practical guy, still working with the same partners, and content with a functional warehouse of a winery, though he has recently bought some of his own vineyards. Local grape varieties like Melnik and Rubin under the Nobile label are an important feature here and are some of Bulgaria's best examples. Hypnose Reserve Merlot is an iconic wine for the country – serious, rich and concentrated. More than ten years ago Peter realized that Bulgarian wine had to switch track, 'We realized that to achieve absolute quality and harmony, the proper place, the proper time and the best people were necessary. It turned out that passion and people are our biggest assets.'

Medi Valley

2641 Smochevo
Tel.: +359 885 552901
www.medivalleywinery.com

Medi Valley winery lies at the northern end of the Struma Valley, officially just outside the Struma region. It's close to the Rila mountains and Bulgaria's world-renowned Rila monastery. The dramatic Stobi sand pyramids are nearby too and it's named for the Thracian Medi tribe who lived in the valley. Established in 2007, its new owners arrived in 2010, along with winemaker Stoycho Stoev and his colleague Ivona Georgieva. Stoev is a renowned character in Bulgarian wine for pioneering the vinification of local speciality Melnik 55 and for his strongly expressed opinions.

The winery owns 40 hectares close by, at 630 metres altitude, probably the highest commercial vineyard in Bulgaria, and a second vineyard near Vidin in the far north-west. Altitude and cool nights mean they pick two weeks after anyone else, meaning flavour development without loss of freshness. Stoev's perfectionist approach includes having his own specially coopered French oak from a mix of forests. 'Oak is like perfume for me. I don't believe in Bulgarian oak,' he says. 'Quality is too unstable, and you don't find out until too late, once the wine has been in barrel at least three months.' The winery's top range is Incanto, with eXcentric for local or unusual varieties and A Good Year in the mid-segment. The winery's flagship is Incanto Black, a blend made with the barrel selection of the best wines of the winery. Stoev's style has evolved from pursuing concentration above all else towards more restrained elegance and purity.

Orbelia

Petrich, Village Kolarovo
Tel.: +359 886 939355
www.orbeliawinery.bg

Orbelia is an ancient Thracian name meaning 'beautiful white mountain' (from the same root as nearby Orbelus though the companies are separate). This is a family project belonging to a couple of food technologists and their children who also run a meat business. The winery began with just 0.3 hectares of Sandanski Misket, a family inheritance. Nikolay (the son) remembers fondly going to this vineyard as a small child to help among the vines and recalls that his grandparents drank wine as medicine. Now the winery has 10 hectares and a well-equipped winery in a former brewery. The idea is to revive local traditions, but in a modern way, experimenting with wild yeast and different oaks. There's a small wine museum too.

Orbelus

Kromidovo village, Petrich municipality, Blagoevgrad
Tel.: +359 2951 5495
www.orbelus.bg

Built to resemble half a barrel dropped onto the landscape, the winery is named after the Thracian word for the nearby Pirin mountains. The owners are a lawyer and a marketer, two friends who wanted to do something in their home village and involve their families. The first vines were planted in 2006 and the winery opened in 2014. It's fully organic and was Bulgaria's first certified winery, so it's good to see an experimental approach continues, bringing in students to do trials here. The concept is to lead with local varieties, especially both Melniks and Sandanski Misket, and blend with international ones. A new single vineyard range shows promise.

Rupel Winery

Melnik 2004 Ltd, 286 Dolno Spanchevo
Tel.: +359 2873 2480
www.rupel-winery.com

Owner Pavel Gramatikov has put his money where his mouth is, living right in the midst of his 30 hectares of vines. 'I feel this is a place blessed by God for vines,' he says. Pavel is originally from this region, and as with everyone here, his ancestors grew vines. A trip to Tuscany inspired him to start purchasing land in 2004 but it took more than 50 contracts to buy the plots he wanted. The winery is named after the Rupel Gorge to the south, which funnels the Aegean climate into the valley. The first proper vintage was 2015. Pavel admits that wine is still part-funded by his other businesses in quarrying and garbage collection, but explains, 'I love the smell of fermenting wine and watching vineyards, it helps me to be human'. So far wines include the fruit-driven Spancha range and more serious oak-matured Gramatik wines, including local varieties plus the more unusual Marselan, Nebbiolo and Sangiovese.

Villa Melnik

2819 Harsovo
Tel.: +359 884 840320
www.villamelnik.com

Owner Nikola Zikatanov was born in the neighbouring village and grew up with the family's tiny plot of vines. He's the son of a rebel mother, who was once condemned by the local priest for daring to wear trousers and drive a tractor. She also had the foresight to encourage Nikola to learn English.

After regime change, Nikola took the chance to study for an MBA in the USA, which led to a career working for US investments funds. Eventually he decided to switch tracks and as he says, 'Dedicate the second, wiser part of my life to reviving family traditions and building a business for the generations to come'. His daughter Militza came back after a few years working for multinational Diageo, 'To put all that effort into building my own family's brand rather than a multinational one,' she explains.

A small piece of restituted vineyard gave Nikola the start in collecting land close to his old home. He reckons it took deals with close to a thousand people across extended families to buy 50 hectares (of which 30 hectares now have vines). The immaculate gravity-fed winery opened its doors in 2013. From the beginning, local grapes and traditions were a key focus, so both Melnik in all its forms, Ruen and even the region's first Mavrud are features. They also grow around 30 per cent international varieties, making intriguing blends plus very good varietal versions such as Reserve Cabernet Sauvignon and Hailstorm Syrah. Recently, they also pioneered orange wine, made from Sauvignon Blanc with a little Keratsuda.

Zlaten Rozhen

2872 Kapatovo
Tel.:+359 879 801300
www.zlatenrozhen.bg

A small hotel close to the historic Rozhen Monastery was the start for this project, as it came with some hobby vineyards. More recently, the family that owns it decided to do wine seriously, opening a modern winery in 2010 in the village of Kapatovo. Today the 'hobby' has expanded from 25 to 70 hectares. Italian Federico Ricci arrived as consultant in 2017, bringing a more natural approach in the vineyards and seeking to select the winery's own local yeast from among its vines. His aim, he says, is 'to reveal the soul of the family and terroir'. Wines from 2017 are showing a step up in quality and interest including local Sandanski Misket, rosé from Sangiovese and from Shiroka Melnishka Loza, and intriguing red blends with local Melnishka Rubin.

THE DANUBE PLAIN

Borovitza

3955 Borovitza Belogradchik, Vidin district
Tel.:+359 887 806200

This tiny winery, founded by industry mavericks Ogy Tzvetanov and Adriana Srebrinova in the forgotten north-west represents something completely different for Bulgaria. It's in the most stunning location in the Belogradchik national park (recently praised as one of the new seven wonders of the world for its dramatic rock formations). Co-owner Ogy liked to claim he was a 318th generation winemaker – underlining how long-established wine is in Bulgaria. He was also an industry maverick, working in the US at a time when almost no one got to travel and bringing back valuable experience to add to his academic knowledge. He and his partner-in-wine were believers in the terroirs of the north-west for red wines, explaining that, 'The hillside vineyards overlooking the Danube enjoy long sunshine hours without baking heat, giving potential for really elegant wines'.

From this philosophy came Bulgaria's first real 'terroir' wine, Sensum, in 2003 (from a plot of 48-year-old-vines), followed by the flagship Dux, aged for five years in barrel and remarkably classy and elegant. 'We can take risks because we're the owners,' said Ogy. At Borovitza, some batches were just a few bottles (they even had special tiny barrels coopered if necessary – a 67-litre barrel for their first MRV, a Marsanne–Roussanne–Viognier white blend). North-west Bulgaria was not well-regarded by the big players of the industry, especially for the rich and super-ripe reds that were their mainstay. However, Ogy and Adriana had found that there were some amazing old plots of vines in this virtually abandoned corner of the country, producing fantastically intense fruit. And because this area is relatively cool compared to the rest of the country (especially at night), the wines have exciting potential for elegance, complexity and long life. After Ogy's untimely death, Adriana is now committed to following their joint vision.

FOUNDING OF A WINERY

Ogy Tzvetanov and Adriana Srebrinova had a long history of research and winemaking in the old Vinprom system. They then set up a business making wine under their own private companies by seeking out parcels of great grapes, often from old vines in forgotten corners of the country, and vinified in rented spaces in other wineries. Along the way, the partners-in-wine produced Bulgaria's first ever icon wine (Maxxima Reserve 1999). Renting space occasionally brought unexpected issues. I recall one story about an amazing Sauvignon Blanc they had made, but every time they went back to check it, it seemed somehow more dilute and they wondered what had gone wrong. Finally, the truth emerged. The winery staff had spotted that this was the best wine in the place and had been quietly siphoning off wine to drink and topping up with whatever else they could find in the winery. This motivated the pair to find a way of owning their own winery.

The dream came true when on a grape hunt in a remote village in the far north-west. A grape-grower happened to mention a derelict, long-forgotten, former state winery that importantly still had all the right licences. Somehow, Ogy and Adriana scraped together the funds to buy this run-down shell among the rocks of the stunning Belogradchik national park and pursue Ogy's dream of making handcrafted wines. A chance encounter over a glass of wine with a specialist in writing EU fund applications meant they even got EU support for their renovations. Some vineyards followed too, but they also kept on buying grapes from whoever had interesting fruit to sell, including some from a vineyard that was more than a century old.

Burgozone

3341 Leskovets, Oryahovsko shose str. 1
Tel.: +359 888 323877
www.burgozone.bg

The ruins of the ancient Roman fortress of Burgozone after which the winery is named lie close to the vineyards, near the town of Oryahovo on the Danube. Owners Svetla and Stefan Marinov had a dream to revive the winemaking tradition that had disappeared around here thanks to the Gorbachev regime. It took them four years to put together their land from over 350 plots, and today the winery has 100 hectares of vines on the southern side of the Danube. All the family threw themselves deeply into the wine world, studying for wine MBAs and other qualifications, and bringing in consultants to help them realize their ambitions to make modern Bulgarian wines that they enjoy themselves.

Daughter Biliana explains, 'In our family, the frontier between business and family is fragile, as we spend all our family gatherings and celebrations talking about the wine business. We even celebrate special family events and births with the creation of special wines. Our Iris Creation was named for the first child from the third generation of the family and made from our most important varieties'. Cuvee Phillippe and Cuvee Eva have followed. The modern winery is inspired by the Roman fort and is rare in Bulgaria for being close to the vines. When they started, viticultural consultant Professor Penkov recommended Chardonnay and Pinot Noir as best for their terroirs, but recently they have planted Gamza. 'As Gamza needs hilly and well-ventilated terrain in a cool climate, preferably close to the river, we have the perfect location,' Biliana points out.

She explains that as a major employer in the region, the family has also recognized the problems of getting young people to work in the vineyards here, one of the very poorest parts of Europe. They have set up a school for vine growing in Oryahovo where their agronomist is teaching young people. They also guarantee them employment after graduation. The wines focus on fresh, aromatic expression of white grapes including Sauvignon Blanc and Viognier, and elegant reds, especially Pinot Noir.

Maryan

St Maryanskata cellar 1, 5084 Maryan
Tel.: +359 888 794449
www.maryanwinery.com

Svetla and Iliya Ivanov are lawyers who decided to make wine in their home village, together with their two sons Petar and Vladimir. The village is connected to the story of Kera Tamara, sister of the last Tsar of Bulgaria, given to the Ottoman Sultan in marriage to keep the peace. The story goes that Dimiat vines sprang from her tears. The project began in 2011, though the vineyards are 18 years old and lie 60 kilometres south of the winery over the mountains. Dimiat is a specialism of the winery, showing the new face of a grape that is traditionally overcropped and mistreated. Petar Ivanov says, 'I'm really proud of Dimiat, I like the high acidity and its ability to mature'. Wines include a part barrel-aged Dimiat and a blend with Chardonnay and a touch of Sauvignon Blanc. There's also a complex, intriguing orange version with 120 days on skins in tanks, cooled by simply opening the cellar doors at night. The reds too are good so far, especially blends based on Cabernet Sauvignon: Ivan Alexander Cuvée and Reserve.

Rousse Wine House

LEVENTA Complex, Rousse
Tel.: +359 8286 2880
www.Leventa-bg.net

One of Bulgaria's impressive women winemakers, Ekaterina Gargova, makes the wine here. Based in a 200-year-old Ottoman fortress with a hotel and restaurant, the winery sources from 20 hectares of their own vineyards as well as long-term growers in Varna, Schumen and Nova Zagora. The brand name is Levent for good Riesling, serious barrel-fermented Chardonnay, attractive super pale rosé from Grenache and grapey Traminer with Vrachanski Misket. Pinot Noir is promising.

Salla Estate

47 Bratiq Miladinovi St., Floor 6 9002 Varna
Tel.: +359 5261 1420
www.salla.bg

Another recent arrival on the scene is this family business owned by two brothers. It launched in 2010 and has a 30-hectare vineyard in Blaskovo village, 60 kilometres from Varna and close to a medieval rock monastery and Stone Age cave. Anelia Hristakieva is the winemaker and winner of top white wine in Bulgaria in 2017. She says, 'I love it here because I can experiment with the grapes from our own vineyards. I think the potential is great'. As well as appealing, elegant whites (especially Riesling, Vrachanski Misket and Chardonnay) there's very good Cabernet Franc and decent Pinot Noir. It's also set up for tourism, with Lipizzaner horses on site.

Santa Sarah

Goritza village, Ivailo street 2, 8225 Pomorie
Tel.: +359 888 908064
www.santa-sarah.com

Ivo Genowski is a Bulgarian who studied robotics and electrical engineering in Germany. As a student he ran short of money while writing his doctoral thesis. Turning to selling wine to pay the bills, he got caught by the wine bug. Fast-forward a few years and he started his own project in Bulgaria with a small team and three caravans, seeking out interesting parcels of grapes and renting space in other wineries. He made his first vintage in 2001 – by following instructions in a German text book. His philosophy from the start has been different from that of most others, avoiding the big capital investments until his wines were established. He arrived on the scene with a bang when he won the first internationally judged wine competition in Bulgaria in 2003, beating all the better-known names.

Eventually he bought land near the historic town of Nessebar, close to the Black Sea, and built a winery. He didn't plant any vines until around 2015, commenting, 'Planting vines is almost like getting married – mistakes are hard to change and last a long time'. The idea is ultimately to use half his own fruit and half sourced from growers, to be able to follow the best grapes from changing people, ideas and climate. Today three women comprise the winemaking team; led by Evgenia Georgieva (with vintages in New Zealand and Bordeaux behind her) they bring a more elegant touch to the wines. The consistently good Bin range is numbered for Ivo's age when he first made a good version of that wine, while Sauvignon Blanc and Privat Red continue to impress. Indeed, Privat has a track record of ageing very well. New labels include supple Petite Sarah and the refined 'We are no Saints' rosé.

Svishtov Winery

5250 Svishtov 33rd Svishtovski polk str. 110
Tel.: +359 6316 0470
www.svishtov-winery.com

Founded in 1948 near the Danube's southernmost bend, this long-established former Vinprom now has new owners and has been completely renovated. It was Bulgaria's first large winery to be self-sufficient, with its own grape supply from 400 hectares of vineyards. It's particularly famous for its Gorchivka rosé, launched in 2003, long before pink wine became so trendy.

Today Italian consultant Federico Ricci is working closely with the winery, in his poetic words, 'To express the sensuality of the ground.' More practically he has insisted on tastings of the latest wines with all the staff from vineyard and winery, so they feel connected to the wines and understand what they are aiming for, 'Otherwise it's just liquid in a bottle,' Federico says. The Aureos range is all about well-made fruity varietal wines, while emblematic Gorchivka is named for one of their two vineyards and includes very good Merlot from old vines. The selected Legio range is named for the Roman legion that had a camp nearby, guarding the edge of the Roman Empire. There's a very good Merlot–Cabernet Franc and a harmoniously oak-aged Chardonnay.

Varna Winery

Varna, General Kantardzhievo village
Tel.: +359 897 009594
www.varnawinery.eu

Based 10 kilometres from Varna itself and 2 kilometres from the beach, this is the project of two friends, Grigor Grigorov, a vine grower and investor, and Tsanko Stanchev, an experienced oenologist. It was the first entirely gravity-fed winery in Bulgaria and processes 300 tonnes of grapes from its own vineyards – all whites except Pinot Noir and Sangiovese. This winery has captured a niche that almost no one else in the country can match, for pure, fresh, crisp, drinkable whites and rosés, and even a simple but pretty Pinot Noir. All are good value too – no wonder they sell out so quickly.

THRACIAN LOWLANDS

Alexandra Estate

28 Knyaz Aleksander Batenberg, fl. 3, office 22 6000 Stara Zagora
Tel.: +359 884 891188
www.alexandraestate.com

Svetlana Slavova is the driving force here. Prior to this she helped to set up Katarzyna and also worked for Midalidare. An economist by training, she is by heart and soul a winemaker. She's self-taught through 'many, many hours in vineyards and wineries,' she says. There are 60 hectares of vines and the first vintage was 2013. The winery makes interesting red blends and a gently fruity Malbec rosé, plus good Vermentino and Viognier.

Angel's Estate

Banya, Sliven district, Nova Zagora municipality, postal code 8914
Tel.: +359 884 246619
www.angelsestate.bg

This ambitious personal project of poultry farmer Ivan Angelov is located near the Zhrebchevo dam (zhrebchevo means 'stallion' and inspired the winery's first label) with 150 hectares on the hillsides of the Sredna Gora mountains. The winery, designed in the shape of an angel's wings, has every possible bit of technical equipment including Bulgaria's only optical grape-sorter. It was relaunched under this name in 2017 with the arrival of superstar winemaker Alex Velianov, who sadly died later that year, a great loss to Bulgarian wine. Ripe, polished and modern wines have taken Angel's Estate into Bulgaria's top 20 producers with a 32 per cent increase in revenue from wine sales in 2016. The Angel range has no oak, Stallion wines range from fruity Young Stallion to intense Stallion Gold, while varietal Deneb reds are impressive. The Angel Rosé is also good.

Bessa Valley

Pazardjik region BG-4417 Ognianovo village
Tel.: +359 889 499992
www.Bessavalley.com

One of the earliest foreign investments in Bulgaria's new era, in 2001, this was named for the Thracian Bessae tribe who lived in the region. French winemaker Marc Dworkin has been involved since the beginning. 'I had a dream and my friends made it come true,' he says, explaining that the chance to do a project like this from scratch would simply be impossible anywhere in Western Europe. The investment is backed by Count Stephan von Niepperg (of Château la Mondotte and Canon la Gaffeliere) and financier Dr Karl Hauptmann, and supported by substantial EU funds. This was fallow land post-Gorbachev but soil analysis showed distinct similarities to Bordeaux's St Emilion, hence a strong focus on Merlot along with Syrah, Petit Verdot and Cabernet Sauvignon matched to the clay-limestone soil. Six hectares of Marsanne, Roussanne and Viognier have recently been added.

The smart winery, faced with local stone, is actually very simple – concrete vats and oak barrels, but meticulous attention to detail by Marc and his team means there's no need for anything more. The cellar has a thousand barrels, all French, and it takes four barrels of wine every month to keep everything topped up – to make up for the angels' share (wine that evaporates). Enira, Enira Reserva and Syrah all impress, while the flagship BV has recently been renamed Grande Cuvée and is on superb form.

Better Half Wines

Zmeevo 6059 Stara Zagora
Tel.: +359 888 678811

Making some wines for friends in a garage is literally how this winery started. It's run by Nikolay Dalakov with his wife (or better half) Yana and son Stefan. It's equipped with tiny tanks up to one tonne in size, plus clay jars and clay eggs. Dalakov says, 'I believe in clay, I am building a new winery which will only have clay.' He started working with vineyards in 1999 and was a bit of an industry 'kingmaker', involved in establishing up to 3,000 hectares of vineyards for various companies, and seeing real progress in understanding terroir. For his personal project, he selects the best wines from his own 10-hectare vineyard and sells the rest of the grapes.

The original idea was to simply make one white and one red, but market demand put paid to that idea. Today the range includes a Sancerre-style Sauvignon Blanc from a 600-metre-high vineyard on an extinct volcano and a complex Chardonnay with 12 months in French oak. He's another producer who doesn't believe in Bulgarian oak; this is due to, 'lack of ageing of the staves, not the cooperage of the oak itself,' he explains. Pinot Noir rosé is elegant while the red Pinot Noir is very much of its place, warm and spicy. Blends are unconventional but work well and include a Syrah–Malbec–Regent and the current star, made from Cabernet Franc, Cabernet Sauvignon and Syrah.

Bratanov

15 Yanko Sakazov St, 6450 Harmanli
Tel.: +359 887 002193
www.bratanov.wine

The tale here is of a father and his two sons, Hristo and Daniel, bringing the family dream to life. It began in 2010, based around land restituted to Stoycho Bratanov. This single hectare had once been the biggest plot in the village (where Stoycho's father had been mayor); it took another

5 years to buy the current 24 hectares. The philosophy is all about low-intervention winemaking, using spontaneous fermentation. There is a very good Chardonnay *sur lie*, an aromatic Tamianka and rich, complex reds, including a Cabernet Franc and the South Sakar Selection.

Dragomir

4000 Plovdiv, 15 'Kuklensko shose' blvd
Tel.: +359 888 325830
www.dragomir.bg

No one can fail to be impressed by the glamorous Nataliq Gadjeva, who can pour red wine all day in an immaculate white top. However, there is more to Dragomir than external appearances. It's the story of a romance between two young winemakers who wanted to change the perception of Bulgarian wines. Nataliq and her husband, Konstantin Stoev, are a couple of trained oenologists who ploughed their fifteen years of experience working for other companies into setting up their own small winery in 2009, becoming partners in business as well as life, a decision made while Nataliq was expecting their second son. Nataliq says, 'As in any family, we have different outlooks on some professional issues, but we always strive through a conversation to reach a solution that will satisfy both of us. I hold my position when it comes to the overall vision of presenting our wine, and Konstantin is more adept at production and solving how to bring it all together.'

They began with a modest warehouse in downtown Plovdiv with careful investments in all the right equipment and the highest quality barrels. Instead of pursuing the complexities of buying land, they worked with growers they could trust to control fruit quality. After years in the original warehouse, they finally have a winery in Brestnik village, close to Plovdiv, with 13 rented hectares of their beloved Rubin, along with Mavrud, and another 24 hectares of their own, just-planted vines of Rubin, Merlot, Cabernet Sauvignon, Syrah, Petit Verdot and Cabernet Franc. Local grapes feature in many of their wines and labels including Sarva, Karizma, Pitos (their first wine, named for a Thracian wine cellar). Rubin, which they source from 40-year-old vines, is their passion, showcased in their admirable Rubin Reserva and Grand Reserve.

Eolis

2W Anton Marchin Str. BG-6001 Stara Zagora
Tel.: +359 888 86 484
www.eolisestate.com

Quietly spoken but committed Swiss couple, Laurent and Kremena, are bringing Swiss viticultural precision to Bulgarian terroir in one of the sunniest parts of the country, near the Greek border. So far, they have just 3 hectares, vinified at Rossidi, but are planning another 5.5 hectares soon. Kremena is switching to biodynamics, explaining, 'I'm not going for certification, but it's about managing the soil better.' Laurent hates over-ripeness, and picking is two to three weeks earlier than their neighbours, giving wines a more restrained and elegant feel. The best so far are the Cabernet Franc, the Inspiration blend and a refined Syrah.

Midalidare Estate

6239 Mogilovo village, Chirpan municipality
Tel.: +359 889 217413
www.midalidare.bg

A Kazakhstani businessman, Eugene Yusupov (from the field of high tech medical equipment), fell in love with this place, nestled among the Sredna Gora mountains in Mogilovo village. His initial aim was to build a summer home: then he saw the vineyards. The result was this small but immaculate winery built in 2009 where the internationally experienced team is allowed free rein to focus on quality. A second winery followed as vineyard area increased to 160 hectares, allowing the winery to pick and choose its best fruit and sell the rest. Bright, refreshing whites and smooth reds are the hallmark here, and brands include Nota Bene, Angel's Share, Carpe Diem and Grand Vintage.

Edoardo Miroglio

Nova Zagora Elenovo, 8943
Tel.: +359 4450 0411
www.emiroglio-wine.com

Edoardo Miroglio is an Italian textile producer and winery owner in Piemonte. In 2002, he discovered the perfect combination of soils and microclimate around the village of Elenovo and has since invested around €22 million here. Over 220 hectares of vines have been planted with 16 varieties, though he had to negotiate with around 1,500 owners to put this land together. The immaculate winery spirals down the hill, and more recently a hotel and spa have been built above.

After much detailed research Miroglio picked the area of Elenovo, near Sliven, for its great soils and has planted both Bulgarian and imported vines. Pinot Noir is a speciality of the winery – appearing as a stylish *blanc de noirs* and a refined red (a more elegant style than seems to be appreciated in Bulgaria, where they like their reds rather macho). The bottle-fermented sparkling is made with utter attention to detail under the watchful eye of another of Bulgaria's impressive women winemakers Desislava 'Desi' Baicheva. There is a notable *blanc de blancs* vintage and an utterly delicious rosé brut. Italian technical director Alberto la Rosa says he is inspired by his background in Piemonte. Elenovo is the top label, with flagships being the powerful Soli Invicto and wonderful Pinot Noir Reserve. There's also a range of organic wines, mainly from Bulgarian grapes.

Neragora

Chernogorovo 4456 Pazardjik, Mogilata St
Tel.: +359 888 201094
www.neragora.com

The Italian Azzolini family found this place to be charming and unspoiled, just like the Italy of their childhood, so the decision to go organic was obvious. It had been an animal farm in communist times but today they have 72 hectares of vines, plus cherry orchards and a business growing wild mushrooms. This is one of only two totally organic producers in Bulgaria and the Azzolinis work with an Italian consultant to ensure close control, especially of hygiene and temperature, so they can bottle unfiltered with lower sulphite levels. Reds are their strength, particularly Mavrud, on its own or blended with Merlot in Ares, or with Cabernet Sauvignon in Cherno.

Rossidi

Southern Industrial Zone, Sliven 8800
Tel.: +359 886 511080
www.rossidi.com

Dressed in immaculate cutting-edge fashion and with designer hair, Edward Kourian doesn't look like a typical winemaker. Indeed, he and his wife Rosie were living in London, where he was a graphic designer, when one day they got a call from Rosie's father, who had bought land and wanted to have a winery. Edward says, 'Our primary objective is to draw attention to the regionality and uniqueness of the wines produced from the vines of this particular region.' He adds, 'And yet, we are in the beginning of this process. We learn things on the go. The first two vintages we counted as purely experimental.' Today, the winery is a small warehouse in industrial Sliven with 40 hectares of vines a few miles away. Together with winemaker Peter Georgiev, they produce just 10,000 bottles under their name.

There's no standard recipe here, as they are constantly experimenting and pushing boundaries. Good wines include a surprisingly elegant Pinot Noir, an unoaked Chardonnay vinified in concrete eggs and a notable Rubin from a plot at 500 metres. 'We are trying not to torture the grapes, Rubin doesn't do well if too stressed,' says Peter. Orange wine is another pioneering line for Rossidi, initially Chardonnay, but now Traminer made with no sulphites, 30 days of skin contact and 7 months in barrel.

Rumelia

4, Bratia Deikovi Str.4500 Panagyurishte
Tel.: +359 3576 3366
www.rumelia.net

This winery near Panagyurishte is now run by Tsveta Kostova. She has taken over from her father who was a textile producer in France, where he fell in love with wine. He had grown up near Pazardjik surrounded by vines and was inspired to revive the traditions that had been lost during communism. He found a piece of land that had been vineyards in the nineteenth century, and soil analyses confirmed that vines would thrive here. They now have 55 hectares at around 250 to 400 metres altitude, mostly planted with red varieties. Mavrud is a particular passion, and from it they consistently produce some of Bulgaria's best, both as a single varietal and in their top blend Erelia. Kostov says, 'My vision in textiles was to follow cotton from crop to end product, so I had the same idea for wine. No regrets – at least so far.'

Terra Tangra

6450 Harmanli 35, Nikola Petkov Str
Tel.: +359 879 966070
www.terratangra.com

Founded back in 1999 by former vegetable grower, Emil Zaychev, the winery now has 350 hectares on the slopes of the famous Sakar Mountains near Harmanli. The red varieties are all certified for organic production as, 'The sloping sites, well-drained soils and Black Sea breezes make this easy for us.' Too much extract and oak have been criticisms levelled at the winery in the past, but 2014 saw a switch in thinking. They began looking more towards pure fruit flavours, uninterrupted by oak, with just fermentation then bottling. An understated but vibrant Sauvignon Blanc, a super-pale Mavrud rosé, a juicy organic Mavrud and a surprisingly good Malbec impressed recently, while Roto and Single Barrel have potential but need patience.

Villa Yustina

Village Yustina, 51 Nikola Petkov Str.
Tel.: +359 876 946480
www.villayustina.com

Here, in a village close to Plovdiv, is a small, modern estate. The owner's other business is a wine technology company, so this is a real showcase for winemaking toys, especially tanks of every shape and size, conical wooden vats and concrete eggs. There are 20 hectares of vines already producing fruit with another 20 hectares of Rubin and Mavrud planted on chalky soil. The estate is best known for its Four Seasons range and the very good Mavrud–Rubin Monogram.

Yamantiev's

District Haskovo, Ivaylovgrad 6570
Tel.: +359 885 400463
www.yamantievs.com

Iulian Yamantiev's story goes back to his ancestors, the Bitanov brothers, who ran a company called Damiat, exporting grapes, wines and brandies to Austria and Germany. He still has certificates for gold medals they won in 1907 in London.

In 1945, the business was confiscated. After independence in 1991, Iulian felt the call of his blood and realized that wine was his destiny.

He worked at Rousse and Targovishte until 1997 to gain experience but says, 'We were so ambitious, young and determined that the people calling the shots at the time decided to eliminate us by sending us to a disused winery in Ivaylovgrad. This is how we came to possess a pearl of terroir with unique climate, neatly sandwiched between three national borders. Our land and winery are exactly where the Rhodope mountains hug the ancient Thracian valley. This is really where our story began.'

To begin with Iulian and his wife Ivana hired winemakers, but after being told by an English customer that their wine was green, Ivana decided that she would learn about wine and take on the winemaking herself. After renting the winery for a couple of years they bought it outright and raised EU funding for restoration, before adding vines in 2006 to close the circle of quality. In the last 25 years Iulian and Ivana have visited lots of wine countries, always continuing to learn, 'Our conclusions were that there are no bad wines, there may be green, underdeveloped, unsupported, misunderstood wines, but not bad wines – just like there are no bad children. It lies within us to correct that. The vineyards and the wine are our children and the role of the parent is to make sure that his child reaches its maximum potential. We are trying to raise our vines and our wines the same way.' Villa Armira wines are commercial and fruity, while their best wines, the exciting Marble Land Red and Chardonnay come from a plot of marble bedrock at 400 metres, where Iulian loves to watch the eagles.

Zagreus
Iglika Str 30 Parvomay 4270
Tel.: +359 3369 8091
www.zagreus.org

In 1998 the first vineyards were planted for this family-owned winery. Today it has 120 hectares, all close to the winery, and since 2013, it has been certified organic. It's close to Plovdiv in the heart of Mavrud country so around half the vineyards are planted to this ancient Bulgarian variety, where it's produced in all styles from white, unusual rosé fermented in acacia barrels, via traditional reds and reserve wines aged in Bulgarian oak, to the much admired Vinica. Vinica uses grapes dried naturally for a couple of months, before being aged in new oak, giving a totally different face to Mavrud, though it benefits from several years' ageing. Owner

Dimitar Kostadinov reckons, 'Mavrud has an image problem in Bulgaria, it's pale like Pinot Noir unless concentrated. We had to start from the beginning and learn its potential.'

Zelanos Winery

Slavyantsi 8460, Oreshaka area
Tel.: +359 5571 5153
www.zelanos.bg

At this family winery, named for the Thracian god of wine, everyone has (figuratively speaking) earth under their fingernails and is proud of what they have achieved. Owner Reni Slavova has been an agronomist for 25 years and manages 600 hectares altogether with 70 hectares under vine, and her mother still works in the vines. The start of the winery itself and the arrival of the quietly effective Svetla Roshleva as winemaker happened more recently, in 2013. Her winery is immaculately clean, reflected in the pristine varietal expression of white grapes such as Red Misket, Pinot Gris and Sauvignon Blanc. Use of oak is subtle, to avoid overwhelming the fruit, with careful selection of the best French oak and larger or older barrels. Experiments with different yeast are another project. The really promising Z label Chardonnay and Pinot Noir are produced in tiny quantities from a selection of their very best fruit.

IN BRIEF

These are vineyards and producers who had only just come to market at the time of writing, are very small or have made big changes recently. So far all have produced something good or interesting, so it's well worth keeping an eye on where the future takes them.

Bendida

12 Velchova zavera Str Brestovitsa
Tel.: +359 887 911188
www.bendida.eu

Led by the bubbling-with-enthusiasm female winemaker Elizabeta Porteva, this slightly quirky, small family winery in the Plovdiv region focuses on Rubin (from 50-year-old vines). There's no crusher or press so everything is free-run juice only, which reduces the tendency for rustic tannins from these native grapes.

Bononia Estate

Gomotartzi 3772
Tel.: +359 882 598901
www.bononiaestate.com

A new project, this has its winery in an old brewery dating back to 1895. It has 13 hectares near Vidin in the far north-west of the country. Its first vintage was 2013 and so far it has produced light, pleasant whites and the popular Ooh La La rosé.

Château Copsa

32 General Kartsov Str., 4330 Moskovets,
Tel.: +359 882 645452
www.copsa.bg

The best wines at this project in the heart of Rose Valley are the whites, especially those based on the aromatic local Misket.

Four Friends Winery

6053, Gorno Botevo, Stara Zagora
Tel.: +359 895 541036
www.fourfriends.bg

This small boutique winery makes handcrafted wines with 40 hectares near Stara Zagora. The first wines were released from 2012, produced from vines planted in 2006, when four friends passionate about wine got together. Recent releases such as Red Cuvée and Cabernet Franc have impressed.

Gulbanis

5100 Gorna Oryhovitza, 1 Han Krum Str
Tel.: +359 6182 0055
www.gulbaniswine.com

The winery name means flower face, inspired by the Azeri wife of one of the owners. It was a family dream to own a vineyard and they now have 45 hectares in Yantra Valley, planted between 2007 and 2011. There is a promising Cabernet Franc and Moscato Bianco and an interesting Kailashki Misket.

Stratsin winery

Stratsin, Burgas
Tel.: +359 885 510620
www.stratsinwinery.bg

This brand-new project released its first vintage in 2016. The 25 hectares in the Pomorie region near the Black Sea are based around family vineyards that belonged to the grandparents of the current owners. There are two smartly labelled brands: Early Bird (no oak) and Soulmate (oaked). So far the whites and rosé have proved zesty and fresh, and there is a delicious unoaked Merlot.

Tohun Winery

Pomorie 8200, 'Kosharite' District
Tel.: +359 888 768464
www.tohun.bg

This small estate near the Black Sea makes clean, modern whites, rosé and a ripe cassis Cabernet–Merlot blend under the Greus and Tohun labels.

Tsarev Brod Winery

Tsarev Brod 9747, Mezarlak area
Tel.: +359 889 266897
www.tsarevbrod.com

Former Santa Sarah winemaker Nikolay Krastev makes his own wines from 27 hectares close to Shumen. So far the whites are good, especially Amber Harvest, local Gergana, Sepage Blend and Riesling. The young Pinot Noir is better than the oaked version.

Ivo Varbanov

Tel.: +44 7956 377705
www.ivovarbanov.com

Here Varbanov, a classical pianist turned winemaker, is making super-ripe reds and sleek Chardonnay from a small plot in the far south-east.

Via Vinera Karabunar Winery

Septemvri, Karabunar 4484
Tel.: +359 888 550140
www.bulgarian-heritage.com

The first vintage was 2008, and currently the winery has 30 hectares. Bulgarian Heritage is the label for local varieties. The winery produces Red

Misket and Dimiat in both white and orange versions with 25 days' skin contact and partial barrel-fermentation. There is a good rosé from Mavrud and Rubin and a decent Mavrud red with one year in French oak.

Yalovo Winery

Village of Yalovo 5056, 2 'Shesta' str.
Tel.: +359 884 088019
www.vinarnayalovo.com

This small winery in an old school near Veliko Turnovo was only built in 2016 and so far the grapes have been bought in. Young oenologist Dimitar Dimov is also winemaker at Suvla in Turkey. He has a passion for local varieties in old vineyards and is trying to locate historic Kokorko. He's also fascinated by Dimiat and produces good Red Misket, which he believes needs more acidity, so he adds some Rkatsiteli. There's also a promising barrel-aged Rubin.

PART 2
ROMANIA

9
AN INTRODUCTION TO ROMANIA

In most countries, people drive on either the left or the right. Not the Romanians. Traffic hazards like horses and carts, flocks of geese or just potholes (I suspect they get left as traffic-calming) make driving anywhere a slow and hazardous experience and safest in the middle of the road. It's best experienced, I have found, with eyes firmly closed. That is perhaps why Romanians have such an apparently relaxed attitude to timekeeping, as journeys are so unpredictable, or perhaps they are channelling their Latin nature. Not sticking to a tight timetable means that visits to wineries in Romania always involve fascinating side trips: Peleş Castle, the salt mines at Prahova and Turda, horse-drawn carriage rides round open-air museums and evening parties where dancing a *hora* (the traditional dance of Romania and Moldova) is required, even if you have two left feet.

Visiting Romania is a distinctly different experience to Bulgaria or Moldova, and by now I've learned, I think, to go with the flow rather than try and stick to the plan. One recent trip took me first to taste wine made by monks in the Cetăţuia Monastery cellar, and visit their secret treasury with its three-dimensional icon, and then in complete contrast tour the high-tech research lab at Iaşi university. On another visit in Miniş, when I wanted to go on an impossible visit into the snow-bound vineyards, a brave driver was found to take me there in a tractor-trailer. I've been lucky enough to stay in castles, creepy Gothic hotels with frozen wind whistling through the window frames, Transylvanian cottages and even a hotel designed by Gustav Eiffel.

This is definitely a country of contrasts wherever you look. Bucharest itself is marked by rather brutal and monstrous architecture, and everywhere you hear the soundtrack of barking dogs. Close to the capital, the flat, fertile plains are more like green concrete, dotted with the rusting remnants of communism and marching rows of pylons. It's a different country when you arrive in the Carpathian mountains and pass through small villages, dark brooding forests, and every so often, snow-sprinkled graveyards between the trees. You can see where the legends for which the country is famous might have sprung from. When you arrive in the heart of Transylvania itself, it's a land-that-time-forgot place of farming by scythe and donkey.

ROMANIA'S VINE ROOTS

Romania is a fascinating and complex country, especially when it comes to wine. The sheer size of the country (covering 238,391 square kilometres) and vast range of climatic zones and topography – from seaside to mountains – makes for a fascinating tapestry woven of different wine styles. Romania is a wine country through and through, with vines grown in just about every corner, from huge estates to tiny plots in back gardens. As with her neighbours, communism broke the links between the Romanian people and their land, but this country's path back to recovery has taken a different route, shaped by its own history, culture, political influences, and landscape.

Romania is a country rich in natural resources. There are deposits of iron ore, Europe's richest gold deposits, and other minerals, as well as oil and natural gas (though not enough for self-sufficiency). It was a supplier of oil to the Soviet Union in the past. Romania is particularly famous for its forested Carpathian Mountains which dominate the centre of the country in a giant horseshoe shape around the Transylvanian plateau. This is home to the majority of Europe's brown bear and wild wolf populations. Fourteen national parks protect some of the unspoilt natural environments, ranging from alpine meadows to lakes; verdant valleys to the Danube delta wetlands. You need to leave the surrounds of Bucharest to see Romania at its best.

In this part of Europe, it's important to understand that the countries as they exist today bear little resemblance to the past, indeed modern Romania only came together as recently as 1918 when Transylvania joined. There are a few geographical features that remain constant – the Black Sea coastline, mountain ranges and the Danube itself – but otherwise national borders have more often been a question of politics than of geography. It seems to an outsider like me that in countries where national identity is more about politics than geography, people become particularly protective about their ethnic identity. Witness the sometimes uncomfortable relationship between ethnic Hungarians and ethnic Romanians in parts of Transylvania and cities like Cluj-Napoca.

Romania is the tenth largest nation in Europe by population, with an estimated 19.6 million people in 2017 according to EU data, and its capital, Bucharest, is Europe's sixth largest city. However, it punches above its weight in terms of area under vine (fifth in Europe after Spain, France, Italy and Portugal), and wine production (sixth in Europe after Italy, France, Spain, Germany and Portugal). However, Hungary has the edge, if production from noble *Vitis vinifera* varieties only is taken into account, and the substantial volume of wine made from hybrid vines is discounted. The problem of Romania's very significant area of hybrid vines (vines crossed with other species of *Vitis* such as *Vitis labrusca*) will be discussed later. Discounting the hybrid vines would put Romania seventh in terms of wine production. Agriculture is still a very significant sector, and grapevines cover around 1.7 per cent of arable land. Around 1 million people make a living from wine, so it has a significant socio-economic role too.

Romania, along with Bulgaria, became a full member of the EU on 1 January 2007 though neither country joined the eurozone. Romania grows 5.7 per cent of the EU's vines but has more than one third of the grower holdings of the whole EU (34.4 per cent) and the smallest average holding size of just 0.2 hectares. In contrast to Bulgaria (where today around 65 per cent of vineyards are in holdings of over 10 hectares), only just over 30 per cent of Romanian vineyard land is farmed in areas of over 10 hectares. Romania is in thirteenth place in global wine production – well ahead of more famous wine-producing countries like New Zealand – but the majority of Romania's wine is consumed domestically. The country has been a net importer of wine since 2006, so its export share is relatively insignificant.

10

ROMANIAN HISTORY

THE PREHISTORIC ERA

The area that is Romania today has been lived in by modern humans for a long time. In 2002, three amateur cavers found a karst cave they named Cave of Bones in Caraş-Severin county in western Romania. In one of the galleries, they found a fragment of jawbone with five molar teeth still attached. Later this was identified as coming from an adult male aged between 35 and 40 years, from at least 40,000 years ago. There were also a part skull of an adult male and remains of a female dated to the same era. These remains were at least 2,000 years older than the previously recorded oldest modern human remains found in Europe at that time. Some of Europe's oldest human footprints have also been found in Romania's Ciur-Izbuc Cave in the Carpathian Mountains. Radiocarbon dating of cave bear fossils found just below these footprints suggests that these early humans left their impressions 36,500 years ago.

The various Neolithic societies in this part of Europe probably had grapevines, and certainly grew a range of crops. These civilizations appear to have had organized agriculture and clear hierarchies (such as that of the Varna culture, see p.12). A culture called the Vinca occupied a large part of the Balkans from 5700 BC to 4500 BC, overlapping in time with both Bulgaria's Varna culture and the Cucuteni-Trypillian culture. This latter group lived in the area that stretched from the Carpathian Mountains to the River Dniester (today's Romania and Moldova) from 5200 BC to 3500 BC and is also believed to have grown grapes, though there's no evidence that these people actually made wine.

THE GETO-DACIANS

The Carpathian-Danube region, in which the Romanian ethnic community evolved, seems to have been settled by around 2000 BC by Indo-Europeans who migrated and intermingled with the native Neolithic peoples to form the Thracians. Legend says that Dionysus, the god of wine, was born in Thracia or Thrace, (in today's Dobrogea region, though Banat also lays claim to his birthplace). Some sources believe that the Early Thracians had a similar god – Sabazios – who could have been picked up by the Greeks and personified in Dionysus.

The Ancient Greeks settled in the coastal Dobrogea region in the seventh century BC, on the Black Sea in what is now Constanța and they may have influenced viticulture by bringing vines of their own. This is when the first records of Thracian contact with the Greek world arose. Herodotus, writing in the fifth century BC, described the people of this land as the Getae who lived alongside the Dacian tribes. Vineyard tools dating back 2,500 years have also been found in the Dobrogea area, while evidence of pottery and vineyard tools from the fifth to the third centuries BC have been uncovered on Cătălina Hill in the Cotnari region.

Rome expanded into the Balkan Peninsula in the third and second centuries BC. Under the leadership of King Burebista, who reigned from 82 to 44 BC, the Geto-Dacians came together in a tribal union to oppose the Roman advance. This powerful union stretched from the Black Sea to the Adriatic and from the Balkan Mountains to Bohemia and threatened Rome's ascendancy in the area. The Roman Emperor Trajan mounted multiple campaigns in the region, finally triumphing in 106 AD. The next century and a half saw the region becoming the Roman province of Dacia. Officials, soldiers and merchants settled alongside the native Dacians and the Latin language became influential. The region remained a Roman province until finally the Emperor Aurelian withdrew the Roman army and his administration in around 271 AD.

We know there were vines and wine during this period. For instance, the poet Ovid was exiled to Constanța in around 8 AD by Emperor Augustus (and Ovidiu is still a popular name in Romania in his honour). He described the Getae as knowing how to produce a kind of brandy by concentrating wine through freezing. The ancient geographer Strabo describes both Dacian men and women drinking undiluted wine from horns, and describes a vine-clearance order from King Burebista – perhaps to make the land less attractive to invaders, or to reduce drunkenness. However, a Roman coin, the Dacian Felix, minted around 106 AD to celebrate Trajan's successful campaign, depicts two children offering grapes and wheat as a symbols of the region's riches, which suggests that Burebista failed! Even today a few important wine words in modern Romanian are inherited from the Dacians: *strugure* (grape), *butuc* (vine) and *ravac* (must).

The Romanian people claim that much of their ethnic character derives from this Roman influence, though this ancient identity has been reshaped continuously by its location at the heart of so many major continental migration routes.

AFTER THE ROMANS

For several centuries after the Romans left, this region was overrun by successive waves of migratory peoples who mingled with the remaining Romanized people. By the early seventh century, the Slavs had arrived in the area. Their occupation of much of the Balkan Peninsula cut Dacia off from the Roman world. It seems that the Slavs and the more numerous Daco-Romans assimilated during this period. The recorded story of wine in these lands is harder to find, though there's no reason to assume that wine did not continue. The first known written historical evidence in the region of Miniş dates to the early eleventh century, when the first Queen of Hungary, Gizella, along with King Stephen, donated 'eight vines' to the Abbey of Bakanybel.

Another story from this time is about the naming of the village of Beltiug in Satu Mare. It dates to around 1085, after a fierce battle between King Ladislaus I of Hungary and a migratory Turkish tribe (the Pechenegs). After the battle, a pumpkin filled with wine was brought to the king. The story goes that he actually asked about the variety of pumpkin, but nonetheless this was proof that wine was being produced. The village name derives from Hungarian words 'bél' for content and 'tek' for pumpkin. Subsequently, in the twelfth and thirteenth centuries, viticulture and wine production is documented in Catholic monasteries in Mocrea, Pâncota and Arad.

In Transylvania, there was believed to be a real renaissance in winemaking in the twelfth century, with the arrival of Saxon settlers from the Rhine and Mosel. We know that King Andrew II (1205–1235) exempted Transylvanian Saxons from paying customs tax on their wine. By the fifteenth and sixteenth centuries, the production and trade of wine became the main source of income for Miniş residents, and around Lechinţa there was documentary evidence of a coopers' guild in 1546, suggesting wine was being made in significant quantities. Cramele Recaş in Banat has documents dating back to 1447 recording sale of vineyards in the area.

Copy of 1447 vineyard sale document at Cramele Recaş

It's not clear whether one of Romania's most famous sons had anything much to do with wine. Vlad the Impaler, son of Vlad Dracul, was born in Sighişoara in Transylvania in 1431 and became *voivode*, or prince, of Wallachia three times between 1448 and his death. He gained his moniker from plundering Saxon villages in Transylvania and then impaling his captives, a trick he also used against envoys of the Ottoman sultan. An echo of his reputation for cruelty lives on in the stories of Count Dracula.

From the fourteenth to the eighteenth centuries, the principalities of Moldavia and Wallachia evolved as part of the Eastern Orthodox religious and cultural world. They kept an allegiance to Constantinople, but unlike their neighbours they spoke a Latin-derived language and recognized the Romans as a key part of their ancestry. Records of wine continue to appear during this period. The first written evidence for vineyards around Cotnari comes in 1384 with a mention by Moldavian ruler Petru Muşat, though the village of Cotnari itself was only first referred to by name in 1448.

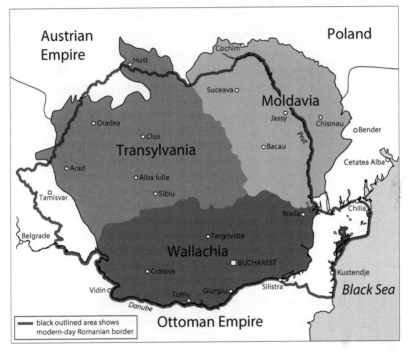

Moldavia, Wallachia and Transylvania c.1600

By 1464 Valea Călugărească is mentioned as a winemaking village. It was described as 'surrounded by vast areas of vineyards' and came under the rule of Vlad the Monk who was appointed by Ştefan Cel Mare, the great leader of Moldavia. In foreign documents of the era, wine from Dealu Mare was described as 'oily, strong and durable'.

The fifteenth century saw mentions of Cotnari wine increase in documents about gifts to monasteries, and even records of its sale in Venice; the famous Cotnari blend is believed to come from this era. Professor Valeriu Cotea in his book *Vineyards and Wines of Romania* describes Ştefan Cel Mare as closely linked to the wine of this region. Indeed, Ştefan Cel Mare's doctor wrote to the Doge of Venice in 1502, stating that, 'The Cotnari wine resembles that of Friuli, Italy.'

A paper by Boc and Dobrei in 2015 mentions a Hungarian chronicler, Anton Verancsis (1504–73) describing Transylvania and Moldavia, saying, 'Hills covered with vineyards and wines arise everywhere, whether you want them strong or weak, rough or sweet, white or red, they are so good in taste and so special in variety that you do not want any Falerna wines from Campania and even when comparing them to these, you love them more.' This is high praise at a time when the wines of Campania in Italy were particularly admired. A century later, in 1646, a Catholic missionary, Marcus Bandinus, mentions that, 'All the southern part of Moldavia produces so much wine that during harvesting they sell a bucket (10 litres) for four bani and during winter they sell it for six or seven bani'. Dimitrie Cantemir (1673–1723), ruler of Moldavia in 1710–11 says that the 'finest wine comes from Cotnari,' and adds, 'Being I daresay finer and better than any European wine and even better than the Tokaj wine.'

OTTOMAN INFLUENCES

The four centuries of Ottoman Turkish domination over the Balkans from 1541 were significant, but by becoming a vassal state under the Sultan, and paying annual tribute, the pre-Romanians (of the principalities of Wallachia and Moldavia) avoided direct incorporation into the Ottoman Empire. This allowed the principalities to preserve their political institutions, laws and social structure, including their leaders and *boyars*. They also avoided a mass Muslim settlement of their land. This was different to the situation in Bulgaria.

However, under the Ottoman Empire, the heavy taxes and duties imposed by the Sultan's administration forced the peasants to sell much of their land. This in turn was bought by members of noble families and *boyars*, often serving in the Sultan's local administration. The economies of the two principalities rested upon agriculture led by these *boyar*-owned estates, as well as monasteries, but with a population of peasants who had sunk to the level of serfdom. Transylvania at this time was dominated by the Roman Catholic nobility, while in the cities the Lutheran German-speaking Saxon classes held sway. The Romanian population here was excluded from public affairs because they were considered to be both peasants and Orthodox. The fortunes of the majority of people finally improved when Transylvania was brought under the Habsburg crown the end of the seventeenth century.

The net effect was that from that point until the First World War, a couple of thousand *boyars* or *chiaburi* (wealthy peasants) owned more than 50 per cent of the agricultural land in the principalities of Wallachia and Moldavia. The other half was owned by around 1 million smaller landowners. A couple of million people worked on the landowners' fields, without owning any land.

During the eighteenth century, although Moldavia remained nominally subject to the Ottoman Empire, Russian influence in the principality increased, becoming a point of contention between the Turks and the Russians. In 1744, Moldavia lost its north-western territory of Bukovina to the Austrians, and in 1812 it gave up its eastern portion of Bessarabia to Russia in the Treaty of Bucharest. Following the Russian defeat in the Crimean War, Moldavia became an autonomous state under the Ottomans.

Then in 1859, influenced by Romanian nationalism, the ruling assembly of Moldavia voted to unite with Wallachia under the *voivode* (prince) Alexandru Ioan Cuza, formally unifying in 1861. He took large areas of land from monasteries to give to private people and in 1865 introduced a civil code on land ownership, including viticultural land, modelled on the French Napoleonic code. The name Romania was used for the first time in 1866 and in 1877 the state claimed independence from the Ottoman Empire. The Second World War was decisive in the development of modern Romania. Greater Romania came into being after the First World War, gaining Transylvania and Banat from Hungary, Bukovina from Austria and Bessarabia from Russia, doubling its territory. However, in 1940 the Soviet Union took back Bessarabia and northern Bukovina while Hungary took northern Transylvania and Bulgaria took southern Dobrogea. In 1947, Western influence ended, and northern Transylvania was returned to Romania and this is the area that is Romania today.

THE PRE-PHYLLOXERA PERIOD AND GRAPEVINE HISTORY

There seems to be little detailed evidence of the grapes grown or wine styles produced in most of Romania up to the nineteenth century. As

Şerban Dâmboviceanu (co-owner of the nineteenth-century royal winery at Corcova) explains, all the historical records of what was grown on the estate were either burnt in the fire that destroyed the winery in the early twentieth century, or destroyed by the communists. After funding to Romania's royal family was cut in 1884, they were given a number of domaines to raise money to live on. One such domaine was the crown estate in Segarcea (which King Karol had planted with grapevines, guided by advice from French experts). Unfortunately everything was ripped out under communism, and no written records remain, so all that was left were a few ancient vines of pink-skinned Tămâioasă Roza. These had originally been brought from France, where they have since died out.

The arrival of the vine-destroying, aphid-like louse phylloxera (see Glossary) in the late nineteenth century seems to have brought more formal attention to the wine sector, and thus academic literature starts to appear. In a research paper by Popa et al. in 2006, there are reports on some historic documentary sources for Romania's pre-phylloxera wine sector. It seems that before 1880, a wide diversity of *Vitis vinifera* cultivars was grown, some localized and others widespread. For instance, G. Nicoleanu, in his work *Introduction à l'Ampelographie Roumaine*, published in 1900, describes 45 local and autochthonous varieties, spread throughout Romania. Specifically, he says, 'On the Oltenian territory were cultivated the ancient kinds Cârlogancă, Braghină, Gordan, Tămâioasă, Corb, Seină, Bebecel, Vulpe, Balaban, Băşicată, Slăvită, Timpurie, Teişor, Rozachie, Cornită, Coarnă albă, Coarnă neagră, Tata vacii, Tata oii, etc.' Cârlogancă is believed to be a historic synonym for Crâmposie.

G. Nicoleanu also collaborated on a work by P. Viala and V. Vermorel, called *Traité Général de Viticulture-Ampelographie*, published from 1902 to 1910. This was a summary of ampelography as it was known at the time, and included a mention of Romanian grapes as Braghină, Crâmposie, Fetească Albă, Fetească Neagră, Gordan, Grasă, Iordană, Negru Vârtos, Timpurie. It also refers to comments on historical Romanian vineyards by French specialist on ampelography J. Roy-Chevrier, who explained that, 'There, the most valuable vineyards were owned by the high officials, the convents and the nobility, producing highly valued, luxury wines, for table and for export purposes.' Reference was also made to Crâmposie wine from Drăgăşani, being, 'Submitted to the champagne obtaining process by N. Benger, at Stuttgart, offering the happiest results.' This is a technique that has been revived by Prince Ştirbey recently with exciting results.

Later on, between 1955 and 1970, Romanian traditional grape varieties were presented in the O.I.V. Journal *Registre Ampelographique International* by Constantinescu and his colleagues. From their reports, it is clear that the viticultural identity of Romania was still led by indigenous varieties – Crâmpoşie, Braghină, Fetească Albă, Fetească Neagră and Grasă are included.

THE MARCH OF PHYLLOXERA

Phylloxera was first spotted near Lake Arad in western Romania in 1880 and officially noted nearly 400 kilometres away in Prahova county in 1884, taking only four years to cross most of the country. In *Dying on the Vine*, it is reported that Romania made a forceful state response and had established a national viticulture service by the end of 1885, though this did not stop damage from the infestation for some time. By 1898, around 29,000 hectares were infested (out of 163,000 hectares at that time, though this stated area almost certainly did not include Transylvania) despite the work that was already going into replanting from the mid-1890s.

Not long after the detection of phylloxera, Romania set up nurseries and research stations with the aim of research into selection of the best varieties of rootstock; to produce and distribute planting material; and to learn about the systematic cultivation of the American vine. For example, the Pietroasa research station was founded in 1893 and was one of the first nurseries in the country with a key role in restoring viticulture post-phylloxera. This was a time when expertise was sought from the French, who brought their own varieties, notably Chardonnay, Pinot Gris, Pinot Noir and Cabernet Sauvignon. Dan Muntean (Domaine Muntean and formerly director of Halewood International) explained:

Pinot Noir was first introduced to Romania soon after the phyl-loxera devastation at Murfatlar Research Station, by French vign-erons from Champagne, not Burgundy, alongside Chardonnay and Pinot Gris. The Research Station was established around 1907. The three grape varieties were accumulating a great deal of sugar in Murfatlar (approximately 300 days of sunshine/year), so they started life in Romania as sweet wines, and for many years the locals considered the grape varieties as producing only sweet wines.

It was around this time that the old mixed plantations and traditional varieties disappeared. Oliver Bauer (winemaker at Prince Ştirbey and owner of Crama Bauer) reckons that:

> Some centuries ago, all of the varieties mentioned were planted and used, but mainly in field blends because a lot of them weren't hermaphrodite, so they needed pollen from another plant to produce grapes (as in the case of the old Crâmpoşie and Braghină). Another advantage of a field blend, and why it was used, was for safer production and possibly to balance deficiencies of each particular variety. During and after the phylloxera disaster in the mid to the end of the nineteenth century most of the existing old plantations were destroyed ... Beside American rootstocks, the French brought also their quality varieties like Merlot, Cabernet Sauvignon, Sauvignon Blanc, etc. at the beginning of the twentieth century. These plants didn't need to be field blends to produce a crop and concerning quality and continuity they also outperformed most of the former varieties. So, their decline began. During the Communist time the focus was more on quantity than quality and these 'boring' varieties guarantee that. So even today they are grown not only in Romania but also in Moldova where high yields (20 tonnes per hectare and more) are gladly embraced.

In the early twentieth century, one of Romania's biggest nurseries belonged to Prince Barbu Ştirbey (great-grandfather of Ileana Kripp, the owner of Prince Ştirbey winery). Between 1905 and 1906, this nursery advertised a wide range of indigenous varieties grafted to a selection of different American rootstocks, and Ileana reports that her great-grandfather was even then concerned about the loss of local varieties. The catalogue also offers a range of foreign varieties including Hungarian grapes like Ezerjó, Bakator, Kadarka and Furmint, as well as several varieties of Muscat, Sauvignon Blanc, Pinot Blanc and Riesling.

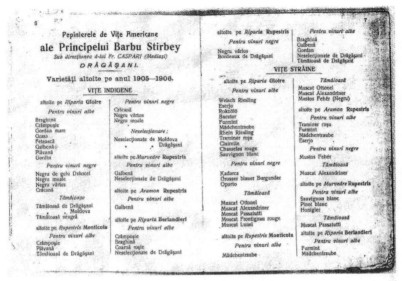

Ştirbey grape catalogue from 1905–1906

Throughout this period, it seems that agriculture remained inefficient, with poor productivity, and there were significant inequities in society. Before 1864, peasants in Wallachia and Moldavia had effectively been serfs. With reforms around this era, it became possible for them to own some land. Further reform in 1889 gave them the right to buy larger tracts, but inevitable lack of finances or education meant that – in reality – land holdings remained small among the peasant class. Another significant agrarian reform came in 1921 with an act that expropriated land from properties of more than 100 hectares. It was redistributed to peasants, in holdings of not less than 2 hectares. This exacerbated the problem of land fragmentation, and by 1930 the average farm size was just 3.9 hectares and small farms accounted for 90 per cent of all agricultural holdings. In the aftermath of phylloxera, the idea of planting cheaper interspecific hybrids (or direct producers, see Glossary), was more attractive to these impoverished growers than buying expensive grafted vines.

However, by the 1930s it seemed that Romania had started to recognize the problem of hybrid vines. In *Science, Vine and Wine in Modern France* Harry W. Paul reports that at that time, 'Romania was a leader in getting the OIV (Office International du Vin) to pass motions hostile to hybrids – the country had been planted with all imaginable varieties of worthless hybrids when the big estates were divided up after the first world war. It required international cooperation to stop Romanian growers being duped [into buying hybrids].' Germany and Yugoslavia went further, banning hybrids completely, whereas anti-hybrid measures seem to have been less effective in Romania. As an indication of rural poverty and meagre funds for investment, in 1938 there were only 4,049 tractors in the whole country.

Between the wars, the foundations of rigorous scientific research were established in Romania and in 1943, there was a report noting high potential from a range of varieties which included Pinot Noir and other international grapes. These research centres continued their work throughout the era that followed, though by the 1960s, programmes had moved on to research into high-training forms to improve yields and to avoid disease, and possibly also to avoid winter frost damage.

THE COMMUNIST ERA

The arrival of the Red Army in Bucharest in 1944 profoundly shifted the political balance in Romania, propelling the communists to power. One of their resolutions was to collectivize agriculture. Jakob Kripp (owner of Prince Ştirbey) explains: 'In March 1945, the government was formed under the *diktat* of the Soviet Union and the Romanian Communist Party, with leaders trained in Moscow before and during the war. It started expropriating – without any compensation – all the agricultural land where people owned more than 50 hectares. An exception were rice fields and vineyards, which were not affected by this expropriation.' All uncultivated land and that belonging to so-called 'enemies of the people' was also expropriated, followed by confiscation of royal properties (the king himself abdicated under duress in 1947). This land was given to peasants in small plots of 1–5 hectares, but only a couple of years later, these peasants were forced to become members of local cooperatives, managed by loyal Communist Party members, and to leave most of their land to these *kolkhozes*.

By 1949, a decision to launch total collectivization was made. Although voluntary at first, it soon became obligatory, claiming the last residuals of the former large farms, plus all vineyards and rice fields. This process was all completed by 1962, apart from some very mountainous areas, where collectivization simply was not feasible.

Collectivization was set up in two ways. First were the CAP (Cooperativa Agricola de Producție) that small growers had to join, though in return they were permitted to cultivate a tiny plot of land themselves (a maximum of 0.25 hectares). Second were the IAS (Intreprinderi Agricole de Stat) which were state collectivized wineries, run by poorly paid state employees. Valeriu Stoica (former Minister of Justice and owner of Avincis) explains:

> According to the communists, private property was an evil of the world, so they aimed to destroy it. Personal belongings such as a house and a car were allowed but all production means were nationalized or moved into a special form of cooperative, except in the mountains where it wasn't possible to organize state farms. So, in effect all land became either state-owned or part of the seven socialist cooperatives. Under communism, households could have the right of use of a small area around the house for their own production of vegetables, grapes, et cetera, but these vines were not noble vines, they were typically hybrids.

All wine was processed through state-owned Vinalcool plants and satellite wineries. There was one for each region, so in effect the plants became both brands and regional designations. This is something that still causes confusion in Romania today, as several of the privatized successors of these plants have retained these regional names. At first, national investment was channelled into industry at the expense of agriculture but by the 1960s there was increasing emphasis on quantity, mechanization and heavy use of fertilizers. A US Department of Agriculture report from 1971 shows that the early part of the 1950s had seen vineyards fall into neglect. However winemaking soon became seen as an economically significant sector. From 1966 to 1970, grape production rose to 1.1 million tons per year while exports increased from 32,900 tons to 67,500 tons (though notably this was still a tiny percentage of production) between 1966 and 1969, particularly to the markets of USSR, East Germany and Czechoslovakia. Winemaking went in two directions, one was making strong reds for the Soviet market, while the other was production of whites from local grapes for the domestic market. Here wine drinking, and indeed any drinking, remained a strong societal habit.

Grapevine plantings in this period were also focused on grapes able to give high yields, as the goal was quantity over quality. This meant many of the historic varieties were abandoned. Traditional vine training systems such as 'gobelet' (or bush-training) were switched to higher-yielding, neatly wired rows using concrete posts and high cordon training. Planting density in the communist era was typically low to allow for mechanization by large Soviet tractors.

EXPORTS TO THE WEST

The Romanian wine industry under Communism was never really set up as an export industry, unlike its neighbours who were designated as wine exporters in the Eastern Bloc planned economy. However, some export business to the West did develop. For instance, in the late 1970s Romania started a contract with PepsiCo in the US, where Romania was buying Pepsi's cola concentrate in exchange for wines. PepsiCo had acquired a wine division called Monsieur Henri Wines that selected, blended, bot-tled and shipped under their own brand, Premiat. The first four varieties were Premiat Târnave Castle Riesling produced at Jidvei, Premiat Valea Blanc (a blend made primarily from Welschriesling), Premiat Cabernet Sauvignon and Premiat Pinot Noir, both produced at the Research In-stitute in Valea Călugărească. Cesar Baeza was PepsiCo's winemaker in Romania from 1977. PepsiCo had hired Professor Maynard Amerine, the so-called 'father of Californian wine' to help with their wine projects in Eastern Europe and he had recommended that they send an oenologist over. PepsiCo wanted someone with an open mind who wasn't afraid to travel to Eastern Europe and the 27-year-old Chilean-born Cesar fitted the bill. He had also worked as a quality controller, dealing with packag-ing, glass and corks as well as being a winemaker, which proved to be use-ful. 'The concept was to bring in varietal wines that were recognizable, the native grapes were nice but difficult to commercialize,' Cesar explained. After travelling around the country, he ended up at Valea Călugărească, where he says he found winemakers who had studied in France and un-derstood what he wanted to achieve. 'They were making sweet wines for the Soviet Union though, so we had to teach them to make dry wines.

We also had to help with glass and corks which were terrible, so I went to Portugal to get corks and bought glass from Italy. The wines were competitively priced because of the barter deal and were a great success. We soon added other varieties like Sauvignon Blanc from Jidvei and sold 300,000 cases in a very short time.' To begin with Cesar found it was hard overcoming objections to young foreigners giving instructions, but he says, 'I made friends with the people at the wineries, who could see I was trying to help and I did them personal favours like getting medicine. I was surprised how much I could understand as Spanish and Romanian are close languages. I spent a lot of time there and it was really rewarding to achieve so much – a good stage in my career.'

Premiat bottles from the late 1970s

In 1967, the notorious dictator Nicolae Ceaușescu came to power, imposing a brutal and repressive regime. By the 1980s, Ceaușescu became obsessed with paying off the country's foreign debts and paying for his egomaniacal, monumental building projects. He decided to export as much agricultural produce as possible to earn money, impoverishing the country's population at the same time. Wine did play a role in this, though it was not a major hard currency earner (especially compared to Bulgaria) because of higher domestic consumption here. Exports accounted for just 7 per cent of wine production in the period 1985 to 1989.

This was a period when exports to the EU developed strongly, especially in the UK, but also in Germany and Denmark. Liverpool-based entrepreneur John Halewood was a key figure in this. He had already seen an opportunity for Eastern European wine in the UK and had been importing Bulgarian wine. Once the Bulgarian state export monopoly, Vinimpex, set up its own UK office in the early 1980s, John was looking for alternative sources of good-value wine. He started to import from Romania (the first shipment was just 365 cases in 1986), with an emphasis on Pinot Noir since this was something Bulgaria could not offer. Initially Halewood imported Premiat wines, purchased through a Spanish subsidiary of PepsiCo, however, he preferred to buy and select the wines from source. He contacted the Romanian foreign trade monopoly Fructexport, who happened to be looking for an agent. Halewood's company was chosen, from a list of 10 other suitors, as sole agent for Romanian wines in the UK, mainly because of his involvement with Premiat. Shortly after, Halewood International designed their own labels under the brand 'Classic'. The major breakthrough came when supermarket chain Sainsbury's decided to import an own-label Romanian Pinot Noir, which stayed on their shelves for another 20 years. Howard Winn (former product quality manager at Sainsbury's recalls, 'The wine was fruit driven and produced in rotary fermenters. They used to do a kind of *vendange tardive* (late harvest) picked in November and so sugary it wouldn't ferment. They added 5 per cent of this at blending, so we got a wine with 9 grammes per litre of sweetness, but all genuine wine.'

The UK picture

Romanian exports to the UK never quite hit the heights of Bulgarian wine, but still reached a peak of 1 million standard cases by 1996. The wines had been good value and offered a point of difference to other Eastern European sources at that time, but by the mid-1990s quality had declined and wine styles were old-fashioned and distinctly variable. There was a period where the question of Romanian identity in branding was de-stressed, with the development of New World-type brands like Willow Hill, River Route,

Black Peak and others (around the same time as Domaine Boyar's infamous slogan 'Does it matter where it comes from?' for their Bulgarian wines). Pressure on pricing meant that corners were being cut in terms of quality (on top of the emerging issues of privatization of vineyards and wineries) and volumes fell rapidly in the late 1990s in the face of the rise of the New World.

One flying winemaker who spent time in Romania recounts stories of trucks that arrived at the winery with a thin layer of Pinot Noir grapes on top, to disguise mostly overcropped Merlot or whatever else could be found. And Romania's own Ministry of Agriculture, Food and Forestry admitted in 2000 that the technical capabilities of the industry remained at the level of the 1960s and 1970s, so production of white wines in particular was non-competitive. Ultimately it became obvious to Halewood International that they needed to control quality directly by investing in upgraded production facilities. Subsequently it became clear that they would only be able source fruit of good enough quality by investing in vineyards.

11

THE NEW ERA

FIRST STEPS IN PRIVATIZATION

By the time of the change of regime in 1989, vineyard area had risen to around 275,000 hectares. In 1990, agricultural land was all still state-controlled through either CAP or IAS. The beginnings of privatization were slow because the communist-leaning party in power immediately after the overthrow and execution of Ceaușescu did not really grasp the need for return of property. As one winery owner explained, 'There was still a lot of backpedalling and worry that a new bourgeoisie would emerge.' But eventually the process began.

The first step was the decollectivization of the former CAP (agricultural production cooperatives) and return of land holdings to their former owners through law number 18, passed in 1991. This only allowed a maximum of 10 hectares of land per family to be reclaimed – even if they owned much more before 1948. There were restrictions on the resale of this land for a minimum of three years. Land was also allocated to people who had worked in these operations for the previous three years. Then in 1997, another law extended this right up to 50 hectares per family, though this amendment didn't come fully into effect until 2000.

Mass privatization of the Vinalcools (winemaking plants) was via a scheme under which vouchers were issued. Sixty per cent of Vinalcool share capital went private by this route, before a secondary market called RASDAQ was established for resale of these shares. Halewood bought a majority holding of Vinalcool Prahova this way. Next the Vinalcools were empowered to sell assets such as satellite wineries.

SUITCASES OF CASH

Angela Muir MW tells a story of a French winemaker she was working with in Romania. He wanted to buy one of these satellite wineries – the first offer was turned down because, with only one bidder, it was not deemed to be an open auction. A second bidder – supposedly in name only – was found, to comply with the rules. But on the day of the sale this bidder turned up with suitcases full of cash and bought the winery.

The next step was the decision of the State Ownership Fund (later Authority for Privatization and Administration of State Stock Holdings) to sell their 40 per cent holdings in Vinalcools (the remaining state holding after the mass privatization through vouchers). This allowed companies like Halewood to purchase the remaining ownership. Finally, state ownership in the former state agricultural enterprise (IAS) landholdings was sold.

As for export trade, during the communist times, with central planned economy, foreign trade in Romania was a state monopoly (and direct export by producers was not allowed). Among these hundred or so foreign trade companies were Fructexport and Prodexport. Fructexport traded in fruit and vegetables, while Prodexport was responsible for processed foods. Until 1983, wine export was a department within Fructexport, then it was transferred to Prodexport as wine was then considered a processed food. After the fall of communism in 1990 the foreign trade monopoly was dismantled and some of the people working in Prodexport decided to leave and set up a new private company dealing in wine export. This new company was Vinexport. At the outset Vinexport was a successful undertaking, with major wineries (Murfatlar, Jidvei, Cotnari, Valea Călugărească) and key customers being stakeholders, but in the end it could not survive the multiple conflicts of interest.

In 2002, and again in 2007, the law was amended numerous times, to finally permit families to claim back the entire area of land that their ancestors had previously owned before 1948. This doesn't apply to land owned prior to 1945 as the expropriation law of 1945 is still in force.

Kripp explains that it would practically be impossible to reverse it, because the expropriated land was distributed to millions of peasants, forced into cooperatives later, and restituted to the peasants. There were special rules for land that was under forests, or indeed where vineyards, buildings or other investments had been undertaken on the land after nationalization in 1948, and in these circumstances the families received compensation.

INTO THE NEW MILLENNIUM

By 2001, private property accounted for 81.5 per cent of the wine industry. Private individuals held 77 per cent of vineyards, mostly in plots of less than 1 hectare; 2 per cent belonged to state research institutes and 21 per cent was in the former state-owned enterprises (IAS) which were just being privatized. The IAS operations proved difficult to sell as the state's valuation was higher than investors were prepared to pay – these were properties with almost negative value as the facilities were so poor. Also, where they were privatized through management–employee buyout schemes, it was difficult to source any additional funds for new equipment or to pay off debts.

Many of these schemes ultimately failed because of this, and were not helped by lack of training nor understanding of how to run a business in a free market environment. In the previous era, wineries had had large workforces, as full employment was guaranteed and the role of senior management was more to do with looking after staff and keeping the authorities on side than anything else. Technical and production directors had to focus on winemaking and bottling according to directions from the state, and there was no such thing as a sales or marketing department, so those skills simply did not exist. After privatization, reducing the payroll became a major issue, and for foreign consultant winemakers, the challenge was to work out who the good workers were. Angela Muir MW points out that, 'Under communism, people just had to turn up to their jobs and the ones who actually worked were seen as the losers. We had to identify these and make them feel part of the elite, with Western cigarettes and dollars.'

Privatization in the two regions of Drăgășani and Dealu Mare was slightly different because there were no huge state farms here. It was possible for new private winery owners to buy bigger areas than in other parts of the country, where privatization was dominated by the extremely large state farms, or by very small fragmented landholdings. One winery owner explained:

> A difference in Drăgăşani compared to some of the other areas in Romania was that there were no big state farms, and the existing state farms were not privatized right away so it was possible to restitution some bigger surfaces. It was similar in Dealu Mare where the maximum owned by single wineries was 200 to 300 hectares compared to these huge holdings of some of the big wineries. Both these areas have benefited from an unexpected effect, in that because there are more owners there has been more competition for producing quality between them.

It is worth noting that vineyard plantings were significantly biased towards high-yielding varieties and almost no replanting had taken place in this phase, so many vines were old and had not been looked after during the uncertainties of land restitution. In effect, there had been a twelve-year gap in viticulture – only 3 per cent of vines had been replanted in any proper way by 2002 according to Guy de Poix of SERVE, one of the first foreign investors. Plantings in 2000 included: Fetească Albă, 42,000 hectares; Riesling Italico, 20,000 hectares; Fetească Regală, 17,000 hectares; Aligoté, 12,000 hectares; Merlot, 12,000 hectares and Cabernet Sauvignon, 11,500 hectares.

PRIVATIZATION CHALLENGES

Today's wine industry has been almost entirely privatized (apart from state research institutes) and most producers with quality aspirations now own land. However to get to this point, there were a number of structural problems that had to be solved around land-ownership, fragmentation of holdings, and the emerging post-communist legal system.

Much of the CAP land was given back to pre-war owners but in very small and fragmented amounts, and these owners were often not interested in farming or not capable of farming to any professional level. By May 2004, 188,630 hectares of vineyards had been registered to private owners in 1.24 million parcels with an average holding of just 0.15 hectares. And in fact, planting of hybrid vines increased in this period.

Guy de Poix (founder of SERVE) reported that he tried to rent some of this land in 1998, but for 28 hectares he had to write 145 contracts, making it impossible to manage realistically. As Guy said in 2002, 'The truth is that if I had known the difficulties encountered since I first arrived in Romania I would have thought twice before investing, not only the money but also the time and energy.'

Land ownership documentation was also an issue. At first temporary documents were issued but these could not be used as security. Formal issue of notarized paperwork was slow, with only a third completed by 1999, and the lack of a formal land register has also been a huge problem in identifying exactly who owned what.

As Valeriu Stoica (former Minister of Justice and owner of Avincis) explained:

> A vulnerable point in the land restitution process is that most of Romania does not have an effective land register which means there is still a lack of clear evidence of land ownership in many cases.[1] The law 18 in 1991 actually created lots of problems because land was restituted with no clear physical limits, it just issued a title to property on a register within a community. In effect just a name and a surface with no clear position. The original aim was to return exactly the previous holdings but this was not always possible. The second option was to give land in a different position from the state reserve (there is still litigation ongoing with this too). Sometimes there would be clear natural borders or marks but generally physical borders were destroyed under communism so nothing precise that could be relied on. There are examples where people's properties overlap entirely or where two owners claim title to the same plot … It is 28 years this year and we still haven't succeeded in rebuilding our country, recovering from communism is proving difficult. Communism destroyed the structure of private property.

---

1 The situation was slightly different in Transylvania where the Austro-Hungarian administration did create a land register and today no one will buy land without a deed.

The Stoica family themselves had to go to court to try and reclaim the family's historic 36-hectare holding at Villa Dobruşa in Drăgăşani. In the end, they had to settle for 24 hectares, as some land had already been restituted to other people, and the vineyards had been destroyed during this lengthy process.

This lack of resolution over Romania's land ownership is a problem still today and has caused significant economic damage to agriculture. Lots of owners are simply uninterested in their land, so it is not cultivated. There are several cases where it's been impossible to track down ownership because of family heritage disputes and owners moving away. At Corcova winery, Şerban Dâmboviceanu mentions a plot of promising vineyard land near his village that belonged to a Romanian princess who was exiled to Paris. She died there intestate and without heirs. It is simply impossible to buy this land because no one knows who owns it today.

Other ongoing issues included a long period with little investment across the industry. Because privatization was such a long process with ownership unclear, this meant that investments were not feasible, except in some former state farms that were bought by new generation capitalists. The rest of the land was returned in such small plots that it was impossible to do modern land management. And because people had been previously collectivized, they were reluctant to join cooperatives again, which meant that it was impossible to unite for better productivity, a situation that remains today.

Balla Géza (owner of Balla Géza winery) was winemaker and then general director of the state farm in the Miniş region. After restitution of the area's 2,600 hectares to around 3,000 people, Géza invited the new landowners to a meeting to discuss organizing themselves together. Géza himself had been visiting cooperatives in France and Italy and thought this model could work in Romania. Unfortunately, 80 per cent of the 2,000 or so new vineyard owners who came to the meeting rejected the idea of cooperating as being far too much like collectivization. So Géza set up his own winery. Two to three years later when growers started to come to him and complain that working vineyards was too hard, he had little sympathy.

A PERSONAL PERSPECTIVE

Philip Cox (owner, Cramele Recaş) explains how he sees the situation:

Obviously all these changes caused an enormous amount of confusion and gave rise to the potential for a lot of corruption. There were thousands of cases of people who purchased land between 1991 and 2007 – that the person selling in fact no longer owned – due to the changes in the law, and even more thousands of cases where the ownership before 1948 was violently disputed by various parts of the same family, grandchildren, nephews, cousins and so on. Apart from nearly 20 years of court cases, the results were that the land holdings became very fragmented with a lot of very small parcels, and many vineyards went out of production because the land was under dispute for many years, and nobody does long-term investments like vineyards on land where you are not sure about the ownership.

Some regions found ways round this by allowing lease or lease-buy arrangements for the land. We ourselves in Recaş entered into a partnership with the former state-owned vineyards, that allowed us to do a lease/buy arrangement after 5 years, and where the former owners of the land received agricultural lands in the areas suitable for general arable farming. Even so, when we were finally allowed to permanently buy the land after 20 years, we had to buy parts of it from 400 families, which was a lot of work. In many regions this has not been possible, leaving numerous small farms that are not economically viable and where the people have lost the know-how of grape farming that is normally passed down through the generations. This is one of Romania's biggest problems in my view.

FOREIGN INVESTMENT

Foreign investment in Romania became possibly as early as 1991 but only under strict conditions. To start with, it was possible to set up a Romanian company with foreign ownership, but this company wasn't permitted to buy land. Romania had to open the door to EU citizens to buy land and property upon EU accession, allowing both individuals and companies to do so. Romania differed from Bulgaria in that the first investors were wine distributors who already had a market for Romanian wines and were seeking to secure a consistent supply base. Early investors included German company Carl Reh, British importer Halewood and Italian-funded Vinarte.

The very first private wine company of all was set up by Corsican count and former dentist Guy de Poix as early as 1994. A significant advantage for Romania of these small to mid-sized investments was foreign expertise and a more flexible mind-set than in some Eastern Bloc countries, so wine quality improved quickly. Indeed, it is these wineries that kick-started a quality revolution in Romania – big enough to be professional but small enough to be flexible. Membership of the EU undoubtedly helped accelerate both foreign investment and the development of a new generation of private estates. These were typically funded with either foreign money (particularly Italian, due in part to language similarities) or non-wine industry money, plus EU funds like SAPARD (the same Special Accession Programme for Agricultural and Rural Development programme as in Bulgaria) in the run up to accession. This was a key financial instrument set up by the European Union in 1999 to support countries in Central and Eastern Europe to bring their agricultural sectors up to EU standards before they became full members.

EU FUNDING

Immediately after the fall of communism, and well into the following decade, the wine industry was burdened with significant structural problems. These included run-down wineries and old-fashioned equipment, lack of motivation to improve, poor understanding of the requirements of global wine markets, lack of supervision or control over small growers to ensure picking when fully ripe, the wrong mind-set for growing for quality rather than volume, wines produced to suit local market demands (low quality sweet and semi-sweet styles) and all the privatization challenges already mentioned.

However, starting with Halewood International (from the UK) and followed by other foreign companies (including Carl Reh from Germany) a wave of investment began. Significant pre-accession funding for the wine industry through the EU's SAPARD programme has also raised standards in both wineries and vineyards substantially (€35 million between 2002 and 2006). In the early days, it wasn't always easy to get funding though – Dan Muntean, formerly of Halewood, explained that a SAPARD funding proposal in 2004 ran to 16,000 pages, a particularly heavy burden for a small winery with limited admin personnel to be able to manage. This continued, with the wine industry receiving €210 million between 2007 and 2013 through an EU-funded national support programme. Further funding continued to be available to the tune of €47.7 million per year until 2018. This programme provided funding for promotion of wines, including advice on responsible consumption, help regarding designations of origin and geographical indications, assistance in restructuring and converting vineyards, harvest insurance (against disasters like hail or frost to ensure steady cash-flow) and investments in winery equipment. The Ministry of Agriculture And Rural Development, that manages the scheme today, expects vineyard redevelopment to take the biggest share of the money.

Today, most wineries have bought land and now own significant, consolidated vineyard holdings, which is a major structural change in the wine industry. In addition recently, especially within the last five years, a number of high quality, small private estates have appeared, many with EU subsidies.

A note of caution needs sounding though: although 42,000 hectares of vineyards had been replanted or redeveloped by 2015, in some cases vineyards have been planted with no winery to process the fruit, or with absolutely the minimum possible cost input so that subsidies could be pocketed. And today there are still 815,582 grape growers with less than 0.5 hectares, and only 220 with more than 50 hectares – these are the ones who can do a truly professional job and afford the right technology to do so. A further 242 grape growers have between 20 and 50 hectares where the investment balance is more marginal, but still feasible.

BETTER VITICULTURE

Vineyards have seen improvements in several ways, including the introduction of higher quality clonal material. For one of the most exciting local grapes, Fetească Neagră, recognized commercial clones have only become available very recently and most improvements have been through the efforts of individual producers in selecting cuttings in their own vineyards … and sending them off to nurseries in France or Italy. Vine training has been returned to systems that favour quality, using guyot and vertical shoot positioning (see Glossary), and vines planted at higher densities (4,000 to 5,000 vines per hectare, and occasionally, such as at Catleya's new vineyard, up to 10,000 vines per hectare). Better rootstocks, cover crops and, in a few cases, investments in irrigation, have been made to reduce stress from more frequent droughts. Older plantings and poor quality vines such as Muscat Hamburg and Chasselas are disappearing.

A number of producers have also replanted with mechanical harvesting in mind. In spite of the capital cost of purchase, there are now several machine harvesters working in the country, allowing wineries to reduce reliance on unpredictable labour sources, and to pick at night for better grape aromas.

There's no doubt that foreign investment and EU money have changed the face of Romanian viticulture. The first phase of vineyard reconstruction involved a lot of international grape varieties, possibly planted because wineries believed that was what the market wanted, rather than necessarily considering matching the varieties to the soils. A decade ago, international varieties were arguably glamorous and interesting to local wine consumers compared to the local varieties that their grandparents had consumed. But more recently, the interest has grown in local varieties, as part of a global search for authenticity and wine that is unique and exciting.

Romania is luckier than its Eastern European neighbours in that it has significant areas planted with good quality local grape varieties. In some cases, local grape varieties remain exactly that because they're difficult to grow or simply not very interesting. But today clients, both locally and internationally, want indigenous grapes. Oliver Bauer reports his frustration at the lack of research into local grapes though, highlighting that EU investment has encouraged spending on international grapes from Western nurseries (along with sales of Western European winery equipment). 'Why support research and production of indigenous vines in Romania with huge amounts of money when the first reliable and credible results won't be visible for more than a decade? Today serious research is almost non-existent in Romania mainly because there is not enough money to pay for it,' he points out. He goes on to explain that, 'I still remember when we started in 2003 with Ştirbey promoting and focusing on single grape, single vineyard wines obtained from indigenous varieties. Back then literally almost everybody (producers, officials, wine writers, etc.) laughed about this idea.'

Some wineries report selling out quickly of grapes like Crâmposie or Negru de Drăgăşani. Livia Gîrboiu of Crama Gîrboiu confirms that when she started to make Şarbă as a higher quality, dry wine, it was a tough sell but now it is her best-selling white wine. Valeriu Stoica says, 'If I had known then what I know now, I would have planted more local grapes.' One solution for Avincis has been to invest in a technique they call green-grafting (or cross-grafting), doing this for the first time ever in Romania, using a team from their Italian consultants. It's been miraculous according to Stoica, allowing them to cross-graft Negru de Drăgăşani onto established Cabernet Sauvignon plants. Rather than waiting years for a crop from young vines, they should benefit from an almost immediate crop production with the advantage of a well-established deep root system. For such an individual winery, it makes sense to focus on their local speciality, as Negru de Drăgăşani looks to be very promising. But with barely 20 hectares in the whole world, it is hard for the wider industry to switch course and build an export strategy on this grape. Avincis has also planted a small plot of a novel local grape called Alutus. Older researchers at the local research institute described this grape as one of the most promising of the crosses ever created here, even better than Negru de Drăgăşani.

WINEMAKING AND WINEMAKERS

Two decades ago, winemaking equipment in Romania was still awful: grim Soviet-scale concrete vats, rusting pipes and decades-old, smelly oak casks, reeking of mould and vinegar. One new Western winery owner in the 1990s had to employ the Romanian army and high explosives to break up their old concrete vats, while another (Carl Reh at Oprişor) repurposed one of their vast vats by turning it into a full tasting room. Since then, winemaking equipment and techniques have also improved considerably, with modern equipment now widespread.

Home-grown winemaking talent is sometimes hard to find, as Romania's winemaking schools find it hard to teach to global standards due, according to one academic, to large numbers of students and a lack of motivation among young people to really get involved in hands-on practical work. Lots of wineries have foreign winemakers or consultants (which is an extra cost burden as they rarely come cheap). Facilities for critical services like complex wine analyses is basic, so some wineries send samples to Italy for full laboratory services.

As recently as the 2000s, there was no specific winemaking degree, so wine was just a part of food technology studies and didn't require any international experience. According to Aussie flying winemaker Stephen Bennett, back then the market taste was still strongly for sweetened wines, so there was no need for any high-level skills. In contrast, good dry wines are less forgiving; faults can't be covered with sugar so better winemaking is essential. Today, the best home-grown talent has improved and will usually have spent time working abroad too.

THE OAK QUESTION

Despite improvements in winemaking, there are still pockets where a fondness for ancient oak barrels remains, though really these have little place in modern winemaking, especially where hygiene standards are less than pristine. Mihai Citic (formerly of Halewood) is proud of his idea to give away more than a thousand old casks as firewood to staff – he even lent them axes to chop them up. In other wineries such as SC Cotnari and Jidvei, such old casks are still used to age some of their white wines.

But overall, use of oak has improved considerably. As in Bulgaria, early efforts at showing that there was a new generation of quality red wine came with hefty concentration, extract, and lots of status-symbol new oak. Today oak use is becoming more subtle, though it is still often the case that cheaper, unoaked wines are more appealing to an international palate than the prestige cuvées that have spent extensive time in barrel. And over-oaking remains a problem in some cases, at least as far as international perceptions go. French oak use is widespread, but Hungarian and American oaks also appear. Increasingly some Romanian cooperages are now making high-quality barrels, though opinions vary about the quality of Romanian oak.

There are two leading coopers, and oak forests in Romania, which are on the same latitude as the great forests of France, grow both species of European oak used for barrel making (*Quercus petraea* and *Quercus robur*). There are even reports that Romanian oak was exported to France for barrel-making back in the seventeenth century. Ultimately it comes down to a winemaker's style preference. Some producers prefer the northern oak of Transylvania Bois, though Davino (one of Romania's top wineries) gets excellent results from Vallach oak from the south of Romania, but is careful to source 36-month-seasoned wood that has been washed and toasted with utmost care to avoid 'greenness'. Dan Balaban (Davino's founder) explains that he finds a different balance of flavours between forest origins: a lower percentage of vanillin in wood from the south compared to the north. He also finds more malted and spicy notes (especially from isoeugenol), which is why he prefers to use mainly southern wood.

LABOUR, BUREAUCRACY AND FINANCIAL PRESSURES

The introduction of harvesting machines in Romania highlights an ongoing issue for viticulture here. Philip Cox explains that the economy is growing strongly and is the fastest growing in the European Union. The country is experiencing a significant labour crisis at present, because 20 per cent of the total population and over 50 per cent of the active population is working abroad. According to Cox, there are more Romanians of working age working abroad than there are Romanians of working age working in Romania. He reckons about 4 million have left the country, about 3 million are working in Romania in the private sector and 1 million work in the state sector, which does not contribute to GDP. This has a particularly notable effect in rural areas (which is pretty much where the vineyards are), where significant numbers of young people have left to work in other areas.

One difference in Romania, compared to countries like Hungary, is that collectivization meant that the ability to work vines was largely lost, though there are some villages where skills were retained because people had vines in their gardens. Labour is likely to be an increasingly significant issue as young people leave their villages and the workers that most wineries rely on for hand labour are getting old. Many workers in Romania still take the opportunity to leave for jobs in places like Spain and Italy where multiple crops mean the harvest is much longer and the pay is higher. The future is not clear, though there are discussions about importing labour, but then wineries have to solve the question of logistics, space and cost for worker accommodation, and indeed where these labourers might come from. In some areas, a lot of seasonal work is carried out by the ethnic minority Romani population. At Corcova, a lack of local workers in the village means that temporary staff are brought by bus from the city of Craiova, and usually set up camp, so the winery doesn't have to find accommodation. The winery itself here employs around 30 people regularly, plus up to 150 for the harvesting season (and this is for a moderate-sized operation with 60 hectares – Romania's biggest vineyards are around 2,500 hectares and so need a lot of people). Security guards are pretty much obligatory too, as theft of both grapes and metal posts and wires can be a real issue.

In 2017, seasonal workers earned just €15 a day, with skilled workers earning a little more, but this will rise in 2018. Romania raised its minimum wage in January 2018 to 1,900 Romanian *lei* per month (around €408) though this is still one of the lowest minimum wages in Europe. For comparison, the poorest country in the EU, Bulgaria, raised its minimum wage to 510 Bulgarian *leva* in 2018 (€260 per month). Vineyard work tends to be seasonal and for quite a short period, so the attraction of longer seasons and better wages in other European nations is strong. Philip Cox notes, 'Last year especially in Dobrogea and Moldovan Hills, there were really big problems in getting enough labour, especially for the harvest. We have had that problem here in western Romania for many years already which is why we automated everything we can and use a lot of machine harvesting.'

In addition to 2018's roughly 15 per cent wage increase, to retain staff and comply with the law, there are inflationary cost pressures from transport and dry goods (glass, cardboard and closures). Wineries also complain about a huge bureaucratic burden. A mid-sized winery has to face up to a hundred inspections per year from multiple different agencies, some of which incur a fee and many of which may impose fines.

12

MARKETS, TRENDS AND CONTEMPORARY ISSUES

ROMANIA'S HOME MARKET

It's hard for a wine industry to develop beyond its culture. In simple terms, there has to be a matching level of appreciation for food and flavour to go with high-quality wines. The domestic market is always the strongest opportunity in any wine producing country, especially in a strong consumer nation like Romania (officially drinking 20.5 litres of wine annually per head, plus more that's unmeasured from the grey market). People are more likely to buy out of a sense of patriotism and it's easier to educate on the doorstep than to try and create a category in another country, where the whole world is already fighting for shelf space.

This is where education becomes very significant and is something that Romanian wine producers need to really commit to. This has to be education at all levels, from qualified professional staff at wineries (including trained winemakers and viticulturalists), to those that are selling the wines into the trade, and perhaps most importantly, those that speak directly to customers (for instance shop and restaurant staff). There is a huge need for education at the business-to-business end of the chain too. Stores, restaurants and their stock controllers need to know that wine is fragile, and stock must be rotated in the right order. It can't be stored too warm, or left toasting under bright lights, or displayed in a sunny window, or it will die a swift death. Wine service in restaurants leaves room for improvement too – red wine served too warm is just one of the common problems for consumers.

ROMANIAN FOOD

It's no surprise that Romanian food draws on influences from her neighbours as well as the abundant fresh vegetables and fruit that grow here.

Meals often start with salad made with whatever is in season – cabbage and carrots in the winter, or leaves, cucumbers and tasty tomatoes in the summer. Bread is always served. A local brined cheese called *brânză* (some argue this is a Dacian word while others think it derives from the Latin *brancia*, and yet others think it may be Celtic or Persian), often made from sheep's milk, accompanies salads.

Soups are also popular. *Ciorbă* is the name for popular soups with a sour note from lemon juice, vinegar, sauerkraut juice or fermented bran (called *borş*). Typical soups include tripe (*ciorbă di burtă*) which is particularly popular as a hangover cure, *ciorbă de văcuţă* (sour beef *ciorbă*) and chicken with noodles (*ciorbă de pui* or *supa de pui* if it's not sour). Flavourings may include herbs like lovage, tarragon, dill and parsley, and sour cream. Other soups include tomato, *ciorbă de perişoare* (meatball soup) and typically near the Black Sea *ciorbă de peste* (fish soup). Fresh or pickled chillies may be served on the side – take a bite between spoonfuls of soup. Bean soups with meat (pigs' trotters are typical), or without, are widely served too. Other popular starters may be based on smoked aubergine or a mixture of peppers, aubergine and tomato stewed together called *zacuscă*, or a paste of white beans. There is a wide range of cured and smoked meats and sausages made from wild boar, pork and sometimes lamb. *Pastramă* is a brined, dried and lightly smoked meat, originally made using lamb in Wallachia and believed to be the original inspiration for pastrami.

Main courses are often a simple piece of meat or fish accompanied by mashed or fried potatoes or the typical staple called *mămăligă* (cornmeal similar to polenta), sometimes served with *brânză* cheese and sour cream (*smântână*). *Mudjei* is a typical garlic sauce as an accompaniment, made from mashed garlic in oil, sometimes with the addition of vinegar or sour cream. *Sarmale* are practically the national dish; stuffed cabbage leaves with minced meat, rice and spices. Other popular dishes include meatballs and a type of spiced, skinless sausage called *mici*, which are typically grilled and served with mustard. Pork is the most common meat – in the past most rural households would have a pig, while cattle are usually raised for dairy products, not beef.

The most famous stew is *tochitură*, a stew of pork or beef, though the exact recipe varies by region. It's often served with an egg on top. At Easter, it is typical to serve *drob de miel* which is a type of lamb haggis and lamb sour soup.

Desserts may be fruit and nuts, or a simple cake, but also pancakes (*clătite*) stuffed with fruit or sweetened cottage cheese. *Papanași* are spheres of fried dough with sweetened curd cheese and jam, and *gogoși* are fried, filled doughnuts. At Christmas a sweet cake called *cozonac* is made with poppy seed or walnuts, and a cake called *pască* made from curd cheese with dried fruit is the typical Easter centrepiece. There's a special sweet dish called *colivă* served at Orthodox funerals; it is made from boiled wheat mixed with honey, and sometimes includes walnuts, almonds, raisins and spices.

History shows that you can't fob customers off with rubbish for too long – they are too smart. Market statistics clearly show that tastes in Romania are changing rapidly, and unless the wine industry responds, it will lose out. Producers need to act together and learn from mistakes made by others. Just one example worth considering is Bulgaria (and indeed Romania itself) in the UK in the mid-1990s, which lost out massively to Australia. The Australians came along offering fruity, value-for-money wines at a time when Bulgaria's quality was falling through the floor, and the various regions and producers joined forces to market themselves really effectively together. Increasingly there are signs that Australia is currently failing to learn from its own history, as it cuts corners on quality to meet the demands of supermarket-led price wars. The example of Austria shows us what happens when a country cuts corners to meet price demands – it took years to rebuild its wine industry after the diethylene glycol scandal.

My plea to Romanian producers is this: treat your customers with respect, and make sure wine is a pleasant experience – whether they are paying €2 or €50, or they will go elsewhere. It's easy in the wine world to get distracted by all the talk of terroir, grapevines and winemaking details and to forget that ultimately, this is a business, and that means people buying and drinking those wines. And ideally coming back and buying again. In some cases, there is a bit of a producer-led mentality, perhaps a hangover from the old days, but market experience proves that simply making the wine isn't enough.

In the light of the rapid appearance of so many new and ambitious wineries, producers need to work out what their unique story is, and tell it. Thinking about who the potential customers are, what wines they might like and how to engage them is still sometimes forgotten.

The good news is that the number of specialist wine stores, wine clubs, online wine magazines and tasting events is growing. The brilliant Rovinhud in Timișoara (run by and for the young disabled people of the Ceva de Spus charity), Wine-Up in Cluj-Napoca and Revino's Bucharest wine fair are just three examples. Wine tourism is another growing sector, with a number of wineries able to host tastings, corporate events and dinners, and even offer guest rooms (and there are tour companies to make this easier). It is also encouraging to see that two new schools have started to offer Wine and Spirit Education Trust courses in the last couple of years (Wine in Business, with national coverage, and TRAWIS in Transylvania). In the on-trade, the idea of a professional sommelier really didn't exist in 2003 when the Romanian Sommeliers' Association was set up, though now Romanian sommeliers have done well on the world stage and Sergiu Nedelea offers sommelier training courses at his Winetaste school. The problem, as is so common in Romania, is that some of the best young people leave for education and experience in other countries and then find they don't want to come back. Dan Balaban of Davino sums up:

> I think the market as a whole is improving for overall quality, in the sense that it is rare nowadays to find bottled anomalies or irregularities, so this is an excellent sign. The public is more and more interested in wine, but in the educational sense as well as consumption. We are seeing many wine bars popping up around Bucharest and the other large cities. Also, more and more educational tastings are taking place, and we can feel a certain buzz around wine at the moment. However, problems still remain with availability (the large retail chains have improved their selections, but there still is a long way to go, and they are mass market shops after all) and from a consumer point of view, with pricing. There's a perception that everyone is producing premium wines at above

average prices, thus leading to a lack of good value for money alternatives in the marketplace.

Encouragingly, a recent Euromonitor report suggests that the Romanian market is becoming more mature, and it is predicted that it will switch from a price-driven model towards more balanced quality considerations. Perhaps wineries will adapt and see the need for more investment in branding, marketing and communications.

A CUSTOMER-FOCUSED BRAND?

Philip Cox of Cramele Recaş recounts what he describes as, 'One of the more odd stories from my time in Romania.' He says:

A few years ago our Japanese distributor asked us for a wine for the 'escort' sector – where there were a lot of young 'working' Romanian women who needed something to entertain their male clients. We came up with a brand for them called 'Te Iubesc', meaning 'I love you'. We still do well with that brand, though today the brothel part has stopped working. Oddly enough, it has now switched to being aimed at priests and people getting married in town halls here in Romania. So now when you get married pretty much anywhere in the west of the country at least, the local registry office or the mayor will give you a bottle of this wine at the wedding ceremony and many priests do too at religious weddings. And it's also very big for Valentine's day too. I was quite surprised when I saw all that was happening!

ROMANIAN DRINKING HABITS

It turns out that if you look at statistics, Romania is actually a beer-drinking country for preference, with beer accounting for more than 50 per cent of alcohol consumption. (In comparison, Bulgaria is culturally a spirit-drinking country.) As Radu Rizea (Premium Wines of Romania explained): 'Taste for quality wine in Romania has been destroyed. First of all, there was virtually no wine between 1881 and 1910 because of phylloxera and its destruction of the vineyards. This was a period when breweries were founded, so beer drinking grew, and then hybrids and cheap spirit arrived on the scene. Under communism, semi-dry and semi-sweet wines were common because the sweetness could be used to hide faults. So, all of this broke Romania's taste for wines with any quality aspirations.'

And to be honest even today, given how bad some of Romania's entry-level wines are, never mind the horrors that are available as home-made wine sold by the roadside, it is no wonder that so many people opt for beer. After judging a wine competition in 2012, my comments were:

> The worst categories I judged were inexpensive wines (in the €2–5 price range) bought from retail stores, and honestly speaking, if I were a Romanian faced with this disheartening selection, I would drink beer. The line-up of faults included wines showing oxidized, volatile, vinegary and dirty TCA characters, as well as the fruitless, over-extracted and dried out. A number of wines had clearly been spoiled by putting them to 'mature' in dirty, unhygienic old wood, so if that's all you as a winery can afford, don't bother – the wine will be better, and cheaper, if you just stick to using clean stainless tanks.

This problem has diminished but has by no means been solved since then, so the question for the wine industry in Romania to consider is why this problem exists, where the fault lies and what to do about it.

At the top end, Romania today is making better wines than ever before, including some genuinely thrilling wines. However, these wines will only ever be afforded by the few, and they will be people who already have a taste for wine. I believe that this means poor quality mass-market wines are a problem for everyone across the industry. I can't see how Romanian winemakers can encourage new drinkers, or even keep drinkers in the category rather than switching to beer, or reliable imports, given the grim lottery of nasty, cheap local wines that can still be found on shop shelves. It's also not just a problem for entry-level wines. More attention especially needs to be paid to boring details of handling and bottling processes – there's no point in investing in quality in the vineyards or winemaking if bad bottling spoils the wine before it gets to the consumer. As an example, in one particularly disheartening line-up in early 2018, out of a dozen samples of premium wines, three showed bottling faults making them undrinkable (cork taint, secondary fermentation and *Brettanomyces*). Most consumers won't identify a fault, instead they will just assume they don't like the wine.

This means there is a huge challenge – and opportunity – in Romania to encourage consumers into the wine category, switching them from home-made wines or cheap beers to commercial wine. Once consumers are open to drinking wine, it is easier to persuade them to spend a bit more for better quality wine. This does require a concerted effort by the wine industry to ensure that whatever consumers pay they get a wine that is clean, pleasant and enjoyable. And with modern winemaking technology there's no excuse for not offering this as a starting point.

SHOPPING TRENDS

Supermarkets have an important role to play here. Supermarket shopping is increasing at the expense of traditional grocery stores (which lost 5 per cent of the market between 2016 and 2017). As everywhere, they make it easy for shoppers to pop a few bottles into their trolleys along with the food shop, so they avoid a special trip out to buy wine. Once people pick up the habit of consuming commercial wine, they will soon lose the taste for home-made nasties. Producers often have a love–hate relationship with supermarkets, which are able to deliver volume sales but also make demands for listing fees, discounts, merchandising support and funding for promotions.

The off-trade dominates wine sales in Romania by volume, where around nine in ten bottles are bought to take home. However, the sector's share by value shows a different picture; it is worth less than 50 per cent of the market due to higher prices and generous margins in the on-trade (restaurant, bar and hotel sector). Both take-home trade and on-trade are forecast to keep growing, at around 9 per cent each year up to 2021. Almost certainly, some of this will be due to time-poor, younger drinkers moving away from home-made wine, and indeed highest wine sale growth is seen among 25 to 30-year-olds. This is an encouraging sign for Romania, differing from much of Western Europe where wine is dominated by both older producers and ageing consumers.

BALANCE OF TRADE

Romania became a net wine importer in 2006, following a short harvest, though this trend has continued ever since. According to the Ministry of Agriculture and Rural Development in 2016, imports reached 50.2 million litres, while exports were only 14.2 million litres. And in 2017 imports were a little lower at 43.5 million litres, while exports reached 14.7 million litres. Despite cheap land and low labour costs, wine production costs are not cheap (the average price of grapes in 2017 was 1.40 lei per kilo, around €0.30). This means that Spanish winemakers have been able to undercut Romanian producers, flooding the cheap end of the market (where it is often sold in plastic bottles or as bag in box) with nearly 28 million litres of wine at an average price of €0.44 per litre in 2016 (less than the cost price of Romanian grapes if we assume 1.5 kilos for a litre of wine). Other cheap sources of wine include the Republic of Moldova and Bulgaria, while Italy and France supply more premium wine from established regions. This should provide an opportunity for newer Romanian wine producers to target the more premium segment through the right education and marketing. And with 2017's difficult harvest in Western Europe bringing significant price rises, this may change the pattern of imports, especially at the lower end of the market. For the first time, Romania has also seen significant exports of grapes and juice going the other way – to Western European countries. One can only speculate what might happen to tankers of Romanian Pinot Grigio juice heading to Italy, as it apparently never reappears as Romanian Pinot Grigio when it gets there.

In 2016, exports reached a value of €20.5 million, increasing to €22.6 million in 2017. At the time of writing, a more detailed breakdown was only available for 2016. Main destinations were: UK 22 per cent, Germany 16 per cent, China 16 per cent, Netherlands 11 per cent, then interestingly Spain and Italy, which took 8 per cent each. Both the UK and Germany have provided big boosts for Romanian wine during 2017, in the face of static or declining markets in these countries. Newer estates are however finding it hard to gain an export foothold. Alfred Binder of Antinori-owned Viile Metamorfosis explained that deals are hard to achieve unless well below the winery's asking prices, and buyers are only interested in the entry-level categories. He goes on to analyse why it is so hard to sell the premium priced wines:

The main obstacle is the lack of image and awareness for Romania as being a reliable supplier of quality wines, though quality is not an issue any more. We are newcomers and we have discovered that we also need to overcome cheap pricing of Romanian producers already present on foreign markets. On top of all these of course we have to accept the fact that we are competing with many other countries and wine regions from all over the world. The modern Romanian wine industry has a big gap to recover and nobody else stands still to wait for us.

Philip Cox concurs:

Any Romanian wine at any price point has to be more competitive in terms of price and quality than a similar wine from an established country like France. The same is even more true for high end wines – it is very hard indeed to sell any wines in the higher price points (over €8 per bottle). Even if you have a really special wine, it is very hard for anyone to take Romania seriously at those levels, when they can get some fantastic wines from Australia, Chile, South Africa, Spain or even occasional good French wines for those kind of prices, that come with much better kudos.

WINE PRICING

One possibly unforeseen downside of wineries investing in their own vineyards is that their own production of grapes can actually be more expensive than buying grapes on the open market. This may be due to lower yields, better management practices and sites that require more labour, for instance if they are on steep slopes. The loyal and patriotic domestic market pays higher prices than are required for most major export markets, where competition is keen, and it is estimated that two producers (Cramele Recaş and Halewood) account for as much as half of all Romania's exports.

Some sources believe there is a surplus of grapes and wine in stock in the market that may help rebalance prices. Another source points out that Romania only produced 1.24 million hectolitres of quality wine (PDO, PGI and varietal wines) in 2017 so the real volume of wine that could be of competitive export standard is only 30 per cent of the total. Many producers took EU money for planting vineyards but were unable to fund wineries, so these grapes are being sold on the secondary market. There is also a lack of sufficient space in the market for all the small new wineries who are producing premium wines, and thus are chasing the on-trade and wine specialist stores. Many have large financial investments and loans to pay back so cannot compete in the inexpensive sector. Many of the new estates are being supported by owners' other business interests as well as substantial EU funds and it is not clear how sustainable many of these are for the long-term.

A QUESTION OF STYLE

Romania's wine market is still very heavily biased towards semi-sweet and sweet wine styles, which is not the sector that most of the newer producers are competing in. According to Nielsen research, dry wine consumption only reaches the heights of a 20 per cent share in the regions around the cities of Bucharest and Timișoara (and less elsewhere). Urban professionals in these cities, as well as Cluj-Napoca, are known to have a higher engagement with wine, and more educated drinkers tend to opt for drier styles and more red wine. So, the dry wine sector is highly competitive and still small, though developing.

As Virgil Mandru, owner of Tohani, explains:

Let's go back to the consumer. In 1999, the Romanian market was dominated by sweet and semi-sweet wines, and most producers focused on volume. Normally, in a mature market, there is a significant consumer segment that choses quite the opposite – dry and semi-dry wines, and prestigious producers focus on quality, not volume. This is how the Romanian market has evolved. Step by step, in nearly 20 years, consumption has become more and more educated; we can now speak of a more discerning consumer in a clearly segmented market that shows a significant increase of the premium and super-premium segment.

Edit Leitersdorfer of Carastelec Winery confirms that more and more consumers are interested in wines and gastronomy. She observes that it is currently trendy to be knowledgeable about wine, but she notes that it is mostly more highly educated people who are the ones who want to learn.

There is a strong preference for white wine in Romania, which takes about two-thirds of the volume sold, but is falling. Rosé is the star category, with an increase of 14 per cent in 2016 and perhaps surprisingly at the drier end of the scale. Looking at the breakdown of wine choice by variety, among red wines it is Merlot that is first choice (29 per cent share), then Cabernet Sauvignon (20.6 per cent share) and Pinot Noir takes just 4.6 per cent (echoing what wineries are saying about how difficult Pinot Noir is to sell in the domestic market). The white category is led by Sauvignon Blanc with 19.8 per cent share, Riesling (16.9 per cent), Chardonnay (14.1 per cent) and Muscat Ottonel (6.1 per cent).

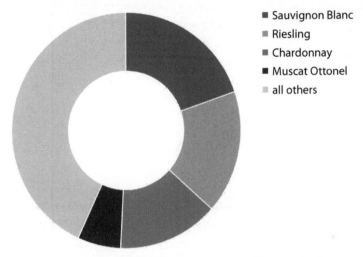

- Sauvignon Blanc
- Riesling
- Chardonnay
- Muscat Ottonel
- all others

White wine preferences in Romania (Euromonitor)

As with Bulgaria, it appears that the trade, and a few educated consumers, regard local grapes as exciting but these are not easy to sell in the domestic market. One reason is their association with inferior quality as well as consumption by older generations so there is no understanding of quality potential in the right hands, never mind the perceived glamour of international grape varieties.

KEY PLAYERS

The domestic market remains strongly dominated by a few big players, with the top seven wineries holding a 65 per cent share in 2016. Jidvei has become the leader of the Romanian wine market and in 2016 registered a turnover of 150 million lei (€32.2 million), up 16 per cent compared to the previous year, with an increase in net profit of 22 per cent, at almost 14 million lei, according to data sent to the Ministry of Finance. Second place is held by Cotnari, whose turnover increased last year by 18 per cent to 139 million lei (€29.9 million). Net profit increased fourfold in 2016 to almost 23 million lei (€4.9 million). Cramele Recaş has moved up to third position (and is also the largest wine exporter in Romania), with a turnover of 120 million lei (€25.8 million), up 20 per cent since 2015 and earning a net profit of 29 million lei (€6.2 million), up 37 per cent from the previous year. All three of the leading companies appear to have picked up market share following the collapse of former leader Murfatlar Winery. Murfatlar, which had held a 28 per cent share in 2015, was in trading difficulties in 2016, but by the end of 2017 had lost its fiscal licence and several senior executives were arrested for financial fraud amounting to an alleged €140 million (over 650 million lei).

ORGANIC, NATURAL AND ORANGE WINE

The Ministry of Agriculture claims that 10 per cent of Romanian vineyards now produce ecological wine and there are a few producers with certified organic vineyards, though detailed records are hard to track down. The potential for successful organic production varies by area, linked to local mesoclimate and rainfall patterns. One previously certified producer, Crama Oprişor, abandoned certification around 2005, since it did not deliver quality fruit nor a good cost–benefit ratio. At that time, the organic market was very weak and Gabriel Roceanu from the winery reckons that even now, the market share of 'bio' wines in Romania is very low. It is also difficult to work organically on small, fragmented plots, so this type of viticulture can only really be undertaken by wineries with consolidated plots. Registered growers include Domeniile Franco-Române's Crai Nou, Viile Metamorfosis, Lechburg, Petro Vaselo, La Sapata and several others. While demand is still low, some Romanian consumers are now in the early stages of being aware of environmental responsibility, and it looks like a trend that is set to grow.

Biodynamic production has not so far received great attention in Romania, possibly because the only significant attempt so far had poor results. Natural winemaking is also very limited, possibly because this low intervention approach to winemaking is often far too close to the home-made wine tradition of the country. One exception, Edgar Brutler at Nachbil, is making intriguing, low-intervention, skin contact whites from an old vineyard (60–100 years old), though wines like this will require careful placement and hand-selling.

The orange wine category is also gaining some attention. These are white wines made in the style of reds, using extended skin contact and often low intervention production techniques. The first producers of orange wines are both small: Liliac (with Chardonnay) and Oliver Bauer (with old vine Sauvignonasse), and recently Cramele Recaș has developed an orange wine for an export customer in the UK. This is now based on organic Sauvignon Blanc, using extended skin contact, no added yeast and low sulphites.

LEGISLATION LOOPHOLES

Until August 2017, DOC wines were taxed at a higher rate than PGI wines (12 lei and 6 lei per hectolitre respectively), and table wines attracted no tax and no need for certification. This was a major disincentive for production of higher quality DOC wines (especially because permitted yields are frequently small). Industry lobbying got this changed from August 2017 to a harmonized rate of 8 lei per hectolitre for DOC, PGI and varietal wines, though table wines remain free of tax or any requirement for certification. Only the top fifteen varieties are permitted for varietal labelling – with the exception of Fetească Neagră and Regală all are international grapes. The criteria were that there had to be at least 500 hectares currently planted, and the grapes could not have varietal names that might be confused with a DOC region, meaning no Grasă de Cotnari, nor Fetească Albă (due to objections from Italy's Alba DOC). Another concern that ought to gain official attention is that half to three-quarters of wine is not taxed or recorded in Romania, so corner-cutting and fraudulent wine are still issues. The state may be losing up to 600 million euro in VAT at up to 5 lei per bottle, but given that much of this will originate with the 815,582 growers with less than 0.5 hectares, there is a significant social barrier to shutting down this sector.

CONTEMPORARY CONCERNS – PUTTING ROMANIA BACK ON THE MAP

Putting Romania back on the world wine map will require some considerable effort by the industry and government. Obviously wine quality must be good (and the best producers are now making wines that can stand up in any company) but making space on wine shelves and lists needs more than that. Considered in comparison to Hungary, Romania doesn't have the advantage of its own Tokaji, that is, it does not have a revitalized world-class wine to create an image, and Bucharest has not got anywhere close to the tourist appeal of Budapest. Nor has the country developed the tourism hooks of cheap skiing or summer sunshine that Bulgaria is targeting. Rural tourism may offer stronger opportunities given the wealth of forested land and protected wetland areas like the Danube Delta, while the current Prince of Wales' interest in protecting rural Transylvania is unlikely do any harm. Romania as a country has not always had the best PR, as news stories in the West often confuse the negatively portrayed Romani people with Romania itself. Several wineries have commented that Transylvania has a more positive image than Romania, though this message is only useful to producers in the region.

Romania needs to identify and communicate its unique selling points, some of which include the fact that this is an island of distinction compared to its neighbours, not Slavic while still being part of the mysterious eastern end of Europe. The country is relishing independence but is open-minded enough to bring in help (from the likes of the UK, Italy, France, Germany, South Africa and Austria). As for industry structure, there is a benefit here because many of the new wineries are medium-sized and thus big enough to do a professional job, but still small enough to retain a human touch. Even the very biggest mostly have owners who show their faces, rather than being shadowy 'businessmen'.

THE STORY OF AN ICON WINE

In the eighteenth and nineteenth centuries, Cotnari was renowned for its sweet wines, which were particularly enjoyed in France. And given that there are some similarities with Hungary's Tokaji, in that both regions were famous for sweet wines created by noble-rot, it is worth a look to consider what lessons, if any, can be gleaned.

The region of Tokaj has been a useful hook on which Hungary has rebuilt its reputation. The wine's legendary status comes from its description by Louis XV of France as, 'wine of kings, king of wines'; by tales of its popularity in royal courts across Europe and through the very early establishment of a hierarchy of vineyards (around 1720, long before Bordeaux or Burgundy had got in on the act). In theory, because Cotnari wines once rivalled those of Hungary for fame, this region has the potential to be Romania's equivalent, but in practice this is unlikely. Both regions suffered from collectivization that caused utter destruction of wine quality in the communist era, and have had to reinvent themselves.

However, Cotnari has emerged following a very different route to Tokaj. Cotnari wine is almost all made by either the former IAS state winery, which was privatized in 2000 through a management buy-out by state employees, or the smaller (but still with 350 hectares) Casa de Vinuri Cotnari, owned by the second-generation of the same families. In contrast, Tokaji has attracted dozens of investments and start-ups including passionate smaller producers and several high-profile foreign investments (such as Vega Sicilia at Oremus, French insurance group AXA at Disznókő, Michel Reybier of Cos D'Estournel at Hétszőlő). The Tokaj region has become a hotbed of competition that has encouraged a focus on quality and is full of like-minded producers who are prepared to work together to tell the story of their region. It has also reinvented its wine styles for today's tastes, with the emergence of a new generation of late harvest, dry and sparkling wines. The one huge state-owned winery in Hungary has lagged behind the times, and this has not helped in the progress of the wine region, though recent changes are improving matters here too. And today, the reputation of Tokaji is now higher than it has been since before the communist period.

It is not clear why other producers and small estates have been unable to develop a foothold in the Cotnari region. Vinarte tried a few years ago but found the project impossible to administer. And the fact that SC Cotnari is so protective of the region's name makes it difficult for incomers to gain a foothold. In 2008, the company took legal action against Carrefour supermarkets for selling wine labelled Cotnari from another producer, claiming trademark infringement. However, they lost because the EU recognizes Cotnari as a PDO, valid for any wine that complies with production regulations, not a brand. Nor is it clear whether it would even be possible to put Cotnari back on a pedestal as an iconic wine and a hook for Romania to hang its marketing from.

It is also increasingly clear that reliance on an iconic sweet wine is difficult in today's market: however good a top sweet wine is, it will only ever be a very niche product, opened on very special occasions, and sipped from small glasses. These are also wines that are seriously expensive to produce, so come with a high selling price, out of reach of all but a few customers. Today, the best Tokaji wines outperform the wines of Cotnari in whatever form they take, and there's been little incentive for Romania's second most successful wine company to change what it's doing. Everyone talks about Cotnari as famous for its rich, sweet wines, but that does not reflect today's reality – almost all Cotnari wines are semi-dry or semi-sweet, with rare dry wines and even rarer noble-rot sweet wines. It's taken Tokaj eighteen years so far to progress from the first serious dry wines in 2000 to where they are today, producing wines that at their best can rival Burgundy. Producers in Cotnari have barely started and have much to do to catch up with their neighbours.

13

ROMANIAN AND MOLDOVAN GRAPES

There is considerable overlap between the grapes grown in Romania and the Republic of Moldova and indeed some debate about exactly which variety originates where. With the exception of grape varieties that have appeared in the last few decades, there are no definitive records. Additionally, the country borders between Romania's *region* of Moldova and the *Republic* of Moldova were different in the past. The European grapevine database Vitis has designated an official origin for many of these grapes, but any concept of native grape varieties must be interpreted in the context that today's Republic of Moldova represents a part of the wider historical principality of Moldavia (which comprised the present-day republic and Romania's north-eastern region). It seems best to cover the native grapes of these two countries together and describe them as native vines of the territory rather than trying to be too exact. Although only a river crossing separates these two countries from Bulgaria, there is almost no overlap among the indigenous grape varieties.

Romania and Moldova have a relatively narrow genetic heritage in production today, limited to, at most, 40 to 50 commercial varieties. Romania has gone a different route to its neighbours and has kept significant plantings of local grape varieties, rather than switching predominantly to international varieties. This is due to a combination of factors, including local patriotism, adaptation to local growing conditions and the fact that the most planted local grape varieties like Fetească Regală and Fetească Albă particularly suit domestic tastes for semi-dry and semi-sweet styles. Different political routes, particularly during the communist era, are important too. Romania's wine industry was not a designated wine supplier in the Comecon planned economy, unlike those of both Bulgaria and the Republic of Moldova, where international grapes that could produce volume and cope with high trellis viticulture were preferred.

One specific feature of the Romanian picture is that viticultural researchers here have also been enthusiastic plant breeders (like the Bulgarians) and many new local grapes appeared in the 1970s, 1980s and 1990s. Apparently, this was a popular route to academic status. For example, an official catalogue from 2005 listing all the varieties created by the Drăgăşani viticultural research stations gives information on 63 varieties, though most of these are not in commercial wine production. (For detailed grapevine statistics by variety in Romania see Appendix II.)

The grapevine (*Vitis vinifera*) is probably one of the first domesticated perennial crops. Current evidence suggests an origin in the Near East at least 6,000 to 8,000 years ago followed by rapid spread into the Caucasus region and beyond. The earliest winery so far discovered is in Armenia and dates to around 5,900 years ago. The evidence suggests organized winemaking and a ceremonial role for wine. Grapevines today are still an incredibly important economic crop and, in many countries, especially in Eastern Europe, grapes and wine provide significant employment and income for the resident populations.

While the primary domestication from *Vitis sylvestris* (the wild vine) probably took place in the Near East, there is some evidence for secondary domestication sites across Europe including Romania and Bulgaria. It is hard to track scientifically though as populations of wild grapevines were also driven close to extinction by downy and powdery mildews and then phylloxera in the late nineteenth century, followed by widespread habitat destruction.

Some researchers argue that some of Romania's local grapes may have been selected directly from wild populations. In the 2012 book, *The Ampelography of the Caucasus and the Black Sea* it is noted that there were two secondary domestication centres in the area (the southern Balkans and the Aegean region during the fifth to the fourth millennia BC, and a north-western area from the Caspian Sea to the mouth of the Danube a millennium later). The origins and parentage of some varieties such as

Fetească Neagră and Albă, and Coarnă Neagră have been suggested to trace back to this Caspian area. Recent advances in grapevine genetics, particularly investigating microsatellite markers (see the Glossary), have revealed a lot more about the heritage and interrelatedness of grapevines (and in several cases this contradicts anecdotal and indeed historical documentary evidence). There are multi-country collaborations in the region to build a more detailed picture of vines that are in commercial wine production or historic varieties that remain in ampelographic collections.

LOCAL WHITE GRAPES

Crâmposie Selecţionată

This is a selection of the indigenous Crâmposie. Crâmposie itself is a full sibling of Plăvaie as its parents are Iordan x Beala Debela; there is no documentary evidence to support claims that it dates back to Roman or Dacian times. The fact that it is a granddaughter of Heunisch Weiss undermines theories that it is truly ancient. Crâmposie has incomplete flowers and therefore needed a cross-pollinator to crop reliably. The Selecţionată version was produced at the research station in Drăgăşani in 1972, and is only grown in this area, covering 451 hectares in 2017. Before the foundation of Prince Ştirbey winery, this grape was regarded as only suitable for simple table wine, but thanks to the inspiration of Prince Ştirbey to explore the potential of local varieties, it is now seen as a good quality grape with notes of green fruit and apple, retaining good acidity and able to age for up to two years though usually drunk young. It can also produce good sparkling wines.

Producers worth trying: Avincis, Bauer, Prince Ştirbey.

Fetească Albă

This is the second most important white grape in Romania, with 12,383 hectares planted in 2017. It is the more common of the white Fetească grapes in the Republic of Moldova too. Although listed in the Vitis database as originating in the Republic of Moldova it appears to be an ancient variety, so it is really anyone's guess as to its exact true origin. There is a theory that it was directly domesticated from wild vines but there is no robust evidence to date to support this. The limited genetic evidence so far shows that there is shared DNA with a variety called Argant (or Gaensfuesser Blau). This is an almost extinct and very ancient variety that is possibly of German origin. Fetească Albă is now generally agreed to be synonymous with Hungary's Leányka and it is not, as is often suggested, a white mutation of Fetească Neagră.

Many growers regard Fetească Albă as the lesser of the two white Feteascăs in quality terms, but some of Romania's best producers prefer it. Dan Balaban of Davino says, 'Fetească Albă has a smaller natural yield than Fetească Regală and more moderate alcohols. Fetească Regală also has a shorter taste and its persistence is lower than Fetească Albă, which also has a richer texture. Even though they have similar names, the difference between them is quite big. Fetească Regală's flavours are also more "vulgar", more in your face, unlike Fetească Albă which, if well fermented, is more elegant with an extraordinary finesse.'

Producers worth trying: Aurelia Vişinescu, Casa de Vinuri Cotnari, Davino, Gramma Winery, Hermeziu Winery, Liliac, Licorna Winehouse, SERVE, Strunga Winery.

Fetească Regală

This is Romania's most widely planted grape variety, covering 12,661 hectares in 2017, accounting for 13.5 per cent of the noble grape varieties in the country, and appearing in most regions (see Appendix II). Its name translates as the 'royal young girl' or 'royal maiden' grapevine (Fată means girl, Fetească is the possessive form) and was first observed in the 1920s in a village called Daneş, near Sighişoara in Transylvania. A nurseryman called Gaspari first distributed this grape under the German name Dunesdorfer Koenigsast (meaning king's branch from Dunes village). He then went on to present a wine made from this variety at the National Wine and Food Exhibition in Bucharest in 1928 using the name Fetească Regală, which was then adopted. It has long believed that Fetească Regală is a natural cross of Fetească Albă with Grasă de Cotnari. However recent DNA analysis (Laccombe et al., 2012) has revealed that the parentage is Fetească Albă crossed with another grape variety from the region of Moldova called Frâncuşă.

Synonyms for this grape variety include Danesana, Galbena de Ardeal and Királyleányka (in Hungary). There is some controversy about this last claim; Jancis Robinson's *Wine Grapes* states that the Hungarian variety is not related to the Romanian one. However, the balance of most recent research evidence indicates that these two grapes are likely synonyms.

In growing terms, Fetească Regală is frost hardy and shows reasonable resistance to both downy and powdery mildew (perhaps all good reasons for its popularity) but is highly sensitive to drought. It is regarded as a semi-aromatic grape variety and it has noticeable phenolics present in the pulp, not just in the skins as in most white grapes, making this difficult to avoid in the juice. Hartley Smithers, consultant winemaker at Cramele Recaş describes its phenolic texture as 'furriness' in the mouth and its flavours as grapefruit and white pepper. It can take judicious oak use because of its phenolic structure and is often vinified with some residual sugar for balance and to suit domestic market taste. Fetească Regală is much more productive and reliable than Fetească Albă.

Producers worth trying: Balla Géza, Budureasca, Cramele Recaş, Gramma Winery, Liliac, Prince Ştirbey, Viile Metamorfosis, Villa Vinèa.

Frâncuşă

The official prime name for this variety is Francuse. There were 353 hectares in Romania in 2017, largely confined to the north-east region, especially the Moldovan Hills and Cotnari. It is fairly productive, with good drought tolerance but is susceptible to extreme winter cold (below -18°C) and prone to powdery mildew. It is claimed that it has been grown for centuries in Romania, though currently its official origin is listed as the Republic of Moldova. It has recently been shown that it is possible that its parentage is a crossing of Alba Imputotato and the prolific Heunisch Weiss. As yet not enough microsatellite markers have been analysed to be certain, but if proven this would make it a full sibling of Hungary's fabulous grape Furmint (assuming Furmint's proposed parentage is also confirmed), and a half sibling of other grapes including Chardonnay, Gamay, Blaufränkisch and Xinomavro. It seems most likely it arose around a similar time a few centuries ago. Heunisch Weiss is first documented in the eleventh century, though it has never been reported in Eastern Europe. It was probably appreciated as the first cultivar with large white berries, but it also attracted nicknames such as Bettschisser (shit in bed), Laxiertraube (laxative grape) and Scheißtraube (shit grape) suggesting reasons for attempts to improve it by crossing. Frâncuşă itself makes wines that are gently floral, fine and elegant, though it keeps good acidity and freshness. It does appear as a dry varietal wine but is also part of the classic Cotnari blend.

Producer worth trying: SC Cotnari.

Grasă de Cotnari

The most famous grape of the Cotnari region, this was grown on 562 hectares in 2017 data. It has large or 'fat' berries, giving it both its Romanian name, which means 'fat from Cotnari' and its Hungarian name of Kövérszőlő (literally fat grape). In Hungary it is one of the permitted grapes, albeit rare, in Tokaj. It is claimed that it has been cultivated since ancient times in the Cotnari region but given that it is another offspring of the promiscuous Heunisch Weiss it probably arose around the same time as its famous siblings. The other parent remains unknown. In the vineyard, it gives moderate yields, tolerates a little more winter cold than its likely half-sibling Frâncușă (down to -20°C) but is susceptible to drought and fungal diseases. One of its useful features is an ability to accumulate very high sugar levels (famously in 1958 it reached 520 grammes per litre of sugar – a level typical of the incredibly syrupy and rare Tokaji Eszencia from Hungary) and its thin skins mean it can get noble rot. These are the characteristics that have made it so famous over the years as a rival to Tokaji, as discussed earlier. Today production of fully sweet wines is relatively rare. Casa de Vinuri Cotnari has recently started to explore its potential for making serious dry wines, with promising results.

Producers worth trying: Casa de Vinuri Cotnari, SC Cotnari.

Iordan

Usually called Iordana in Romania, other synonyms are Gordan and Zemoasa. It is grown particularly around Alba Iulia and Apold, on an area of 304 hectares in 2017. Neutral and high in acidity, it is used in sparkling wines (e.g. at Jidvei, Halewood). Perhaps more significant is its role as a parent of both Plăvaie and Crâmpoșie. These are both full siblings, with the other parent being a grape of Bulgarian origin called Beala Debela (in turn a sibling of Turkey's Papaskarasi). Popescu et al. (2017) suggest that Iordan has a parent–offspring relationship with the prolific Heunisch Weiss, along with so many other notable grape varieties.

Producer worth trying: (in blends) Jidvei.

Mustoasă de Măderat

Little is known about this old Balkan variety, though it may be a parent of a Hungary's Kövidinka. It is first mentioned in writing at the beginning of nineteenth century, so was certainly present pre-phylloxera. It grows in the Miniş area, on approximately 282 hectares in 2017. The vigorous vine gives generous yields and is noted for high acidity, gentle aromas and moderate alcohol levels, so wines are best drunk young. It can also be used for sparkling wine.

Producer worth trying: Balla Géza.

Plăvaie

The prime name for this grape is Plavay and it is listed as originating in Moldova, where it is not currently grown. It shares parents with Crâmpoşie (Iordan x Beala Debela). In Romania in 2017 154 hectares were grown. Noted for being a late season grape, picked in mid-October, it has neutral aromas, moderate sugar levels and medium acidity. Only one producer makes it as a varietal wine, also using it for their Cuartz sparkling wine, along with Fetească Albă.

Producer worth trying: Crama Gîrboiu

Şarbă

Şarbă is the name of a Romanian dance, a hill in Vrancea and this indigenous variety. Records show it was created at the research centre in Odobeşti in 1972 from an open crossing of Graševina (Italian Riesling or Riesling Italico). Recent genetic analysis shows that the pollen donor was in fact Muscat Hamburg (which in turn is the offspring of Muscat of Alexandria and Schiava Grossa). It is only found in this part of Romania and is currently only vinified by two commercial growers – Crama Gîrboiu and Senator. Best drunk young, it produces gently grapey wines with light, floral aromas, green notes, refreshing acidity and moderate alcohol. It is a vigorous and productive vine and covered 282 hectares in 2017.

Producers worth trying: Crama Gîrboiu, Senator.

Tămâioasă Românească

Regarded by many as a unique Romanian relative of Muscat Blanc à Petit Grains, scientific research has now proved that most Tămâioasă Românească in Romania is in fact genetically identical to Muscat Blanc à Petits Grains. The Muscat family is complex though and some research collections do hold other Muscats that have turned out to be distinct grapes (one such has been renamed Tămâioasă Bucureşti to avoid confusion). There are stories that this grape has been grown in Romania for over 2,000 years, and it appears conceivable that it arrived directly in Romania with the Ancient Greeks, who had a colony on the Black Sea coast from around 700 BC. It suits areas with long, warm autumns, gives medium yields but can accumulate high sugars. It's often vinified as a sweet or semi-sweet style, but good dry versions are now being developed. It covered 1,668 hectares in 2017.

Producers worth trying: Aurelia Vişinescu, Avincis, Budureasca, Casa de Vinuri Cotnari, Halewood, Licorna Winehouse, Prince Ştirbey.

Zghihară de Huşi and Galbena de Odobeşti

Zghihară is an old native variety with unknown origins. According to Costantinescu writing in 1960, the variety belongs to the same group as 'Galbena de Odobeşti' and in fact research published in 2017 shows that it is genetically identical to Galbena de Odobeşti. In 2017 the variety was grown on just 63 hectares in Romania (and on 406 hectares as Galbena) and is only found in ampelographic collections in the Republic of Moldova today. Zghihară is reported to be relatively resistant to frost, but susceptible to fungal diseases. It is high yielding, low in sugar and neutral in character so at best produces simple, refreshing wines that should be drunk young.

Producers worth trying: Crama Avereşti

LOCAL PINK GRAPES

Busuioacă de Bohotin

Busuioc means basil, which gave its name to this aromatic pink-skinned grape variety, grown on 448 hectares in 2017, mostly in north-eastern Romania and Dealu Mare. It is known for moderate yields, high sugar accumulation and good acidity. There are differing opinions about its origin, which variously suggest that it was cultivated directly from wild vines along the river Prut; that it was brought by the Ancient Greeks; or that it was selected in the village of Bohotin. Unfortunately recent research by Popescu et al. (2017) shows that its genetic profile matches Muscat Blanc à Petits Grains so the conclusion, much less romantically, is that it is a somatic colour mutation of this Muscat (though still possibly brought by the Greeks directly). There is another pink-skinned Muscat grown near Craiova, which the producer claims is a distinct cultivar and describes as Muscat de Frontignan Rose, but given that this is another synonym for Muscat Blanc à Petit Grains, this seems hard to argue, though it is possible that some minor differences come from clonal selection and different growing conditions. This grape is traditionally vinified as semi-sweet, or sweet, but drier versions are now appearing. It is currently booming in popularity in Romania as a dry or semi-dry rosé, and several producers are making good sparkling versions.

Producers worth trying: Casa de Vinuri Cotnari, Crama Basilescu, Hermeziu Winery, Domeniul Coroanei Segarcea, Strunga Winery.

LOCAL RED GRAPES

Băbească Neagră

This old Romanian variety possibly originates from Galați county near Nicorești. Its Romanian name literally means grandmother's black grape from Baba, meaning old woman (thus Băbească means 'belonging to an old woman'), and Neagră, meaning black. Another theory is that the name means 'black from ancient times'. It is also known as Rară Neagră in the Republic of Moldova where it is seen as a speciality of the country, not least for its role in Moldova's most famous wine, Negru de Purcari. The first written mention goes back to the fourteenth century, but it is believed to be a very old native variety, and no parentage or other close genetic relationships have yet been identified. There are several biotypes including pink and white-skinned colour mutations called Băbească Gri and Băbească Alb. There were 2,615 hectares of this variety in Romania in 2017, compared to 6,313 hectares in 2006, so it is showing considerable decline. It is a late ripening grape requiring at least 180 days from bud-burst to harvest and is high yielding and vigorous. This thin-skinned grape is susceptible to drought and fungal diseases but has good frost resistance. Usually drunk young, it produces pale-coloured reds that are not generally regarded as high quality in Romania, where the fashion is for deep-coloured reds. A few producers are working on improving its reputation and when done well, it can produce lightly spicy wines more like Pinot Noir in structure. The best examples to date are from the Republic of Moldova and are covered more in that section of this book.

Producers worth trying: Senator, La Sapata.

Fetească Neagră

Its name literally means 'black maiden' grape – Fetească means belonging to a girl or maiden, and Neagră means black. Fetească Neagră is Romania's most important red native grape (though officially its origin is the Republic of Moldova). It has received a lot of attention in recent years as the country's best hope for a flagship variety and is now appearing in almost every region of the country, and is the subject of academic research into the best ways of growing it and formally identifying its flavour profile by region. There were 2,950 hectares in 2017, showing a sharp increase from the 1,270 hectares reported in 2006.

It seems to have been grown in this region for a very long time, and is claimed to originate around Uricani near Iași, though there is no documentary evidence for when it first appeared. Older reference books (such as Constantinescu in 1959) suggested that this variety was selected directly from wild grape vines. As yet nothing is known about its parentage, while the fact that there are several natural biotypes supports the theory that it is a very old variety. It is definitely not a colour mutation of Fetească Albă as has been claimed. It can be tricky to grow well as it has very vigorous canopies but with low bud fertility, meaning it needs careful canopy management (so producers like Balla Géza prune it to two canes in the hope of getting sufficient fruitful buds). It ripens slightly after Merlot, needing 160 to 170 days from bud burst to cropping. It can ripen unevenly and is prone to inadequate quality and lack of colour if overcropped. Most producers reckon yields must be kept under 6 tonnes per hectare for high quality wines. Fetească Neagră can also have problems with high total acidity alongside high (in wine terms) pH. It shows good resistance to frost and drought as well as downy mildew but is susceptible to powdery mildew and grey rot. The official catalogue of plant varieties cultivated in Romania for 2016 shows that there are now seven approved clones, all certified since 2005, though various producers are working on their own selections, as well as undertaking research into matching it with appropriate rootstocks and the best approaches to canopy management. Currently Fetească Neagră is produced in a huge range of styles, varying from unoaked, light and fruity to more serious oak-aged styles, and it is also used in blends to add a sense of place and local identity. Dan Balaban of Davino explains why they grow it: 'It gives our own personal touch. At best it is exceptional but will never compare to the best Cabernet Sauvignon or Merlot grand vins.'

Producers worth trying: Alira, Aurelia Vişinescu, Balla Géza, Bauer, Casa de Vinuri Cotnari, Corcova, Crama Avereşti, Crama Gîrboiu, Crama Oprişor, Cramele Recaş, Davino, Domeniile Tohani (Apogeum), Halewood, Licorna Winehouse, Petro Vaselo, SERVE, Viile Metamorfosis.

Negru De Drăgăşani

Literally 'black from Drăgăşani', this crossing was carried out at the Drăgăşani research institute and released in 1993. According to the literature it was a cross of an old variety called Negru Vârtos with Saperavi, though this has not yet been proven by DNA analysis. Jakob Kripp of Prince Ştirbey insists that a conversation with the scientist who carried out the work indicates that it was in fact a crossing of Negru Vârtos with Băbească Neagră. It produces grapes with good levels of sugar but only moderate acidity and has medium vigour and yield potential with good resistance to frost and mildew. It was only grown on a very small area of around 18.8 hectares in 2017 but is already showing great promise for deep coloured, richly fruity and high quality red wines.

Producers worth trying: Avincis, Viile Metamorfosis, Vinarte, Cramele Recaş.

Negru Vârtos

Although this old variety only exists in research vineyards it has been identified by some producers as worth investigating for revival. DNA analysis has shown that it is an offspring of Prokupac and may be a synonym for a rare Bulgarian grape Mavrud Varnenski (which has nothing to do with Bulgaria's true Mavrud). Jakob Kripp notes that Negru Vârtos is a grape variety that suffers from poor fruit set and uneven ripening due to having flowers that are functionally female only. Traditionally it was always planted with Negru Moale as pollinator, but this didn't entirely solve the problem, so the variety fell out of favour.

Novac

Another crossing from the Drăgășani research institute of Negru Vârtos and Saperavi, released in 1987. It ripens about 10 days ahead of Merlot and is potentially a highly productive vine. The fruit has balanced sugar and acid levels at ripeness, and high levels of anthocyanins giving deep coloured wines. One practical problem is that it has a very narrow picking window of just one week, before it loses quality. It is only grown by a very limited number of producers (74 hectares in 2017) including Prince Știrbey, which reports that, 'it is a bit of a prima donna in the vineyard', while Ghislain Moritz (winemaker at Avincis) reckons, 'It is even trickier to grow and handle than Pinot Noir'. It can also be used for sparkling wine.

Producer worth trying: Prince Știrbey.

OTHER LOCAL VARIETIES

There is a long tail of other local grape cultivars that are either historic varieties, largely confined to research institution collections, or new varieties produced in the 1970s and 1980s which may have potential but are not widely planted. These include Alutus (Băbească x Saperavi bred in Drăgășani, now being trialled by Avincis); Columna (Pinot Gris x Grasă de Cotnari, produced in 1985, grown in Dobrogea) and Amurg (Muscat Hamburg x Cabernet Sauvignon bred in Blaj). The list of historic varieties, some of which are reported to have potential for high quality wine, includes Ardeleanca, Armas, Basicata, Bătută Neagră, Berbecel, Braghina Roz and Alb, Creață (a.k.a. Rizling de Banat), Negru Moale and Vulpe.

INTERNATIONAL GRAPE VARIETIES

Aligoté

This Burgundian grape has long been widely planted in Eastern Europe. In 2017, it covered 5,545 hectares in Romania making it the fifth most important white variety. It rarely appears in wines destined for export and it is not clear why it retains its popularity. The story goes that it arrived in 1912, in Dobrogea, brought by a boyar (a Romanian nobleman), Constantin Mimi, from France as a present for his friends in the country. It was also planted in Oltenia, and in Dealu Mare but apparently showed the best potential in Dobrogea.

Producers worth trying: Gramma Winery, Via Viticola, Sarica-Niculițel.

Blaufränkisch

This grape was called Burgund Mare (literally meaning 'big Burgundian' in Romanian). For some time it was believed to be Pinot Noir or possibly Meunier because of presumed links between Burgund and Burgundy, though it is almost certainly named after its Austrian heartland, Burgenland. It was Eugen Ungureanu, Director General in the Ministry of Agriculture of Romania in the 1970s, who took the decision to import Blaufränkisch from Austria, at a time when the main objective in viticulture was greater productivity. There were 698 hectares as of 2017.

Producers worth trying: Balla Géza, Nachbil.

Cabernet Sauvignon

This was grown on just 5,406 hectares in 2017 as it has nothing like the appeal or reliability of Merlot in Romanian conditions, though there are still good quality wines to be found. It is arguably at its best in Bordeaux-style blends, particularly with the inclusion of a local variety.

Producers worth trying: Alira, Avincis, Aurelia Vișinescu, Crama Oprișor, Domeniul Coroanei Segarcea, Halewood Hyperion, Licorna Wine House, Petro Vaselo, SERVE, Viile Metamorfosis, Vinarte.

Chardonnay

Chardonnay arrived in Romania after phylloxera, in the early twentieth century. It was noted for sweet versions in the warm Black Sea coast region of Murfatlar and is still popular in the domestic market. Today better versions are dry. There were 2,005 hectares grown in 2017.

Producers worth trying: Crai Nou, Crama Gîrboiu, Cramele Recaș, Domeniul Coroanei Segarcea, Halewood, Liliac, Petro Vaselo, SERVE, Strunga Winery.

Merlot

Romania's most important red grape variety is Merlot, with 11,367 hectares in 2017, making up 12.6 per cent of noble grape plantings. There is evidence that it arrived in the country along with other French grape varieties after phylloxera. It produces reliable and consistent wine in Romanian growing conditions and is more predictable here than Cabernet Sauvignon, which sometimes ripens rather later and tends to run into early winter weather in some years.

Producers worth trying: Avincis, Domeniile Tohani (Principele Radu), Liliac, Prince Ştirbey, Rotenberg, Vinarte.

Pinot Gris or Pinot Grigio

This variety arrived post-phylloxera in western Romania, under its German identity of Rulander. There were 1,589 hectares in 2017 and it is in particularly high demand today for inexpensive Italian-lookalike, own-label brands for markets such as the UK and USA where this variety is popular. Rumours abound of large bulk shipments to Italy in years where that country has a poor harvest, and export data confirm that 8 per cent of Romania's exports go to Italy.

Producers worth trying: Cramele Recaş, Halewood, Jidvei.

Pinot Noir

Pinot Noir has been associated with Romania for more than a century and has been particularly important in the export sector since the 1980s (see box, p.187). It arrived soon after phylloxera in the Murfatlar area, brought by French advisors from Champagne, so it was not red wine planting material but sparkling clones. In 2017, it covered 2,024 hectares; the last decade has seen some significant plantings of genuine red wine material (often Dijon clones) and the quality of Pinot Noir emerging from the country is much improved. Export markets collapsed in the 1990s and local demand at the time was not strong as Romanians are reported to be obsessed with dark-coloured reds. It is currently enjoying resurgence due to both growing export demand (Romania is still a good value source for this notoriously expensive grape) and a local market with strong trends for Pinot Noir rosé and even sparkling wines. Dan Muntean notes: 'Compared to our neighbours, Pinot Noir has had quite a long history in Romania, and along with Pinot Gris, has spread to Dealu Mare and other wine regions of Romania. The local consumption of the variety was (and still is) very low and the grape notoriously difficult to grow, hence the small acreage (about 1,000 hectares in the mid/late 1980s, at a time when the total vineyard area was in the region of 300–350,000 hectares).'

Producers worth trying: Avincis, Carastelec, Cramele Recaş, Halewood, Liliac, Petro Vaselo, SERVE, Viile Metamorfosis.

THE PINOT NOIR STORY

The Romanian Pinot Noir story started in earnest in the late 1970s. Romania started a contract with PepsiCo, whereby Romania was buying Pepsi-Cola concentrate in exchange for wines, under the Premiat label shipped by its wine division, Monsieur Henri Wines. Dan Muntean recalls that it was John Halewood who encouraged the Romanians to go with Pinot Noir in the 1980s as that was what the UK market demanded (see also p. 140). He explained that it was easy in the centralized economy for him, along with Professor Stoian (Director General of the Research Institute at Valea Călugărească) to collect all the Pinot Noir produced in Dealu Mare by other companies and create one 'big batch' blend for all the customers in the UK, and to a lesser extent, US. It was clearly quite a surprise for the male-led hierarchy to have to comply with Western quality control standards though. Dan tells the tale of the first visit of a Sainsbury's technician, a very young woman, to Valea Călugărească where Professor Stoian was also the winemaker. 'As he was showing the bottling line to the young JS technician, Viorel nonchalantly lit a cigarette … only to be told in a very brusque and imperative manner to put it down by the so-young technician! Viorel was in shock.'

Dan Muntean became managing director of Halewood's investments in Romania. He recalls: 'Owing to this success in the UK, when Halewood started planting their own vineyards, it was my decision that the first vines to be planted in 2001 were top clones of Pinot Noir from Burgundy (114, 115, 667 and 777, and 292 for sparkling). Pinot Noir is still the most planted variety in Halewood vineyards. Pinot Noir remains the most successful export grape variety.'

> There has been criticism that there wasn't enough Pinot Noir in Romania to meet all the supermarket demand in the 1980s and 1990s, but Philip Cox (Cramele Recaş) explains:
>
> *I wouldn't say there was no Pinot Noir! There was definitely some, although a lot of Burgund Mare got sold as Pinot Noir [author's note: at that time Burgund Mare was believed to be a clone of Pinot Noir]. You have to remember that in 1986 there were 300,000 hectares here, most of which totally disappeared in the early 1990s due to the botched privatization process. When I came in 1991 there was still a fair bit of Pinot Noir especially in Murfatlar and Dealu Mare, but it then largely died out by the late 1990s.*

Riesling

This is the name used in Romania for Graševina (a.k.a. Welschriesling, Italian Riesling or Riesling Italico). There were 7,520 hectares in 2017. There was very little true (Rhein or German) Riesling at one time, though by 2017, there were 330 hectares of genuine Riesling (usually labelled Riesling de Rhin for domestic sales).

Producers worth trying: Vinarte (Riesling), Carastelec (Rhein Riesling), Lechburg (Rhein Riesling), Villa Vinèa.

Sauvignon Blanc

There were 5,614 hectares in 2017, reflecting the domestic popularity of this grape, often vinified with some residual sugar and without the aromatic intensity of a New Zealand or Loire style. Several producers now make acceptable commercial dry styles.

Producers worth trying: Avincis, Budureasca, Corcova, Davino, Jidvei, La Salina, Viile Metamorfosis, Villa Vinèa, Vinarte.

Syrah

This is another international grape that needs no introduction. It was first planted in Romania by Carl Reh in around 2001, when it was not a registered grape variety for the country. They initially produced it as a very limited selection of 2 to 3 barrels in a magnum bottle sold on allocation only. It has since become a permitted grape variety, planted on 503 hectares according to 2017 data. Several other producers are also now making successful examples as it seems to suit some of the country's warmer locations.

Producers worth trying: Catleya, Corcova, Crama Oprişor, Nachbil, Viile Metamorfosis.

OTHER INTERNATIONAL VARIETIES

These include Neuburger (in Transylvania due to its popularity in German communities and its ability to accumulate sugar in low sunlight), Furmint (in Miniş, notably Balla Géza), Viognier, Kerner, Zweigelt, Roşioară (2,661 hectares, Bulgaria's Pamid), Rkatsiteli, Portugieser, Sangiovese, Kadarka (known in Bulgaria as Gamza and usually spelt Cadarcă here), Cabernet Franc, Malbec, Gewürztraminer, Marselan, Muscat Ottonel (4,898 hectares due to popularity in the domestic market), Petit Verdot and Dornfelder. (See Appendix II for the full list.)

THE BLEND STORY

In Romania, as in Bulgaria, blends have become important and often feature as flagship wines, usually made in small quantities. SERVE's Cuvée Charlotte was the first super-premium Romanian red, released by the influential Corsican Count Guy de Poix in 2000. It was a wine that put Romania's potential on the wine map and inspired many others. Today Cuvée Charlotte, with its blend of Bordeaux varieties and Fetească Neagră continues to be a standard bearer, though it is no longer alone. White blends are less common but there have been notable successes in a small number of cases.

Red blends worth trying (in alphabetical order by producer): Aurelia Vişinescu Red Artizan, Avincis Cuvée Grandiflora, Balla Géza Stone Wine Fetească Neagră/Cabernet Franc, Budureasca Noble 5, Catleya Epopée, Crama Oprişor Ispita, Crama Oprişor Smerenie, Cramele Recaş Cuvée Uberland, Davino Reserva, Davino Flamboyant, Domeniul Coroanei

Segarcea Simfonia, LacertA Cuvée IX, Petro Vaselo Ovas, SERVE Cuvée Charlotte.

White blends worth trying (in alphabetical order by producer): Cramele Recaş Solo Quinta, Davino Reserva, Davino Revelatio, Domeniile Tohani Siel, SERVE Cuvée Amaury.

THE HYBRID ISSUE

One subject that most Romanian growers don't want to talk about is that of the significant plantings of hybrid vines (also known as direct producers) that remain. These are crosses between non-European (usually American) grape species such as *Vitis labrusca* and unknown *Vitis vinifera* to try and improve the flavour, as American vines are notorious for their unpleasant 'foxy' aroma and taste. There were still 83,204 hectares of these so-called interspecific hybrids planted in 2017 according to Ministry of Agriculture data, producing 1.47 million hectolitres of wine. However, prior to joining the EU, Romania had agreed to remove all its hybrid vines by 2014 and in return gained the right to replant 30,000 hectares with *Vitis vinifera*. This requirement seems to have been quietly dropped for reasons that are probably more social than anything else, though it always seemed an impossibly large task to achieve in the timescale. These hybrid vines are largely grown in tiny back garden plots and used for home consumption. Wine from these vines is not permitted for commercial production within the EU, but is commonly sold on the grey market by the roadside, or through informal networks within families and friends. Over the border in the non-EU Republic of Moldova, there are still commercial bottlings from hybrid vines, especially Isabella, and also Lidia. Hybrids are easier to grow on a small scale, being more disease resistant, higher-yielding and tolerant of phylloxera so they are popular for home winegrowers.

Even as recently as 2017, I was greeted at the airport with a bunch of fresh Isabella grapes by the owner of an expensive and very premium winery. For him, Isabella was the authentic taste of his childhood. This harms the country's wine market for proper wine in several ways. Producers of premium wine are competing against wines perceived as more authentic, genuine and from the heart. Another problem is that people who drink these wines don't have a taste for commercial wines, having grown up with the weird, foxy flavour of hybrids and their grandparents' home-made wines. The third problem is that these consumers are simply not buying commercial wine. One solution that Jidvei winery has come up with is to offer grape juice for sale in their 'Must from Jidvei' campaign. In 2017 they sold over 900,000 litres of juice to local people who want to preserve their home winemaking traditions. On the face of it, this undermines Jidvei's business of selling bottled wine, but if it helps move people towards the flavours of wine made from noble grapes, it is arguably a positive step in taste education.

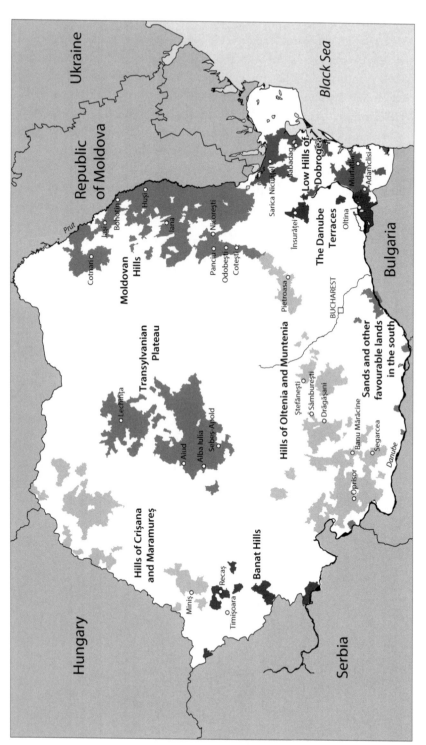

Ukraine

Republic
of Moldova

Black Sea

Prut

Bohotin
Iaşi
Huşi

Cotnari

Iana

Nicoreşti

Panciu
Odobeşti
Coteşti

**Moldovan
Hills**

Sarica Nicuiţel

Babadag

**Low Hills of
Dobrogea**

Murfatlar
Adamclisi

Insurăţei

Oltina

**The Danube
Terraces**

Pietroasa

Lechinţa

**Transylvanian
Plateau**

BUCHAREST

Bulgaria

Aiud
Alba Iulia
Sebeş-Apold

Ştefăneşti

Sâmbureşti
Drăgăşani

Hills of Oltenia and Muntenia

**Sands and other
favourable lands
in the south**

Hungary

Banu Mărăcine
Segarcea

Danube

Miniş
Recaş
Timişoara

**Hills of Crişana
and Maramureş**

Oprişor

Banat Hills

Serbia

Romania's wine zones (information courtesy of ONVPV)

14

ROMANIAN REGIONS

GEOGRAPHY AND CLIMATE

Romania has a very wide range of climates, regions and different zones with the potential to offer considerable diversity in its wines. Although there is a coastal plain on the Black Sea, the country is dominated by mountains, with the eastern Carpathians running north to south across the country and the Transylvanian alps running west to east, at an average altitude of around 1,000 metres. The Wallachian plain stretches south to the River Danube and Bulgaria, while the Pannonian plain lies between the Carpathian foothills and Hungary to the west.

Romania lies on much the same latitudinal span as southern France, ranging between 44 and 48°N. Its climate is temperate continental and it can suffer from harsh winters. Recent research on the impact of climate change here shows an increased frequency of extreme winter cold during the grapevine dormant period (along with increased risk of cold injury or grapevine death) over the last 20 years. From 1888 to 1963, this occurred once in 10 years, but now temperatures drop below -20°C in four or five years per decade. Typically, vineyard land is on sloping sites or in favourable microclimates in valleys to avoid harsh winter temperatures, and this is part of the reason why there was less of a wholesale move of vineyards from hills to plains under collectivization in Romania compared to Bulgaria. The Black Sea helps to moderate winter temperatures in Dobrogea by the coast. Summer temperatures can be high, and are starting to cause drought stress in warmer regions and hotter seasons; there has been a recent increase in the number of hot (>30°C) and very hot (>35°C) days in summer. The average July temperature is 23.5°C and typical annual rainfall is 400–600 millimetres. Currently most vineyards are not irrigated but several irrigation projects are in progress in drier areas.

WINE LAWS

Romanian wine law is fully compliant with EU regulations. PDO (Protected Designation of Origin) wines must be made from *Vitis vinifera* and in 2017 accounted for 819,510 hectolitres or 29.3 per cent of the harvest (the total crop from noble vines was 2,798,979 hectolitres). This is a significant increase over PDO wine production in 2016 (564,060 hectolitres). In Romania, DOC (*Denumire de Origine Controlată*) is the recognized traditional term for PDO wines, that is high-quality wines from a delimited area, produced within that area and subject to certain other controls such as yield and grape variety. The basic DOC category is supplemented by further classifications according to maturity of grapes:

- DOC-CMD (*Cules la maturitate deplină*) for wines harvested at full maturity
- DOC-CT (*Cules târziu*) for late harvest wines
- DOC-CIB (*Cules la înnobilarea boabelor*) for noble late harvest wines.

Romania currently has eight wine regions and 33 PDO wine areas (though 38 are registered with the EU because some regions have multiple PDO registrations for different wine styles), and one of the eight major regions has no PDO wines. There are two DOCs (Adamclisi and Însurăței) that, at the time of writing, are protected under national law but are still in the process of approval by the EU for PDO status. (See Appendix II for a full list of classifications and permitted grape varieties for each.)

In Romania, the term for PGI (Protected Geographical Indication) wines is *Vin cu Indicație Geografică*. This category accounted for 262,869 hectolitres in 2017 and showed an increase over 2016 (212,165 hectolitres). At least 85 per cent of the grapes must be produced and vinified in the specified, delimited area. Currently, 12 PGIs are recognized by the EU (see Appendix II). Actual alcoholic strength must be a minimum of 9.5 per cent or 10 per cent depending on the wine-growing zone. Other protected traditional terms include *Rezervă* for wine matured for at least six months in oak and six months in bottle and *Vin de Vinotecă* for wine matured for at least one year in oak and four in bottle. Another term is *Vin tânăr* (young wine) which is a wine sold before the end of the year of production.

This still leaves a substantial volume of wine being produced with no quality status – just over 1,557,692 hectolitres in 2017 – plus wine from hybrids, as already mentioned. Production by colour from noble vines is still significantly biased towards white wines. In 2017, red volume was 709,933 hectolitres, white was 1,883,169 hectolitres and rosé 205,477 hectolitres (a huge rise from the 2015 volume of 65,237 hectolitres). Part of the significance of the rise of DOC wines may be because to declare a region on the label, a wine must have DOC or PGI status. It may also be due to EU subsidies for these categories. A new category of varietal wines has been added to the wine law recently, and accounted for 158,943 hectolitres in 2017.

Compared to her Eastern European neighbours, Romania has ended up with a lot of DOCs and PGIs (in comparison Bulgaria only has two PGIs and Moldova three). Perhaps these are a necessity to reflect the bigger vineyard areas and diverse climatic zones, but it does add complexity in a market where grape variety and brand are the key drivers. Most consumers are simply not aware of the implications of DOC status. Some sources reckon that Romania ended up with so many DOCs as it was useful in EU negotiations for planting rights, rather than genuinely reflecting what was useful for the wine industry.

WINE REGIONS

Romania is divided into eight distinct wine zones (see map, p. 192): Podişul Transilvaniei (Transylvanian Plateau) in the middle of the country; Dealurile Crişanei ai Maramureşului (Hills of Crişana and Maramureş) to the west of the mountains; Dealurile Moldovei (Moldovan Hills) on the eastern slopes of the Carpathians; Dealurile Oltenei si Muntenei (Hills of Oltenia and Muntenia) in the southern Carpathians; Dealurile

Banatului (Banat Hills) towards the borders with Hungary and Serbia; Colinele Dobrogei (the Low Hills of Dobrogea) between the Danube and the Black Sea; Terasele Dunarii (Danube Terraces) and Nisipurile din Sudul Țarii (the unwieldy 'Sands and Other Favourable Lands in the South'), the last two being relatively unimportant for quality wine production.

Transylvanian Plateau (Podişul Transilvaniei)

This high central region lies in EU growing zone B. Typically the vegetation period lasts 177 days between budburst and first frost, and with an active heat summation (see Glossary) of 2,789°C (April to September). It is relatively cool, especially at night, and altitudes range up to 600 metres. Lower lying vines are often buried or earthed-up to protect them from the winter cold, which can fall as low as -30°C. DOCs within this region are: Târnave (with its sub-regions of Jidvei, Blaj and Mediaş), Alba Iulia, Aiud, Sebeş-Apold and Lechinţa. These are some of Romania's coolest vineyards and produce mainly white wines, which can have fresh acidity and good aromatic expression when well made. Evidence of the medieval immigration of Saxon settlers from the Mosel valley to the region is still seen in the architecture and in the wine styles.

One of the most important DOCs in production is Jidvei, after the village of the same name, which is mentioned in documents dating from as early as 1309 (it is called Seiden in German and Zsidve in Hungarian). Winemaking has been important throughout its history, and Jidvei is also the name of the privatized former state winery (also Romania's largest single vineyard at over 2,460 hectares). Other DOCs in use include Lechinţa, noted for its brown alluvial soils, rich in calcium and iron. The zone had fallen out of favour for wine production due to humid summers but new wineries, notably Liliac, have planted at 300–500 metres, where there is good exposure to sun and breezes to keep vines healthy. Foggy autumns also allow for slow ripening and good freshness and flavour development. Other DOC areas with presence in the market include Târnave, produced by Villa Vinèa.

Crişana and Maramureş (Dealurile Crişanei ai Maramureşului)

This north-western region lies in EU growing zone CI, where there are typically 187 days between budburst and first frost, and an active heat summation of 3,049°C (April to September) making it a little warmer than Transylvania, despite being the most northerly region in Romania, lying at 48°N. There are two DOCs within this region: Miniş in Arad county, influenced by Lake Arad, and Crişana (with sub-denominations of Diosig, Biharia and Şimleu Silvaniei). Total vineyard area was around 9,693 hectares in 2017. The Miniş DOC itself has a temperate continental climate with Adriatic influences, bringing long warm and dry autumns so red grapes can ripen well. Soils are low in humus but high in iron and may have volcanic or limestone bedrock. Vines are predominantly planted with southern exposure and vineyards grow as high as 500 metres in altitude. Miniş is particularly famous for the creation of a sweet red wine first made in 1744, using the Aszú method (using dried berries affected by noble rot) and Cadarcă grapes. To everyone's surprise, it was an overnight sensation, and soon became a favourite of the Habsburg Court.

Moldovan Hills (Dealurile Moldovei)

This is the eastern part of the old Romanian principality of Moldavia and is much the biggest region in Romania in terms of grapevine area, with 69,154 hectares in 2017. Located east of the Carpathians, it stretches southwards for several hundred kilometres from the hills of Cotnari at 47°N, so climate and growing conditions vary considerably. Vineyards are typically sited on the slopes of south and south-west facing amphitheatres that protect the vines from the harsh north winds. Altitudes can vary from 200 to almost 500 metres. The region has 183 days from budburst to first frost, while active heat summation is 3,154°C (April to September) and rainfall is relatively low at only about 500 millimetres. Soil types include chernozems and sands. The DOC regions include Bohotin, Coteşti, Cotnari, Dealu Bujorului, Huşi, Iaşi, Iana, Nicoreşti, Odobeşti, Panciu. DOCs of commercial significance include Cotnari (see Box, p.214) and Coteşti located in Vrancea county (location of the historic Ştefan Cel Mare Cellars, dated to between 1457 and 1504). In official documents, Coteşti vineyards were first mentioned in 1580, when they were referred to by Muslim convert Mihnea Turcitul. Grapevine growing and wine production have always been two of the main activities of the people of Vrancea so almost every household has a few vines. There is good potential for quality here due to altitudes of 100 to 300 metres and mineral-rich soils based on clay, sand and marl. Recent investments are starting to turn this potential into reality, though it is still early days for this investment phase. Iaşi itself is considered the cultural capital of Romania; it is the former capital of the unified principalities of Wallachia and Moldavia, and was the first location to have a university. Today, it is still dotted with historical buildings, including more than 20 monasteries and even more churches.

Oltenia and Muntenia (Dealurile Oltenei si Muntenei)

This large area in the Carpathian foothills, north of the capital Bucharest, covered 53,601 hectares in 2017. It crosses the EU's CI zone (Oltenia) and CII (Muntenia), benefiting from a vegetation period of 195 days from budburst to first frost and an active heat summation of 3,192°C. The DOC areas include Dealu Mare, Drăgăşani, Pietroasa, Ştefăneşti, Sâmbureşti, Banu Maracine, Mehedinţi, Cernăteşti-Podgoria and Segarcea.

Most famous is the historic and extensive Dealu Mare, meaning big hill, which stretches for 65 kilometres across the counties of Buzau and Prahova. It lies on the forty-fifth parallel, along with Bordeaux and Tuscany. It has a temperate continental climate and iron-rich red-brown soils. Summers are hot, while autumns are mild and dry, and vineyards are typically planted on south-facing slopes. The first written documents about the existence of a vineyard culture in this part of the country date back to the fourteenth and fifteenth centuries, when Ceptura and Valea Călugărească are mentioned. Later, Transylvanian princes came here to buy wine from Wallachia. Today, it is best known for its reds and for being the source for some of Romania's most exciting wines. Vineyards are at altitudes of between 130 and 550 metres and protected from winter freeze by high hills and forests above the vineyards. Annual rainfall averages around 640 millimetres. Another notable DOC is Pietroasa with its outcrop of calcareous soil at 300 metres, making the district particularly famous for its lusciously sweet late harvest wines, especially Tămâioasă and Busuioacă, and in some years noble rot occurs. Archaeological finds suggest a long history of wine production in the DOC of Ştefăneşti located at the eastern end of the hills of Oltenia. Vineyards are planted on south-facing slopes at around 250 to 300 metres, typically on brown forest soils with limestone bedrock. Whites and full-bodied reds from Cabernet Sauvignon are particularly famous.

Towards the south-west and river Olt basin, the history of wine in Oltenia becomes almost impossible to follow. Since the Middle Ages, Oltenia has been the theatre of an almost uninterrupted series of wars, revolutions, uprising, or battles for land and power between the Austro-Hungarian and Ottoman Empires. At the heart of this region lie the historic DOC vineyards of Drăgășani. The legend of this region dates back to the reign of Dacian king Burebista with a love story between his daughter, Bagrina, and the fearless Dacian warrior, Gordan, immortalized in the naming of two grape varieties (Braghină and Iordan). The Drăgășani vineyards are first officially mentioned in the sixteenth and seventeenth centuries, during the reign of Prince Michael the Brave (r.1593–1601), who apparently appreciated the wine produced by monasteries here. There are later royal connections with Princes Știrbey and Bibescu who had properties here, while Leo Tolstoy was said to have enjoyed wines from Drăgășani while travelling through Bucharest in 1877. The vineyard area stretches for around 50 kilometres and plantings range from 200 to 500 metres in altitude. Soils are varied and include brown forest soils, alluvial deposits and limestone. Average rainfall is around 640 millimetres and hail is a frequent summer hazard. This is a dynamic region of small estates that have recently set up a growers' association. There is particular focus in the region on local grape varieties: white varieties include Fetească Regală, Tămâioasă (sweet and dry styles) and local Crâmpoșie Selecționată, while local red specialities such as Negru de Drăgășani and Novac show promise.

Twenty kilometres to the east lies the smaller DOC of Sâmburești, which specializes in Cabernet Sauvignon and other reds. It's a hilly, sunny area with predominantly clay soils and moderate rainfall of 555 millimetres per annum. About 30 kilometres south of the university town of Craiova lies DOC Segarcea, on the Oltenia plain at around 100 to 150 metres. Soils are largely chernozem with good levels of calcium carbonate and iron oxide. The climate is temperate continental with minor Mediterranean influences and good sun exposure, while vines are largely planted on gentle, south-facing slopes. The region was mentioned as early as 1557, in a document in which Pătraşcu cel Bun, the father of Michael the Brave, gave 'the lands of Segarce to his daughter Mary', as a dowry.

The DOC Mehedinţi covers the vineyard areas of Plaiurile Drâncei and Severin county and has sub-divisions covering Severin, Corcova, Golul Drincei, Vânju Mare and Oreviţa. This is a sunny and warm region, with a temperate continental climate and mild Mediterranean influences. Producers here tend to concentrate on red wine production. There are varied soils including outcrops of iron-rich 'terra rossa' as well as brown forest and alluvial soils, pebbles and sand. The region was first mentioned in writing in 1407 when Mircea cel Bătrân is recorded as giving wine and wheat to the Cozia monastery. Much of this area was substantially grubbed up in the 1980s and has only recently been replanted.

Banat (Dealurile Banatului)

This is Romania's smallest wine region with 2,845 hectares under vine in 2017. It lies towards the west of the country and has a mild Mediterranean climate with Adriatic influences. It is in EU zone CI and there are typically 200 days from budburst to first frost and an active heat summation of 3,207°C (April to September). Soils include clay with sand and limestone, and iron-rich outcrops. There are two DOC regions including Banat (sub-regions: Moldova Nouă, Dealurile Tirolului, Silagiu) and Recaş (the latter is more commercially notable). Vineyards have been planted in the Recaş region since Roman times, with documented evidence of a sale of grapevines for 32 forints in 1447. The arrival of Saxons from the middle and lower Rhine in the early Middle Ages may have shaped wine growing here too. This is a region that was part of Hungary and the Habsburg Empire for around three centuries, a period when Schwabian German settlers moved here and developed the vineyards further, staying until 1948 when all their vineyards were confiscated. Vines planted show both Hungarian and German influences (including Cadarcă, Riesling Italico, Furmint and Kékfrankos). In 1948, the region had just 277 hectares, though by 1989 it had grown to 2,500 hectares, mostly planted under communism. The disastrous privatization process meant that many vineyards disappeared in the region so there were just 600 hectares by the late 1990s. It is the closest wine region to the historic Timişoara, a city that dates back to Dacian times. Its strategic location has made it the scene of many battles but today its architecture largely reflects its Habsburg history. The city was notable for pioneering telegraphy in 1853, followed by gas street-lighting. It became the first European city to have electric streetlights in 1884. More recently, in December 1989, Timişoara became renowned as the place where the Romanian uprising against Ceauşescu began.

Dobrogea (Colinele Dobrogei)

This region lies in the south-west, between the Danube and the Black Sea and is in EU zone CII at a latitude of 44°. Altitude is low, averaging just 71 metres. The vegetation period lasts 196 days with an active heat summation of 3,311°C from April to September. It can have as many as 300 days of sunshine each year and rainfall between April and October averages only 150 to 200 millimetres, which can cause problems with drought. Winters are mild due to the close proximity to the Black Sea, but the climate is distinctly warm. There were 16,948 hectares of vines in 2017, across 4 DOCS: Murfatlar, Babadag, Adamclisi and Sarica-Niculiţel (which includes the sub-region Tulcea). Murfatlar, with its two sub-regions of Medgidia and Cernavodă, is the most important wine region here, and gave its name to Romania's former top-selling winery. In the past, the zone was best known for sweet whites, especially from Chardonnay, but today it is better known for reds. The dry climate is allowing some producers to farm organically.

Danube Terraces (Terasele Dunarii)

This region stretches along the lower banks of the Danube, opposite the Bulgarian border. It is in EU zone CII and has the longest vegetation period of any region at 202 days, but can suffer from extreme winter cold due to its low altitude of just 72 metres. Active temperature summation is 3,466°C. There were 11,210 hectares of vines in 2017. Table grapes are more typical here and the only DOCs are Oltina and Însurăţei. Oltina is an outcrop at 130–200 metres with clay, black soils and loess. Vineyards are planted facing northwards, on terraces close to the Danube, in an area known to have been colonized by the Romans, due to remains of a fortress found at Aliman.

Sands and other favourable lands in the south (Nisipurile din Sudul ţarii)

This is an area of deep sandy soils and a warm climate similar to the Danube Terraces. It has a vegetation period of 198 days and an active heat summation of 3,441°C. There were 12,943 hectares in 2017 and there are no DOC wines here.

15

ROMANIAN PRODUCER PROFILES

It would be an impossible task to profile every one of Romania's producers, not least because they change faster than they can be written about. So as with Bulgaria, this section will focus on those who have made an impact either through significant market presence, current export success or because quality has impressed. Producers who are very new and have not yet had the chance to show consistency over several vintages but have produced at least one good wine so far are mentioned in brief – and are well worth keeping an eye on as this is such a dynamic sector. The bigger producers in Romania have largely kept close touch with their regional origins – and are usually still named after the original state farm. While some multi-region sourcing is now happening, such producers still largely identify with a specific region, so they will be covered on that basis.

BANAT REGION

Cramele Recaș

Complex de Vinificatie CP1, Recaș 307340, Timiș Co
Tel.: +40 256 330 100
www.recaswine.ro

Today Cramele Recaș is one of Romania's biggest producers, managing over 1,100 hectares, and is also the country's most successful exporter. It's run by Elvira and Philip Cox and their Romanian partners. The story of how a Bristol man got so involved in Romanian wine is fascinating as it parallels the development of the post-communism industry (see Box, opposite). Since 2005, the winery has worked with Hartley Smithers, a Sydney-born winemaker with over 40 vintages under his belt. He splits his time between Romania and Casella Wines in Australia (producers of Yellowtail), where he locates himself in the European winter. Smithers has been very important in instilling a consistent commercial style, regardless of whatever the weather brings for each vintage. Basque-born Nora Iriate arrived in 2010, bringing a more European perspective, and marrying Smithers soon after. It's hard to keep up with the enormous range of labels and own-labels produced by the winery, most of which are aimed at the value and volume end of the market, though there's a philosophy of over-delivering on quality to make up for the lack of recognition for Romania as a wine country. Premium wines are a developing sector for Recaş. Solo Quinta is one of their most famous wines, though it started as an accident in 2008. Someone had ordered 5,000 litres of white Cabernet Sauvignon but went bust and never paid for it. Smithers was then given the task of making a premium blend of whatever he liked as long as he used this abandoned white wine, and so Solo Quinta was born. The idea of five varieties, and always one red grape in the blend, has stuck ever since and it is now Romania's top selling premium wine. Other premium ranges include Selene, for red wines, inspired by collaborating with famous European producers (Planeta for the first Cabernet Sauvignon, now joined by a Fetească Neagră) and Sole for white wines, plus the impressive Cuvée Uberland as the red flagship.

Cramele Recaş continues to grow and recently invested another €4 million in production facilities. They have also developed partnerships with wineries in the east and employed more winemakers (Peter Valeri from Australia and Matteo Lappi from Italy) to supervise these sites as demand was up 20 per cent in 2017. Philip Cox credits Elvira with all this success, saying, 'She is the author spiritually because she does most of the selling, so it's all her hard work.'

FROM BRISTOL TO BANAT

PHILIP COX – HOW AN ENGLISHMAN CAME TO RUN ONE OF ROMANIA'S BIGGEST WINERIES

I came to Romania in 1991 – straight after finishing a degree in Humanities and Philosophy at Greenwich. In my summer holidays, I had worked for a London advertising company, and made a few Romanian friends, so they badgered me to visit them. As soon as I arrived in Romania I could see a lot of potential business opportunities, as the country basically had nothing back then. After experimenting with a running a cinema, eventually I ended up importing Heineken beer, because I could see the local beers were poor quality, and this turned out to be a huge success.

The problem was that we had heaps of Romanian currency, which was very difficult to change into hard currency, due to the national bank restrictions at the time and hyperinflation (over 1,000 per cent in the early 90s). In the end, I decided we had to export something to be able to turn Romanian money into something useful. My cousin had a wine shop near Bristol, and I had helped him out in my school holidays so my idea was that Romania had wine and I should be able to export it.

I did a couple of wine courses to find out a bit more about the industry, then I headed out to a few of the larger Romanian vineyards, to try and get some samples. This turned out to be hard, as they weren't very interested in exporting back then, plus there was still a state monopoly on wine exports. Anyway, in the end I managed to get some samples from a few wineries and set off to the UK to try and sell them. After a few people just laughed at me, I eventually ended up meeting Angela Muir MW, who was working for German wine group Reh-Kenderman, famous for Black Tower. The Germans were looking to get into Eastern Europe as their Liebfraumilch sales were declining, so Angela came over to Romania and we went on an epic trip across the country in a 20-year-old Opel Ascona. We ended up finding some decent bulk wines and selling them to Kwik Save and Sainsbury's (bottled in Germany by Reh-Kenderman). The first one actually came from Recaş winery [Cramele Recaş in Romanian]– state-owned at the time in 1993.

Things went well with the wine, and after a while the Germans asked me to work for them full time, with the idea of setting up a subsidiary in Romania. I was managing director of Carl Reh Romania from 1994 till 2000. The business grew quickly, we were making wine with flying winemakers, with grapes bought in from all over the country, and using rented wineries. Eventually Carl Reh purchased their winery in Oprişor, in southern Romania. It was a very good time for me. I learned a lot about wine production and grape sourcing but also got to meet big UK supermarkets and learn about the business. Last but definitely not least, I met Elvira in 1995 when she came as export manager, though I wasn't the one to hire her!

In late 1998, I took the decision to try and do something on my own as I could see the future would need us to plant vineyards. In 1999, Recaş winery came up for privatization. Elvira and I, together with Gheorghe Iova and Ioan Georgiu (director and winemaker for the state operation), decided to try and buy part of it to make a small company, ideally producing no more than 100,000 litres a year. That didn't work out as the government insisted that we buy the whole company, but luckily, we managed to convince them to let us pay for it over five years.

This pretty much defined our business model for the next 15 years because we suddenly had a big company with 650 hectares of vineyard, and no business. So we had to create new markets, and totally new products, taking a flexible approach with customers and developing innovative wine styles and packaging. We become the first winery to develop modern, fruit-forward New World-style wines, at entry level price points, which proved a big success. Since the 2008 financial crash, we have put a lot more effort into international markets, as we felt the Romanian market was stagnating. This effort has paid off, and we have managed to grow our export sales to match local market sales of bottled wine, with the UK being the most important market, closely followed by Holland and the USA, and a total of 25 export countries.

Petro Vaselo

Petrovaselo no. 230, 307346 Timiş County
Tel.: +40 256 307 048
www.petrovaselo.com

Italian owner Nella del Tio, a world leader in producing espresso coffee machines, set up a subsidiary in Romania. In 2002, having decided to learn more about Romanian culture he set off on a trip to explore the country, but got lost and found himself at Petro Vaselo. When he saw the unspoiled green hills, he was transported back to his childhood, and the idea was sparked of producing wine. The village name dates back to as early as 1359, when the place was described as the village of Petru the Serbian. Between 2005 and 2009, 42 hectares were planted with the philosophy of being as green as possible in this unspoiled region, and the vines have been certified organic since 2013. The vines grow in a natural amphitheatre at 170–220 metres and are planted at the high density (for Romania) of 6,250 vines per hectare. The climate is similar to that of southern Italy, with plenty of rain (800 millimetres) but very little in summer. The first two vintages were even shipped to Italy in refrigerated lorries to be vinified, followed anxiously by the winemaker in her car. Today's winemaker, Marco Feltrin, is a quietly spoken but passionate young Italian. His concept is all about working as naturally as possible in the cool underground cellar, using gravity rather than pumps, wooden fermenters, natural fermentation and no filtration. Entry-level wines include fruity Alb and Roşu de Petro Vaselo and Bendis tank-fermented sparkling wines, while premium wines include the very good Melgis Fetească Neagră, named after a Dacian noblewoman, and Ovas. The weighty PV Grand Cru and complex Kotys bottle-fermented sparkling wine complete the range at the top end.

CRIŞANA AND MARAMUREŞ

Balla Géza

583 Păuliş, Arad Co
Tel.: +40 257 388 045
www.ballageza.com

Balla Géza is a Hungarian, born in Transylvania, who has more or less single-handedly put the wine region of Miniş back on Romania's wine map. He studied winemaking in Cluj and took a job as a trainee at the state winery near Arad in 1984, where he rose through the ranks to become general manager. Back then, he oversaw winemaking for the region's 2,600 hectares, and when the state company closed down he initially tried to persuade the local growers to form a cooperative. When that idea was rejected, he said goodbye and went to start his own winery. His previous job meant he knew exactly where to find the best vineyard areas. He admits it was a slow process at first to persuade owners to sell immediately after land restitution, but after agreeing contracts with more than 200 people Géza eventually ended up with 120 hectares in three relatively large plots in the dramatic Miniş hills. Back in 1999 when he started with just 5 hectares, a Hungarian name was a distinct disadvantage in Romania, so he christened his winery Wine Princess, but is now switching back to using his own name. Géza's Hungarian spirit shows in his choice of grapes like Furmint and Cadarcă, and also Cabernet Franc, as his land is on the same latitude as Hungary's Villány, where this grape does so well. He is also a believer in reviving the fortunes of Romanian varieties like Mustoasă de Măderat (he makes good still and sparkling versions) and Fetească Neagră. Géza himself is rather a dark horse – such a generous and warm host at the winery that you would never guess that he is also a serious academic, earning his doctorate in 2002 and now teaching viticulture at the university.

The best wines are sold under the Stone Wine label – named for the large stones under the vines which reflect sun back to the fruit. They come from hilly vineyards where altitude reaches 500 metres and the rocky shallow soils particularly suit red grape varieties. Stone Wine Cabernet Franc on its own and also blended with Fetească Neagră particularly impress, as does Furmint. Cadarcă here has more depth and colour than is typical in Hungary, perhaps due to different clonal selections but it is charming and elegant.

Carastelec Winery

Carastelec 604, Sălaj County
Tel.: +40 740 040 777
www.carastelecwinery.com

Carastelec, a village first mentioned in 1241, lies in the north-western corner of Romania. Documentary evidence of vineyards here dates to 1650 when Princess Zsófia Báthory of Transylvania rebuilt the Roman Catholic church in the village and donated some forests and vineyards to pay for it. The region of Carastelec has particularly mineral-rich soil and was historically renowned for high-quality sparkling wines, which appealed to the owners (Hungarians who also have wineries in Tokaj and western Hungary), who set out to focus on 'traditional method' sparkling wines. The vineyard is planted in a south-facing natural amphitheatre near the village, at the top of a slope. The site was selected a few years ago by the legendary Hungarian winemaker Tibor Gál. There are 22 hectares on a plot that had been pulled out 15 years before. With the sparkling wine mission in mind, around half the slope is planted with Pinot Noir, along with Fetească Regală as a local variety and Riesling (the true Rhine variety) because it suits the cool climate here. Carastelec Winery is quite a pioneer in Romania as it is the first estate aiming to focus on sparkling wine. Its first vintage was 2013, and today it makes tank-fermented frizzante as well as 'traditional method' bottle-fermented sparkling wines, especially Pinot Noir rosé. There are some premium still wines, including a ripe smooth Pinot Noir too.

Nachbil

SC Weingut Brutler & Lieb SRL, Beltiug, str. Pieţii nr. 428 Satu Mare
Tel.: +40 261 870 200
www.nachbil.com

This old cellar has a new face, Edgar Brutler, son of the winery's founders. Edgar explains that his family was originally from Swabia in Germany. In the middle of the eighteenth century his ancestors moved to Transylvania where they lived as farmers. It was also a wine region and in fact wine was virtually a religion for his grandparents and everybody else there. The family moved back to Germany in 1982, when Edgar was three years old, in the hope of a better life. They visited friends and family in Romania every year, which kept the connection to their old home. In 1999, the Brutler family decided to plant vines on land that had been restituted to them. This was called Nachbil. The original plan was to manage it all by phone but eventually it became a company, as so many Romanian family friends in Germany wanted to drink wine from their homeland. Unfortunately, the business proved too much to manage remotely. Serendipity played its part with a new partner, and in 2009 the family sold up in Germany and moved back, planning to make the best wines in Romania. The project has had its ups and downs, but now Edgar is making his mark, even though it was an accidental career move. He says:

In 1999, I didn't have any ambition to go into wine. I wanted to study music, but I was too lazy to practise so the university said no. In search of something I could study I noticed that there was a university in Geisenheim where you could study oenology. I knew that my parents had a vineyard in Romania, but wine was never a thing to think about. But studying winemaking sounded interesting. The decision was made in one minute. In 2006 I finished in Geisenheim and got a job as winemaker in Austria. 2017 will be my last year there. After 11 years I have decided to run the winery that my parents built and fulfil that plan to make the best wine.

Edgar's vision is a winery with minimal technology to emphasize the unique location. The Nachbil Label is for very natural, intriguing, unfiltered wines, using ancient steep vineyards, 60 to 100-year-old field blends, and lengthy skin contact for the whites such as Grand Pa and Grünspitz (an ancient variety from grandfather's village). La Capella wines come from a bigger plot and the emphasis here is on fruity, easier-to-drink styles.

TRANSYLVANIA

Jidvei Winery

34 Garii Street, Jidvei, Alba Co.
Tel.: +40 258 881 881
www.jidvei.ro

The sheer scale of Jidvei cannot fail to impress. With over 2,400 hectares of vineyards in one location, this may be the largest single vineyard in Europe, and managing all this is an industry in itself. The winery has its own vine nursery and divides its vineyards into parcels to be managed by 26 vineyard managers, each with their own cost centre. It also has a bakery and dairy to provide bread and cheese to staff. Most of the regular workers (of which there are more than 700) come from local villages with a strong German population, who have good knowledge of winemaking requirements. A lot of vineyard work, including harvesting, is mechanized though, due to the challenge of getting enough workers in some years. For the 2017 harvest, 1,100 manual workers were employed, alongside 13 harvesting machines. The climate here is distinctly cool, with a 15°C difference between day and night, rainfall between 800 and 1,200 millimetres per year and low sunshine levels. Lower lying vines need to be earthed-up to protect against winter cold and red varieties don't ripen well enough, so the winery also has 230 hectares in Dobrogea.

Jidvei was a former IAS which was privatized in 1999 with 700 hectares and has since expanded considerably. It has four cellars: Jidvei, Blaj, Balcaciu and Tauni (which is where the premium Owner's Choice wines are made by French consultant Marc Dworkin). And on the main site, the challenge for the team of twelve winemakers is working with such large volumes (300–500 tonnes per day during harvest and a total of 22,000 tonnes in 2017) to give consistent results. The most successful wines are the fresh whites, especially where they don't go near the old barrel cellar (with its 45-year-old barrels). The Jidvei winery is named for the village, first mentioned in 1309, and winemaking seems to have been important throughout its history. The thirteenth-century castle Cetatea de Baltă was offered as a gift to Ştefan Cel Mare in 1489, along with some vineyards, to seal a friendship. It was sold along with the winery in 1999 and has since been renovated, with plans to turn it into a luxury hotel in the pipeline.

La Salina Winery

10 Dealul Viilor, Turda City, Cluj Co
Tel.: +40 742 908 311
www.cramalasalina.ro

A new winery on the scene since 2014, this was funded by two friends from the energy sector who loved wine and were inspired by friends in Montalcino. With the help of EU subsidies, 70 hectares have been replanted on long-abandoned land, on slopes close to the dramatic Turda salt mine, though luckily the salt is too deep to bother the vines. The wines are sold under the brand ISSA, still young but fresh and clean, guided by Austrian consultants. The winery has a restaurant and guest rooms too.

Liliac Winery

41 Principala Street, Batos Vlg, Mures Co
Tel.: +40 732 733 062
www.liliac.com

The Austrian owner of Liliac, Alfred Michael Beck, came to this region in the heart of Transylvania to look for forests and ended up buying a plot of beautiful young vineyards near Lechinţa, a region that had a history in winemaking going back to Roman times. However, in recent years it has pretty much been forgotten about, regarded as too cool and damp to make anything but table wines. The first full vintage to be released was 2011, which came to the market as a complete surprise. Today there are 52 hectares on two sites at Batoş and Lechinţa, bringing together Transylvanian grapes and Austrian expertise guided by Rudolf Krizan. Liliac has an innovative approach to winemaking and is possibly best known for fine, crisp and precise dry whites, but it has also pioneered sweet wines made from grapes dried on straw (Recioto style), made the country's first orange wine (from Chardonnay) and made its first ice wine too. There are increasingly competent reds, and the very good Pinot Noir rosé is another winery strength. The name Liliac means 'bat' and the bat is not just a symbolic namesake but also a partner in helping to control insect pests, nesting in old church towers and bat boxes around the vineyards.

Villa Vinèa Winery

243 Principala Street, Mica, Mures Co.
Tel.: +40 365 505 107
www.villavinea.com

This story of the winery goes back to 2001 when owner Heiner Oberrauch from Bolzano in Italy came to build a textile factory in Târgu Mureş and fell in love with the place. Vines were planted in 2006 and the first wines released in 2011. The winery has 32 hectares at 330 to 350 metres on south-facing slopes. Still relatively unusual for Romania, it is a proper estate, with a winery built in the shape of a traditional Transylvanian watchtower, overlooking the vineyards in the Târnave valley. Grapes grown include both local and international varieties, including a couple of favourites of Heiner: Kerner and Zweigelt. There's a shared vision between Italian winemaker Lucin Celestino (a winner of Gambero Rosso's winemaker of the year in 2009) and local cellarmaster Mihaly Denes, crossing the bridges between modern winemaking and Transylvanian tradition. There's a Sud-Tirol precision about the expressive, fresh whites, and a sweet passito from Muscat Ottonel too.

MOLDOVAN HILLS

Casa De Vinuri Cotnari

Castel Vlădoianu, village Cârjoaia, Cotnari com., Iași County, 707120
Tel.: +40 232 761 669
www.vinuricotnari.ro

This represents the vision of a new generation to do things differently from their parents (the major shareholders in SC Cotnari winery itself, see below), but with their parents' blessing and encouragement. Casa de Vinuri Cotnari (CVC for short) was launched in 2011 and is run completely separately, headed by Victor Deleanu. Victor studied economics and law, but when he failed his bar exams (by just 0.1 per cent), he changed tack and went to work at the family winery, where he got a taste for the wine business. He is helped by his brother Remus who is the lawyer for both companies. CVC has its own 350 hectares of vines, planted with local grape varieties only (in their eyes Tămâioasă Românească is a local grape), picked at low yields, and with the focus on premium dry and semi-dry whites. They have recently added rosé from Busuioacă de Bohotin, reds from Fetească Neagră and 'traditional method' sparkling. The winemaker is George Măluțan, who won winemaker of the year in Romania at the age of only 27. The head office and the red wine cellar are situated at the historic Belle Époque Vladoianu mansion built in 1901, bringing together memories of Romania's history as well as a new direction for Cotnari wines. Labels include Domenii and Colocviu (meaning Colloquium) for the best selections and a good limited edition Fetească Neagră called Castel Vladoianu.

SC Cotnari SA

Cotnari – Main no. 1, Cotnari village, Iași county
Tel.: +40 232 730 392
www.cotnari.ro

A former IAS, this was founded in 1948, rebuilt in 1968 and privatized as one unit by a management buyout in 2000. It is Romania's second most successful wine company, so undoubtedly is doing things right as far as local market taste and demand goes, but has paid little attention to exports as a result. Out of the region's roughly 1,700 hectares 1,360 are owned and managed by SC Cotnari, all within 8 kilometres of the winery. Most of these were replanted during 2006 and 2007, with the winery renovated to the tune of €15 million. Unusually for Romania, local grape varieties were replanted here after phylloxera and there are no international grapes in the region (apart from Tămâioasă Românească). The winery processes around 15,000 tonnes of grapes and has a mixture of modern stainless steel and oak from the 1960s in its 15 underground *hruba* (an old Romanian word that translates as dungeons rather than cellars). The chief winemaker here is a Moldovan who is a firm believer in the benefits of using these old wooden casks for micro-oxygenation of the winery's sweet and semi-sweet white wines.

COTNARI

Cotnari's golden history

The Cotnari region is historically famous for its sweet white wine. At one time, it rivalled Hungarian Tokaji for renown and was sought after in the royal courts of northern Europe, with one Parisian writer in 1875 describing it as better than wines from the Rhine.

Cotnari wine may be made from any of the four white grape varieties grown in the region, or as a traditional blend (containing a minimum of 30 per cent Grasă de Cotnari). Grasă provides the body and sugar, Tămâioasă Românească provides its aroma (it can give sweetness with losing acidity in this cool climate), Frâncuşă provides acidity and backbone (at least 30 per cent in a blend) and Fetească Albă gives mid-palate fruitiness. Grasă famously can accumulate very high levels of sugar and develop noble rot. SC Cotnari is renowned for its collection of wines made from Grasă in better years (going back to the 1950s), and usually produced with botrytis. These can age well and show attractive complexity but typical sweetness is not in the same league as Tokaji Aszú from Hungary (where minimum residual sugar is 120 grammes per litre, and usually much higher). The 2000 vintage Grasă collection wine has 76 grammes per litre of residual sugar.

Left: Ogy Tzvetanov.

Below: Neglected grapevines near Karabunar village, Bulgaria.

Above: Inside Better Half winery, Zmeevo, Bulgaria.

Below: Melnik's sand pyramids, south-west Bulgaria.

Above: Autumn colours in Villa Melnik's vineyards in the Struma Valley region, Mavrud in the centre.

Below: Preparing grapevine cuttings in Dealu Mare, Romania.

Above: Cramele Recaş vineyards, Romania.

Below: The historic Prince Bibescu building at Corcova Roy and Dâmboviceanu Winery.

Above: The historic Villa Dobruşa mansion at Avincis Winery, Drăgăşani, Romania.

Below: Balla Géza's vineyards at Miniş, Romania.

Above: Vineyards in Moldova's Valul lui Traian region.

Below: Cabernet Sauvignon at Et Cetera Winery, Moldova.

Left: Vinaria Purcari, Moldova.

Below: Soviet-style 'reactor' tanks at Vinuri de Comrat.

Above: The beautifully restored Castel Mimi in Moldova.

Below: Historic wine tanks at Asconi Winery, Moldova.

Crama Gîrboiu

SC Mera Com International Srl, str. Dealul Cramelor nr. 43, Dumbrăveni, Vrancea
Tel.: +40 237 232 079
www.cramagirboiu.ro

This is a genuinely family business, now headed by Livia Gîrboiu, whose mother is Cotești born and bred. The wine part of the business started in 2005 (the family also farms cereals and owns over a thousand hectares of forest); Livia took over from her father aged just 29. The winery itself had been restituted to a woman living in France, and was awful and rundown by the time the Gîrboiu family bought it, so they decided to knock it down and start afresh – something Livia sees as an advantage: 'We don't know the bad old ways,' she says. There are 250 hectares in the DOC zone of Cotești at around 170–200 metres, and one of the features of the winery has been to reinvent forgotten local grapes like Șarbă and Plăvaie. Livia admits this was hard work at first, though today Șarbă is first to sell out. The winery's brands like Tectonic (young varietal wines), Cuartz (sparkling) and Epicentrum (the premium label) are inspired by the fact that this is the most tectonically active area in Europe, where three continental plates collide, making earthquakes a frequent occurence.

Gramma Winery

Visan Vlg, Barnova, Iași Co.
Tel.: +40 735 930 832
www.grammawines.ro

The only small family winery in the Moldovan Hills, this is not far from the dramatic and historic city of Iași. Its strength is crisp white wines from Aligoté, Fetească Albă and Fetească Regală, which all also appear in their very good flagship blend Cuvée Vișan, and recently a bright rosé has also been added. It's now headed by the second generation, Marian Olteanu, who has a new vision about increasing quality through picking into crates and using smaller tanks, and is getting help with winemaking from Iași University. In due course, he wants to replant part of the estate's 17 hectares of 50-year-old vines. He admits quietly that a lot of producers, including his family, took EU funds to build wineries without considering the market but Marian is changing all that. He sold out of his bottled wines last year, helped by their distinctive, memorable labels.

Hermeziu Winery

Bivolari Vlg., Iaşi Co
Tel.: +40 232 259 051
www.cramahermeziu.ro

This new winery came on the scene with its first vintage in 2014. The wine business is now run by Loredana Lungu, who originally studied law but returned home to help her father with branding and marketing. A bit of a workaholic, she then went back to university to study agriculture and wine, before coming back to the family business permanently. As she cheerfully points out, she has made both parents happy (her mother is a lawyer and her father has 35 years of experience in agriculture, running 2,500 hectares of arable crops and fruit). The cellar has 150 hectares of vineyards in production, in an area that was historically vineyards. It was previously owned by the family of the famous Romanian poet Constantin Negruzzi, but abandoned after communism. Modern equipment and an experimental approach to viticulture and winemaking take priority here, with C'est Soir rosé in several styles becoming a tremendous success for the winery. Loredana was the first in Romania to use glass stoppers for this range. Hermeziu is for international varieties, Vladomira for local grapes and Thrubilo for sparkling wines.

OLTENIA AND MUNTENIA

Dealu Mare

Budureasca Winery

472 Gura Vadului, Prahova Co.
Tel.: +40 730 585 555
www.budureasca.ro

The story of how a lad from the former coal-mining heartlands of north-east England ended up running a winery in Romania takes place over a couple of decades. Self-styled 'wine troubleshooter', Stephen Donnelly graduated in winemaking from UC Davis in California and set off on a career as a flying winemaker which took him to countries as far flung as India, Hungary, South Africa and England. Connections in Romania began in 1995, then in 2000 he helped design a winery for the UK-based Hanwood group, on the site that is Budureasca today. The name changed in 2007 when new Romanian owners wanted an identity that fitted their place on the terraces of the Budureasca valley, also the location of many historical sites. Donnelly is now technical director with 250 hectares to manage, and a new avant-garde winery, added in 2013, that reflects his New World winemaking approach. Labels include Budureasca, Origini, powerful red blend Noble 5 and export label Vine in Flames that refers to King Burebista's decision to destroy the country's vineyards in Dacian times. Fumé Blanc and Tămâioasă Românească have impressed recently.

Davino Winery

59 Ceptura de Jos, Ceptura, Prahova Co.
Tel.: +40 318 053 746
www.davino.ro

Davino is Romania's wine aristocracy, consistently one of the country's very top wineries and so reliable that the universities of Bucharest and Iași use its wines for reference samples. Owner Dan Balaban started out as a wine distributor in 1991, working his way up to around 10 per cent market share by 1999. He admits that the role gave him the opportunity to get to know and understand all the vineyards and terroirs in Romania, as well as gaining commercial knowledge by actually selling wine. This meant he spotted the future need for higher quality products in Romania. Balaban started producing wine himself in 1997 as only the third private winery in Romania after the revolution, and in 1999 he quit the distribution business. He explains, 'I bought my first vineyard of 4 hectares and built up to 36 hectares by 2004, still buying grapes until 2007. Now we have a little more than 70 hectares and we rent and work another 17 hectares.'

Winemaker Bogdan Costachescu came in 1998 (after studies in Champagne) and was recruited just in the nick of time before he left the country to emigrate to Canada. In 1999 he became a partner in the business, and is still there today. This has been a no-compromise approach from the start, with over 60 hectares replanted with the best clones available (whites grown are Fetească Albă, Sauvignon Blanc and Italian Riesling, with three red varieties, Fetească Neagră, Merlot and Cabernet Sauvignon) and hiring experts for every step of the journey. A new microwinery in the vineyards was completed in 2017. Balaban adds, 'We continue to improve our work, hoping that in a few years (after more than 20 years of production activity) we'll reach our goal, to be able to make one of the best Romanian wines.'

The very good Domaine Ceptura label is all about blends. The idea is bringing together local and international varieties to showcase the quality potential of the terroir, in a way that anyone can understand but with a local touch too. Excellent examples of single local varieties appear under Plai and Monogram for the local market and Alba or Purpura Wallachia for export. Flagship wines include the fantastic Revelatio white, and intense complex reds in the form of Flamboyant and Rezerva which repay leaving to age for a few years.

Domeniile Franco-Române

143 Scolii Street, Sahateni, Buzau Co.
Tel.: +40 238 594 303
www.domeniilefrancoromane.com

Another French investment here comes courtesy of Burgundian winemaker Denis Thomas (along with partners from Belgium and Romania). Its 44 hectares lie in the heart of Dealu Mare on gentle slopes at 125 to 250 metres altitude. It's close to Pietroasele, which is famous for its Visigoth gold treasure buried in the fourth century AD. Unsurprisingly, given the Burgundian connection, Pinot Noir is most important here, with 16 hectares planted. The vineyard is certified organic, describing its approach as 'lunar-organic' rather than full-on biodynamic, allowing the winemaker to 'vinify as naturally as possible'. Crai Nou and Terra Pretiosa are the labels for organic wines from the winery's own grapes.

Halewood Wineries

92 Gageni Street, Ploiesti, Prahova County
Tel.: +40 748 880 605
www.halewood.com.ro

The story of Halewood's beginnings in Romanian wine back in the 1980s has been told earlier, with Halewood's first wholly-owned Romanian subsidiary founded in 1997. Today, €10 million of investment later, the group has five subsidiaries in the country. Investments include 240 hectares of vineyards in Dealu Mare and Dobrogea. The company owns several wineries including the historic Rhein and Co. sparkling cellar at Azuga, nestled in the Carpathian foothills. This was built in 1892 and supplied sparkling wines to the Royal Court between the wars, including wine for the coronation of King Ferdinand in 1922. It is believed to be the oldest site in Romania where sparkling wine has been produced continuously. Rhein & Co. sparklers are made by the traditional method and still undergo riddling by hand (one of their workers has been riddling bottles since the 1970s). Another historic location is the 1922 mansion at Urlați, restored by Halewood in 1999 and now used as a red wine ageing cellar.

Chief winemaker Lorena Deaconu is quietly passionate about bringing more elegance to her wines, especially with Pinot Noir and Chardonnay. She has had to be clever in developing techniques to manage the growers that supply grapes for a lot of Halewood's wines. In the bad old days, growers would queue up for several days in the sunshine while their grapes started fermenting or going bad in the back of trucks or trailers. It took Lorena three months of sleeping at the winery so she could keep watch around the clock to get the message through that this won't do, and she will only accept grapes picked on her say so or they won't get paid. As a result, wine quality has improved considerably under her watch. The best wines appear in limited quantities and include Kronos Pinot Noir, Theia Chardonnay and Hyperion, while the new Collina Pietra Alba range consists of well-made, modern varietal wines.

LacertA Winery

Fintesti, Buzau Co., Romania
Tel.: +40 378 600 244
www.lacertawinery.ro

Co-owned by an Austrian, Walter Friedl, and a Romanian, Mihai Baniță, this estate is in a stunning location, surrounded by low rolling hills, with a grand neo-Romanian manor house dating back to 1901 at its heart. It's named for the lizards that dart around the landscape here. The winery has 82 hectares under vine – 70 per cent are reds, planted with Austrian material and it is proud of planting the first Rhein Riesling ever south of the Carpathians – and launched its first wines in 2011. Mihai, who makes the wines, spent eight years at a research institute then five years in viticulture, bringing an experimental approach, shown by unusual but very good blends (Cuvee X white and Cuvee IX red) and oak from five different origins.

Licorna Winehouse

Gura Vadului Vlg, Mizil, Prahova Co
Tel.: +40 372 710 710
www.licornawinehouse.ro

This boutique winery opened its doors in 2013 on the site of a century-old cellar. It is a proper estate, surrounded by its own 22 hectares of vines. Winemaker Florin Gabriel 'Gabi' Lacureanu arrived in 2014, attracted by the idea of making his own wines in an area that he sees as having great potential. Gabi reckons he first developed a sense of taste by cooking for his mother and always wanting to get the best flavour in every meal. His winemaking philosophy is the same – maximum flavour but without tampering too much. He opted for horticulture at university in Iași where Professor Valeriu Cotea (who teaches winemaking and viticulture) gave him a love for wine. Next came a master's degree in Burgundy, followed by a doctorate. Gabi has a special focus on Romania's local varieties, making fine, elegant Fetească Albă and very good Feteasca Neagră under both Serafim and Anno labels. There's a pretty, sweet Tămâioasă Românească, well-made Bon Viveur blends and a classy Cabernet Sauvignon too.

Rotenberg Winery

509 Ceptura de Jos, Prahova Co.
Tel.: +40 244 445 365
www.rotenberg.ro

Merlot is what this small winery is all about. Owner Mihail Rotenberg switched to wine wholeheartedly after a lengthy career with computers and telecoms. He owns 23 hectares of vines of up to 50-years-old in Dealu Mare, almost all planted with his favourite grape, plus a tiny bit of Cabernets Sauvignon and Franc. For him, the soil is similar to that of St Emilion. He bought an old ruined winery and redesigned it to use gravity flow, making his wines as gently as possible and bottling unfiltered after 12 to 24 months in a mixture of French, Romanian and Baltic oak.

SERVE Ceptura Winery

125C Ceptura, Prahova Co.
Tel.: +40 244 445 750
www.serve.ro

SERVE has pioneered new standards for high-quality wine in Romania since the beginning of the new era, and is still among the very top wineries in the country. Owner Mihaela de Poix explains: 'A visionary man established our winery back in 1994 when he decided to bring his Corsican know-how of fine wines right to the heart of Dealu Mare, and so we became the first private winery in Romania. He was Count Guy Tyrel de Poix.' Guy had been a dentist for six years when he took over his family's historic estate on Corsica (Domaine Peraldi). One day he picked up Hugh Johnson's *World Atlas of Wine* and read six lines about the great quality potential in Romania, which persuaded him to go and see for himself. And so, SERVE (Societe Euro Roumaine des Vins d'Exception) came into being.

The first winery was a functional warehouse and used purchased grapes. However, the constant struggle of trying to get the right fruit in a system where communist attitudes still reigned meant the winery started to invest in the tedious process of buying vineyards. It now owns 110 hectares in Dealu Mare and Babadag, Dobrogea. A new wine cellar followed in 2000, designed for flexibility in using both modern and traditional techniques and equipment. Total investment amounted to €2.5 million largely raised from the shareholders of the company.

What really put SERVE on the map was the first vintage of Cuvée Charlotte in 1999, the inspiration for so many wineries that followed. It was a selection of the best parcels to show what could be done in Romania, and the addition of Fetească Neagră in the blend with Cabernet and Merlot made it uniquely Romanian. Cuvée Amaury arrived as a white flagship blend in 2001. Other labels are the Vinul Cavalerului (Knight's Wine) for simple, honest, everyday wines and Terra Romana for more complex, serious versions. Tragically Guy died in 2011, a sad loss to the wine industry. His widow Mihaela, along with winemaker Aurel Rotarescu (who had been with Guy since the beginning and had caught his attention with a Fetească Neagră back in 1993) continue Guy's vision, and produced a 100 per cent Fetească Neagră in his name in 2014 to celebrate twenty years of the winery.

Domeniile Tohani

Tohani Vlg., Gura Vadului, Prahova Co.
Tel.: +40 244 251 231
www.tohaniromania.com

Records of wine in Tohani go back to 1773 and it was the location of the secret wedding of Prince Nicolae of Romania to the love of his life, a commoner named Ioana Doletti in 1931. The owner today, Virgil Mandru, was only 24 when he started out in the wine industry in 1991, coming up with the idea of a brand called Edelweiss, a sparkling wine that captured 40 per cent of the market at its peak. He says: 'Edelweiss was the project that launched me in the wine business, and also the project that prepared me for the Tohani moment. I grew up and matured in the wine industry alongside the market, I stayed close to feel the changes in perception, how people refined their tastes and began to slowly recognize quality.' In 1999, he took over the Tohani winery, investing €5 million and now has 350 hectares of vineyards. During the 2000s, Virgil says, 'I understood, at the very beginning, that if I wanted to grow – as a business and as a man – I needed to learn to have patience, build slowly, taking small, coherent and tested steps, going after quality at all costs, because this industry depends on a variety of factors that you can't control.' Two winemakers, Ion Marin and Albertus Van der Merwe from South Africa guide the range, the idea being to make Old World-influenced reds and New World-style whites and rosé, all in the premium sector. Apogeum, the serious flagship Fetească Neagră, was launched in 2014 and the newest white is a blend, the deliciously aromatic and expressive Siel.

Viile Metamorfosis

Unguren Vlg, Vadu Săpat, Prahova Co.
Tel.: +40 371 184 796
www.vitis-metamorfosis.com

It was a holiday in 2001 that brought Romania to the attention of the world-renowned Antinori family with their mere 26 generations of winemaking history. Giancorrado Ulrich was so impressed with how closely Dealu Mare resembled Tuscany that he returned home full of enthusiasm. Indeed, he was so committed to bringing his vision to life that he went on to become president of Viile Metamorfosis. Italian winemaker Fiorenzo Rista, who was already living in Romania, was persuaded to join the team, and the company was founded in 2008. Its aim from the start was quality-without-compromise premium wines. Vineyards came first with 67.5 hectares planted or replanted in three different locations, all close to the winery, and this was followed by a new cellar in 2012, totalling over €5 million of investments.

Sustainability has been a watchword all along, with 15 hectares certified as organic since 2013 and several organic wines now in the range.

Giancorrado explains, 'The best sites were selected for the planting of Metamorfosis vineyards in order to fully express the diverse terroir of Dealu Mare. The vineyards are planted on gently sloping hills reminiscent of Burgundy, even though the region is situated on the same parallel as two other famous wine regions of the world, Bordeaux and Piemonte.'

Ranges include the entry-point Fluturi for fresh, fruity, easy-drinking styles. Viile Metamorfosis itself is the core brand, offering well-made varietal wines and blends. Single vineyard wines include Via Colțul Pietrei and Via Marchizului (especially notable is the juicy and generous Negru de Drăgășani, the first example of this variety in Dealu Mare). At the premium end, Cantvs Primvs is both a vineyard selection and a barrel selection in the very best years, originally just Cabernet Sauvignon but more recently an excellent organic Fetească Neagră too.

Vinarte

Villa Zorilor Wine Cellar , Vernești commune, Zorești village, Jud. Buzau, 127687
Tel.: +40 213 233 803
www.vinarte.ro

Born in 1998 as a joint project between Italian, French and Romanian investors, today Vinarte has three different vineyard sites adding up to around 344 hectares (Zorești in Dealu Mare, Bolovanu in Sâmburești and Stârmina in Mehedinți), but its Dealu Mare site is possibly its best known. It will be celebrating two decades in 2018 and has worked with the same Italian supervision all along. The winery is quietly conservative, continuing to do what has worked from the beginning, which is complex, structured wines with body, made using a traditional winemaking approach. It was also the first winery to make premium wine in Romania with Prince Matei and Soare (both of which are still made today).

Production is 85 per cent reds (both local and international varieties imported from France are grown), and the top labels have a real track record of being able to age well. An advantage of being established for so long is really understanding the vineyards – so the top wines can genuinely come from the same sites every year. Prince Mircea Merlot comes from an amphitheatre of vines near the Danube where it is sunny for 6 months of the year, and is named for Mircea the Elder, a prince of Wallachia at the beginning of the fifteenth century who brought stability to the region. In addition to Soare and Prince Matei other flagship wines include Nedeea (a blend of local varieties: Novac, Fetească Neagră, Negru de Drăgăşani) and Sirena Dunării, a botrytised sweet wine from late-picked grapes. Terase Danubiene is the mid-market range of both local and international varieties and Castel Stârmina is the fruity good value range.

Aurelia Vişinescu (Domeniile Săhăteni)

Sahateni, Buzau Co.
Tel.: +40 212 110 9 7
www.aureliavisinescu.com

Aurelia Vişinescu is possibly Romania's most famous female winemaker, one of the first women to become a production director in the new era. Her love of flowers and nature sent her to study horticulture at first, until she fell in love with wine. She graduated in 1993 and started work at the still state-owned Prodexport which gave her the chance to travel and taste all over the world as well as doing winemaking internships in South Africa and Australia. During her subsequent time at Halewood, she put her name on the map by producing the first ever dry Fetească Neagră aged in barrique. She also produced the first Romanian wine of the new era to win a grand-gold medal at an international wine competition (in Brussels in 2002). Her own winery project began in 2003 thanks to the persistence of her cousin's Canadian husband, who she describes as an incurable wine enthusiast.

They bought a former state farm in the 'very heart of Dealu Mare because of the great potential of the terroir here,' and started acquiring vineyards from scratch, piece by piece. The first vintage was 2006, made with her family. Aurelia admits that her previous role as office-based production director had not prepared her for actually having to operate machines, instruction manual in hand. She says she lost 10 kilos, working every day till after midnight with her brother to sort fruit and check it for stones (it was all bought-in grapes back then). Today the winery has 82 hectares, all close to the winery, and a mixture of local grapes and international ones, including Fetească Albă, Tămâioasă Românească, Fetească Neagră and international varieties – Sauvignon Blanc, Chardonnay, Pinot Grigio, Merlot, Syrah, Pinot Noir and Cabernet Sauvignon.

Aurelia's main brands include the modern, fruity Nomad, Karakter for international grapes and Artisan, for wines that always feature local varieties. Anima is the top label in better vintages, 'the spoilt children of the cellar,' says Aurelia, always unashamedly rich and structured wines, aged in mostly Romanian oak from three different forests. Given Aurelia's history it is no surprise that Fetească Neagră remains her spiritual grape and she makes a very good multi-vintage blend called '3 Fete Negre' (meaning three black maidens) to reflect the three vintages in the blend.

Mehedinți

Domeniul Catleya

293 Principala Street, Corcova, Mehedinti Co.
Tel.: +40 252 383 541
www.catleyawine.com

This is the personal project of Laurent Pfeffer, supported by his two French partners. Laurent trained in Bordeaux as a winemaker and discovered Romania during a period of study in the Moldovan Hills wine region. With the encouragement and support of his friend, Frederic Vauthier from St Emilion, he came back to Romania in 2007 to look for some vines. He decided to settle in Corcova, where he is also technical director at Corcova winery. He was attracted by the potential of the terroir as well as the fascinating history from the Bibescu era and his connections with Marcel Proust when they drank wines from Corcova together. In Proust's most famous works, the Catleya orchid was a symbol of love – which is why Laurent chose it as a name. Laurent's approach is to plant his vines at a very high density (6,600 to 10,000 vines per hectare) and manage the vineyards as naturally as possible, including working with a horse and using only organic sprays since 2014. Laurent's personal style is quite different to Corcova's. Freamat meaning 'tremor' or 'leaves rustling' is the main line, with the very pure and refined Épopée from the best grapes in the best vintages.

Corcova Roy & Dâmboviceanu Winery

293 Main Street, Corcova, Mehedinti Co.
Tel.: +40 252 383 541
www.corcova.ro

Șerban Dâmboviceanu definitely has an air of 'I-still-can't-quite-believe-this-place-is-mine' about him. He left Romania aged eighteen to study law in Strasbourg and discovered wine while living in France. Ten years later he came back with the idea of looking for a small vineyard as a hobby, no more than 2 to 3 hectares. He travelled all over Romania and found himself in Corcova where he was utterly seduced by the place. In the summer of 2005, Şerban and his French co-owner (Michel Roy) bought 12 hectares of vineyard from Corcova IAS and approximately 50 hectares of abandoned vineyards in Jirov village nearby. A successful application for EU subsidy funded replanting of 40 hectares in 2006 and 2007, using varieties that were known to have been grown here before communism. This included Cabernet Sauvignon, Merlot, Pinot Noir, Muscat Ottonel and Chardonnay, plus Syrah and Fetească Neagră which Şerban thought might do well here. The wine cellars were fully renovated and modernized in 2008 to 2009.

This is a place filled with history. Wine here dates back to sixteenth century though there is then quite a gap in the records up to the era of Prince Antoine Bibescu. Bibescu was a Romanian prince, diplomat, writer and landowner, who inherited around 2,000 hectares of farmland and forests around Corcova. Bibescu split his time between Paris and Romania, rubbing shoulders with famous composers and writers like Debussy, Saint-Saëns and Marcel Proust (who wrote about Corcova) and eventually marrying Lady Elizabeth Asquith.

In the early twentieth century he decided to expand his vineyards and build a winery too. The first version of the winery burned down in 1907 in a peasant's revolt so Bibescu had it rebuilt in less combustible concrete by an Austrian firm. This concrete remains in good condition today (unlike the heavy and vast tanks built by the communists) and is still in full use. Bibescu also employed a young French agronomist called Aristoteles Sauget with whom he entrusted the planting and maintenance of the French vines, the construction of the winery and the management of all his property. And coming full circle today, the winery again has a French technical director and winemaker, Laurent Pfeffer.

The vineyards here are some of the most beautiful in Romania, growing above deep deposits of fossil oyster shells (which you can see by scrambling into the forest that surrounds the vines). Birds of prey also enjoy these forest fringes and help to protect the vines from bird pests. Vineyard management is all about sustainability, so no herbicides are used, and the winery takes its role of providing jobs to the local community seriously. Sauvignon Blanc is fresh and citrussy, and there's an appealing rosé too, but reds are the main focus with the appealing unoaked Fetească Neagră selling out within a couple of months of release, attractive Cabernet/Merlot blends and good Syrah in recent vintages.

Domeniul Coroanei Segarcea

108 Dealul Viilor Street, Segarcea, Dolj Co.
Tel.: +40 251 210 516
www.domeniulcoroanei.com

Segarcea means 'land of dream' and the place has made a dream come true for owners Mihai and Cornelia Anghel. It was one of twelve domaines given to the royal family to support themselves when parliament cut off their funding back in 1884. The estate started out as a rootstock and vine nursery and then became a 300-hectare vineyard.

The original winery was built around 1906 to 1908, one of the first buildings in Romania to be built in steel-reinforced concrete, and in a pioneering move, it was designed for gravity flow. The area was recognized as a DOC as early as 1929. Decades of communist rule focused on yield and then everything was abandoned until the Anghels took over in 2002. Cornelia was born nearby and didn't want to see a legend destroyed, though as a cardiac surgeon (while her husband was a mechanical engineer), she didn't have much idea about wine, apart from the vines in her grandfather's garden.

In 2005, the couple met French winemaker Ghislaine Guiraud by chance, persuading her to become their consultant for the next fifteen years. The winery was renovated, keeping its historic heart. The vineyards were totally replanted, including rescuing their famous Tămâioasă Roză of which just 300 plants remained. The winery may have the largest non-commercial rose plantation in the world – there are roses at the end of every vine row. Labels include Principesa Margareta (good Marselan and a Viognier-based white blend), Minima Moralia (good Cabernet Sauvignon) and Simfonia, for a warm, spicy blend of eight red varieties.

Crama Oprişor

Carl Reh Winery SRL
Comuna Oprişor, 227335 Jud. Mehedinţi,
Tel.: +40 252 391 310
www.crama-oprisor.ro

German wine group Reh-Kendermann (operating here as Carl Reh Romania) came to Romania in 1994 in search of wines for their brands like River Route and Val Duna. By 1997, they had decided to buy their own winery, purchasing the 1970s cellar in Oprişor in Mehedinţi and refurbishing it, including turning one of the massive concrete tanks into a tasting room. Vineyards had been recorded in this region since the fifteenth century, but much of the land was grubbed up or abandoned by the 1980s. To begin with, the idea was to buy grapes and control picking time by insisting on growers using only the company's own picking bins – delivered on the day the winemaker felt the grapes were ready. But by the early 2000s, it became clear that owning vineyards was the surest way to deliver quality, and so planting began. This included grapes as diverse as international varieties like Sauvignon Blanc, Chardonnay, Shiraz, Merlot, Cabernet Sauvignon and the first Zinfandel and Dornfelder in the country.

Today the winery has 252 hectares and was renamed Crama Oprişor in 2008. The winery's labels, for instance Măiastru, Caloian, Rusalcă Albă or Drăgaică Roşie (a lake goddess who steals away young men), aim to reflect the soul of the place and link art, folklore and wine together. Many of the wines are blends including the excellent Smerenie and very limited Ispita, but there are also good varietal wines under Crama Oprişor for Cabernet Sauvignon (their 'king of the vineyards' grape) and La Cetate (meaning from the citadel).

Drăgăşani

Avincis Winery

Vila Dobruşa, 1A Valea Caselor Street, Drăgăşani, Valcea Co.
Tel.: +40 751 199 415
www.avincis.ro

This stunning winery must be a contender for the most beautiful in Romania. It sits on a plateau, surrounded by vines in every direction, and is the old family home of one of the owners, Cristiana Stoica. The family connection here began in 1927 when Maria and Iancu Râmniceanu (an officer of the Romanian army), bought a beautiful Neo-Romanian mansion surrounded by vineyards – all managed by Maria herself. It was confiscated by the state in the communist era, but in 2007, their great-granddaughter Cristiana (together with her husband Valeriu) returned to the family estate.

The couple are both high-flying international lawyers and Valeriu is also a former Minister of Justice, where he played a significant role in the land restitution process, as well as helping to reform the judicial system. The ruined mansion has been restored to its former glory, while a dramatic winery has also been built in local stone, with a grass roof to fit into the landscape and be as eco-friendly as possible. The first vintage of the new era was 2011, made by a young Alsace winemaker Ghislain Moritz (who is now the winery's consultant, along with Italian firm Giotto Consulting).

Today there are 40 hectares of vines in production, and each parcel is handled separately, with picking done by hand. Low yields, a fanatical attention to detail (Ghislain sorts the fruit himself as he doesn't trust anyone else) and a pristine winery combine to produce wines that are improving every year. Local varieties including Crâmpoşie Selecţionată and the largest area of Negru de Drăgăşani in the world (the aim is 6 hectares), while a small plot of incredibly rare Alutus was planted in 2017. Labels include simple, fruity Villa Dobruşa and the main Avincis line with very good whites from Crâmpoşie and Pinot Gris–Fetească Regală. Pinot Noir can be good but is fickle and tricky to sell as a red wine. Excellent Negru de Drăgăşani, Cuvée Andrei (Cabernet Sauvignon) and superb red blend Cuvée Grandiflora complete the range.

Bauer Winery

Dealul Olt Street, Dragasani, Valcea Co.
Tel.: +40 751 252 272
www.cramabauer.com

This is the family winery of Oliver and Raluca Bauer (both of whom also work at Prince Ştirbey just up the road). One of the reasons Oliver made his home in Romania was meeting Raluca at a tasting where he was pouring Ştirbey wines for the first time. The idea of their own winery started in about 2010 when Oliver produced his first ever Petit Verdot. At that time, the Kripps didn't want to extend their portfolio as there were already nearly 30 different Prince Ştirbey wines, but Oliver says, 'I didn't want to stop exploring and exploiting the potential of our region, vineyards and grape varieties.' The idea is that Crama Bauer is complementary to Ştirbey, producing wines that aren't made at Ştirbey, and vice versa.

At Ştirbey, the wines are all produced from estate vineyards but the concept with Bauer is different. Oliver explains, 'I especially seek out older vineyards (more than 30 years old) and rare varieties. We purchase each batch of grapes from one place so that means all our wines (still and sparkling) are single vineyard wines, most of them in very limited quantities.' Oliver has also been buying grapes in other regions if he finds an interesting vineyard, so his first Riesling will appear in 2018.

Oliver is exploring various vinification methods, including extensive skin contact – up to four months – for the orange, skin-fermented Sauvignonasse, semi-sweet Crâmpoșie Selecționată in a Mosel style, whole-bunch pressed Sauvignonasse and using Negru de Drăgășani for rosé. Unsurprisingly his Fetească Neagră is excellent. He is also taking a more natural approach by using spontaneous fermentations and no small barrels.

Prince Ştirbey Winery

Dealul Olt Street, Drăgăşani, Valcea Co.
Tel.: +40 751 252 272
www.stirbey.com

This small and beautiful producer in Drăgăşani pioneered the concept of a true small estate in the modern era of Romanian wine. Today, it has 25 hectares of vines surrounding the century-old mansion and winery. In 2001, Jakob and Ileana Kripp were lucky enough to get Ileana's grandmother's 20-hectare property returned, in good condition with vines that had been looked after. The first actual vintage was 2004 and in a few short years, Prince Ştirbey has developed a reputation as one of the country's top wineries, bringing together German precision and Romanian passion and landscape.

From the start, the concept was unusual – all about single varietal wines, with an especial focus on local grape varieties, to allow them to express their individual personality (the winery pioneered the first Crâmpoșie varietal wine, the first dry Tămâioasă Românească and the first Novac). The Genus Loci (or spirit of the place) range adds a real concept of terroir. Crâmpoșie (still and sparkling), Negru de Drăgășani, Novac (red and sparkling), Fetească Regală and Tămâioasă Românească are all elegant and refined with lovely purity of expression. There is also good Sauvignon, Merlot and Cabernet Sauvignon.

A ROYAL CONNECTION

It's not often you get actual blue-blooded royalty cooking for you but offering a warm welcome to visitors has been important at Prince Ştirbey from the start. The effortlessly gracious Ileana Kripp comes from a long line of Romanian nobles. The Ştirbey family is of Wallachian origin and their records go back to the fifteenth century. A particularly notable family figure was Prince Barbu Ştirbey who was elected reigning prince (Domnitor) of Tara Românească after the 1848 revolution. He guided the country from being a feudal agricultural country to an enlightened nation, with roads, industry and education. His grandson Prince Barbu Alexandru Ştirbey (1873 to 1946) was also a significant figure, counsellor to the king and a business pioneer too, opening Romania's first canning factory. He had 200 hectares of vineyards, including 20 in Drăgăşani and huge cellars under the Ştirbey Palace in Bucharest, and Ştirbey became a very strong brand under his watch.

Ileana says, 'We have found advertising for Ştirbey wines from 1904 to 1940 and after, but also for Ştirbey-conserved vegetables and fruits, honey and mustard. Ştirbey wines were also served on the Orient Express. We found a menu from May 1925 with all the details.' In the early twentieth century, Ştirbey was also owner of the biggest vine nursery in the country, actively promoting local grapes grafted onto American rootstocks.

On his death in 1946, his eldest daughter Princess Maria Ştirbey (Ileana's grandmother) inherited the 20-hectare estate in Drăgăşani. This land had belonged to the family since 1713, along with 5 hectares bought in 1804 by Ileana's great-grandfather, born Bibescu (a relative of the Bibescu of Corcova fame). It was all confiscated by the state in 1949. Many of Ileana's relatives – like hundreds of thousands of Romanians – ended up in prison or in forced labour camps, and many died there of famine or lack of medical treatment. Therefore, Ileana and her parents – like many other Romanians – tried to escape from this country. They finally succeeded in 1969, with the help of a friend of her family, Henri Coandă (Romania's famous inventor of the first jet aircraft), then living in France. He invited Ileana to a French language course, and she obviously 'lost' her return ticket. She was aged just fifteen and thought she would never go back.

Ileana met her husband Baron Jakob Kripp in a vineyard in Germany, where Jakob's sister was married to a winegrower, and love blossomed among the Grauburgunder (the German name for Pinot Gris) vines. Jakob was fascinated by her lost background and intrigued by tales of the unspoilt wildness of Romania, so he took her back to her homeland on honeymoon. Ileana says, 'Jakob and I married in July 1997 and we went to Romania for four weeks as Jakob wanted to know my country, my roots. For me it was the first time in the 28 years since I left. I was excited, anguished, happy, sad, curious, all together.' Wine is also in Jakob Kripp's genes – his brother Sigmund von Kripp runs the family's wine estates and 470-year-old castle at Stachlburg in South Tyrol, and had also ventured into the 'wild east' to renovate the Füleky winery in Hungary's Tokaj region.

Perhaps inevitably, the idea came to Jakob of recovering Ileana's inheritance. The pair went back in 1999 in an old Lada, with Jakob ready to buy the property back if he had to. It turned out that the state IAS was really helpful and indeed they were lucky that their vines had been looked after. Today their vineyard manager is still the same guy (Dumitru Nedelut) who had worked in the state winery tending these very vines. In 2001, the estate became theirs once again.

It was through Sigmund that the Kripps met their winemaker-to-be. Oliver Bauer had grown up in a winery in the Baden-Württemberg region of Germany, learning early about the importance of practical experience in winemaking. Formal qualifications, and jobs in several renowned German wineries followed. A meeting with Jakob over a beer in Munich persuaded Oliver to go to Romania for a couple of months to train the local team. Not long after, the Kripps asked him to manage the winery. For Oliver, the chance to rebuild a historic winery from scratch and work with such passionate people was a no-brainer. He explained, 'Thus I quit my job and moved in 2004, a step I do not regret, not even for a second.' Fourteen years on, Prince Știrbey is firmly established as one of Romania's most consistent and exciting wineries, and always offers a warm welcome to visitors too.

Danube Terraces

Alira

Str. Gladiolelor nr. 9b, Comuna Aliman, 907025, jud. Constanţa,
Tel.: +40 21 637 2273
www.alira.ro

A decade ago, Karl Heinz Hauptmann and French winemaker Marc Dworkin saw an opportunity to bring the forgotten arid lands around Aliman back to life. Marc had been making wine at Bulgaria's Bessa Valley (and still does), where Karl is also an investor, and they came to look for opportunities in Romania.

The first spot they looked at proved to be too salty, but passing through Aliman, Marc was inspired by the potential in the place. After detailed soil and climate analyses, the project was on its way, with the first vintage appearing in 2009. The winery gets its name from the nearby towns of Aliman and Rasova and the centaur on the label is inspired by a sculpture discovered in a Roman temple close to Aliman. There is also a legend that the Greeks (who had a colony nearby) called the Thracians 'centaurs' because their famous warrior spirit was maintained by constant wine drinking.

The vineyard lies on a plateau close to the Black Sea with very low summer rainfall, but good soil moisture as it is close to the Danube. The 80 hectares of vineyards are planted with Merlot, Cabernet Sauvignon and Fetească Neagră. The wines reflect their place with notably warm, ripe reds, and highlights include the ripe and complex Feteasca Neagră Grand Vin and the deliciously elegant, super-pale, dry rosé from Fetească Neagră and Cabernet Sauvignon.

IN BRIEF

Below are some small or new wineries that have not had a chance to establish a track record of consistency yet, larger ones which have made very recent changes and made progress in improving quality, and big ones that are significant in terms of domestic market presence, but haven't convinced with quality.

Crama Avereşti

Bunesti – Avereşti, Vaslui Co.
Tel.: +40 235 484 830
www.cramaaveresti.ro

The cellar here dates back to 1874 and was connected to the famous Romanian author Negruzzi, who set up a vineyard of French varieties, and also pioneered irrigation. Today, it has 550 hectares of vines in the cool climate of the Huşi region at an average altitude of 380 metres with a focus on local varieties such as Zghihară and Busuioacă de Bohotin, and promising Fetească Neagră Nativus.

Basilescu Winery

23 Valea Nucetului Street, Urlati, Prahova Co.
Tel.: +40 754 092 030
www.cramabasilescu.ro

Nicolae Basilescu was born in Urlaţi in 1860. His family had vineyards but he grew up to become an important political and business figure. In the 1920s he converted a brewery in Bucharest into a sparkling wine cellar, in partnership with a champagne house. This all came to an abrupt end at the hands of the communists, when the property was all confiscated in 1949 by the state. It was privatized in 2003 and relaunched as a wine estate in 2008. The winery now has 100 hectares in the heart of Dealu Mare.

Crama Ceptura

Ceptura de Jos Vlg, Prahova Co.
Tel.: +40 372 771 038
www.crama-ceptura.eu

Under the same ownership as Bostavan and Purcari in Moldova (and listed on the Romanian stock market since February 2018), Crama Ceptura has 180 hectares, opened a new winery in 2005, and relaunched branding with improved quality as of 2016. Labels include a mass-market, sweet red 'bear's blood' Sangele Ursului as well as more premium Cervus Monte and Cervus Cepturum.

Clos des Colombes

Olimp Street, 23 August com., Constanta Co.
Tel.: +40 732 007 200
www.closdescolombes.eu

Among the smallest commercial estates in Romania with just 4 hectares, this has a strong tourism business based around the winery as it lies just 1 kilometre from the sea. It was the dream of the owner Anne Marie Rosenberg (who comes from a long line of champagne growers) to have her own small winery.

Dagon Winery

Urlați City, Prahova County
Tel.: +40 757 091 663
www.dagon.ro

This small and experimental estate and winery, with just 8 hectares of their own, was set up by a group of winemakers, led by Australian Mark Haisma (previously of Yarra Yering and projects in Burgundy and Rhone). The unusual Pinot Noir/Fetească Neagră red has some real Burgundian complexity about it and there's a good gastronomic rosé from old Cabernet Sauvignon vines blended with Shiraz.

Elite Wine

Misca Vlg, Siria, Arad Co
Tel.:+40 720 934 491
www.elitewine.ro

Walter Szikler set up this small wine estate with an Austrian partner in 2005. He brought the local expertise and his partner (who is a doctor) helped with the finances. There are 25 hectares with a renovated house in the centre of the vines, where the wine is made and visitors are welcomed. Walter replanted all the land around six to seven years ago and is working on finding his direction for bottled wine. A fresh Sauvignon Blanc and Merlot–Cabernet Sauvignon blend are the best so far.

Lechburg Winery

334 Principala Street, Lechinta Vlg., Bistrita Nasaud County
Tel.: +40 748 101 674
www.lechburg.com

The former wine cooperative in Lechința was bought by an Italian family in 2015. The 1962 winery has been renovated and the vineyards are managed organically. Early days as yet, with some inconsistent results, but decent crisp Riesling, Sauvignon Blanc, Gewürztraminer and Pinot Gris rosé so far.

Senator Wine

5 Maior Gheorghe Pastia Street, Focsani, Vrancea Co.
Tel.: +40 21 410 80 87
www.senatorwine.ro

Founded in 1991, Senator owns 850 hectares across four regions of Romania (Huși in the Moldovan Hills; Tirol in Banat; Cotești, Odobești and Panciu in Vrancea, and Însurăței on the sandy soils of the Danube Terraces. It has been certified for organic grapes from Însurăței since 2010, and with 246 hectares here, this is the largest organic vineyard in Romania. The Omnia label is for organic local grapes from this vineyard. The Monser label features ten different Romanian grapes, while Varius features international varieties.

Strunga Winery

707465 Strunga, Iași County,
Tel.: +40 769 003 950

This brand-new winery has 90 hectares planted four years ago. The winery building is still all about functionality, but the first vintage in 2017 looks promising (especially Fetească Albă, Chardonnay Sunburn, Busuioacă and Fetească Neagră) made with the help of Doctor Catalin Zamfir from Iași University.

Via Viticola – Sarica Niculițel winery

DN 22, Niculitel Vlg., 827165, Tulcea County
Tel.: +40 314 251 934
www.viaviticola.ro

This large estate with 400 hectares in the oldest vineyard area in Dobrogea has had a difficult history in recent years, initially doing well under Spanish ownership as a privatized winery. However, it was hit hard by the financial crisis in 2008, which came on top of a decision to replant the vineyards. Without income for several years, it declared bankruptcy in 2013. Current general manager and co-owner Marius Iliev was asked to help out and arrived with the intention of selling it, but explains: 'After looking closer and understanding more about the story of this place, we decided that we should not sell but develop it into a significant business. So, with a friend of mine, we took the company out of bankruptcy by paying all debt and started an investment plan in the vineyard and the winery as well.' There are sound, clean wines under Caii de la Letea label.

Vincon Vrancea

Strada Avântului 12, Focşani, Romania
Tel.: +40 237 222 100
www.vincon.ro

This is mentioned for its sheer size, as Romania's third biggest producer in terms of market presence, with an 11.7 per cent share. However quality leaves room for improvement. Sweet red and pink wines are still huge sellers here. Founded in 1949 and privatized in 1999, it started to invest in vineyards in 2002 and is now owner of 1,500 hectares and eleven wine cellars.

PART 3
MOLDOVA

16

MOLDOVAN HISTORY

Poor little Moldova, literally and figuratively. This small country on the eastern fringe of Europe tends to get forgotten by writers and travellers alike. Quite apart from knowing anything about its wine, few people even know where to find it on a map. Today, it is the poorest country in Europe, and the country that is the most economically dependent on wine in the world. It also has the highest density of grapevines per person anywhere. In most places, wine is a luxury, a nice-to-have product; in Moldova tens of thousands of people utterly depend on it for a living, so here the economy balances on vine roots. The land that is the Republic of Moldova today has been battered by politics, as it lies right on the boundary of east and west, between capitalism and communism, democracy and autocracy. This is a place where wine has borne the brunt of economic and political warfare. Indeed, this sliver of land between the rivers Prut and Dniester has changed hands at least nine times in the last 200 years.

EARLY HISTORY

The earliest grapevine fossils in the Republic of Moldova date from the Miocene era, around 10 million years ago. Fossil leaf impressions belonging to a species called *Vitis Teutonica* were found in 1958 in the village of Naslavcea right on the northernmost tip of Moldova. Other *Vitis* remains from the Miocene era were also found in Bursuc village, near Nisporeni in central Moldova, in 1967. These finds show that grapevines and their relatives are very ancient in this area. Earliest records of domesticated grapes occur from Neolithic sites in the sixth to fifth millennia BC (at the Sacarovca site) and grape pips have been found at multiple Cucuteni–Trypillia (5200 to 3500 BC) sites in Moldova and Romania. This culture was centred on Moldova and included parts of north-eastern Romania and western Ukraine, at its peak building some of the largest settlements in Neolithic Europe. The species of grape found has not been confirmed, but the pips resemble cultivated grapes in morphology, with elongated pointed tips like modern varieties. Later, there are Iron Age traces of grape growing at Etulia in the tenth to twelfth centuries BC. The Roman province of Dacia (later Lower Moesia) left its mark on Moldova's southern territory as the ancient defensive structure of Trajan's wall still exists and has given its name to the country's south-western region.

The land that is present-day Moldova was also populated by the Dacians, so it shares much of its history with Romania and the stories told in Chapter 10 about King Burebista and the Geto-Dacians and Romans. This region's shared history continues with the foundation of the principality of Moldavia itself in 1359, when Bogdan I of Moldavia succeeded in wresting this territory from Hungarian control. Chronicles of the land of Moldavia by Grigore Ureche mention vineyards during the rule of Alexander the Good (Alexandru cel Bun 1400–1432) and record the appointment of a steward of the royal vineyards at Cotnari and Harlau, who had to provide wine on important days. There are various references to trade and consumption of wine during the fifteenth century. For instance, records show that wine from Moldavia was being requested alongside Greek Malvasia by the King of Poland in the fifteenth century. It seems winemaking became significant in this principality until the Ottoman occupation. The legend of the storks of Soroca fortress dates to this time, under the rule of Ştefan Cel Mare (1457–1504), the great Moldavian ruler who fought so hard to hold back the Ottoman tide. The story is that soldiers trapped inside the fortress were starving until storks flew over carrying grapes in their beaks, giving the warriors strength to survive. Since then storks have become the symbol of the nation, an important part of the wine story in Moldova.

Despite the efforts of Ştefan Cel Mare, Moldavia became a vassal state of the Ottomans early in the sixteenth century, though wine production continued. In 1560, a gift by Alexandru IV Lăpuşneanu to the Capriana monastery was documented. He offered eight villages by the River Dniester, including Purcari and Olaneşti, both of which are today highly regarded wine areas in the Ştefan Vodă region. Because the Muslim Ottomans allowed some religious freedom among their subjects, Christianity helped to keep a continuity of wine throughout this era, and wine found its way to Moscow and Poland, as well as Ukraine and Transylvania. In 1596, an Italian traveller named Giovanni Bolero noted that Moldavia's second most important export (after grain) was wine to Russia and Poland. In the seventeenth century, a Turkish traveller called Evlie Celebi wrote about well-cultivated vineyards in Moldavia including regions such as Chilia (on the southern border) and Tighina (on the Dniester in eastern Moldova). Today's Transnistria has also historically produced renowned wines. Wine was produced around Camenca in 1703 and Russian army commander Piotr Wittgenstein took possession of a domaine at Camenca in 1804. He invited six German families to help with winemaking and produced around 400 tonnes a year from vineyards facing the Dniester. He also founded the first sanatorium (a type of hospital for people convalescing from illness) using grapes and wine.

However, wine production appears to have slowed down under the Ottoman regime, not least due to five wars with the Russian Empire between 1711 and 1812. Then in 1812, the eastern part of Moldavia was annexed and became the Russian province of Bessarabia.

1812 ONWARDS

A new period began after the separation of all of Moldavia's land east of the River Prut from Romania. Russia encouraged vines in the new province and introduced high taxes for imported wine to encourage local production. Tsar Alexander I (1777–1825) set up a campaign for repopulation of the empty Budjak steppe lands in southern Bessarabia. This brought in colonists from Germany, Poland, Switzerland and France. Gagauz people (Turkic Orthodox Christians) and Bulgarians were also encouraged to move to the area, and one Moldovan historian noted 950 acres of vines in Gagauzia in 1827. The Russians recognized that the richness of this area was in its soils, so there was a special requirement for colonists to be good agriculturalists, winemakers or orchard growers. In return, they were given religious freedom and an exemption from taxes and military service. Many of the colonists who were accepted, especially the Germans (around 9,000 families mostly from Württemberg) and Swiss had strong winemaking experience. The Swiss Colony in southern Bessarabia at Chabag (today Shabo in Ukraine) was particularly notable for its influence on winemaking throughout the area. Every settler household was given land (around 66 hectares) and encouraged to plant vines.

Around this time, it was fashionable for Russian aristocrats and army generals to own vineyards and they often brought in specialists and grapevines from France. This was a period when the Russian market opened, and as a result there was a huge development in wine production. The School of Viticulture, Gardening and Viniculture of Bessarabia was founded in Stăuceni in 1842, making it possibly the earliest in Europe. By the second half of the century, Bessarabia was sending wine to all corners of Russia, and settlers were reported to be earning more than Western European winemakers.

THE FIRST WINE ESTATES

The early nineteenth century saw the founding of the first estates and industrial wineries in Moldova. The winery that is Vinaria Purcari today was founded in 1827 and run by German colonists for most of the nineteenth century. Eventually, it was taken over by the state in 1940 and turned into a *Sovkhoz* (a Soviet era state-owned farm). Romaneşti winery was also founded in 1850 in the village of the same name, apparently by the Romanov family. This winery sent wine to the rest of Russia until 1917, becoming a *Sovkhoz* in the Soviet era. The last of the three major nineteenth-century wineries was founded at Bulboaca in 1893. This was led by Constantin Mimi, the last governor of Bessarabia, who was also a winemaker and had studied at Montpellier. Mimi had been born in Chişinău and originally studied law. When Mimi returned he created a dramatic winery, which sent wine to Russia and France. The archives in the dramatically restored Castel Mimi winery hold a bottle of the oldest wine in Moldova, a liquor wine from 1727, as well as a bottle from 1893 rescued from a collection in Germany. Only Christine Frolov (Castel Mimi's general manager) and her brother have keys to the cellar where these ancient bottles are kept. Vinuri de Comrat was also founded in 1897, though at that time it produced spirits and vodka, only becoming a wine producer in the mid-twentieth century; it still uses the 1897 cellar today.

In 1878, a bottle of Negru de Purcari famously won a gold medal in an exhibition in Paris, attracting the attention of the Russian imperial family, who started to drink it. By 1883, 20 per cent of the Russian Empire's wine came from Bessarabia and exports to Western Europe, where phylloxera was already causing huge damage, were also strong. The nineteenth-century colonists apparently had a strong influence on wine styles around this time. One source complained in 1891 of Bessarabian wines losing their character 'as a result of different fermentations and mixing in wines with French names'. Around this time, wines from regions like Purcari and Răscăieţii in the Ştefan Vodă region of south-east Moldova were highlighted as excellent and the best wines from the whole of Bessarabia. But then phylloxera arrived.

PHYLLOXERA: THE GREAT DEVASTATOR AND THE BESSARABIAN RESPONSE

The tale of the fight against phylloxera in Bessarabia illustrates quite how different it was to be within the Russian Empire, compared to the situation in Romania.

It's hard to imagine quite how devastating this tiny insect pest was across Europe – but devastating is the right word. The damage it caused in France alone is estimated to have cost more than twice the expense of the Franco-Prussian war (10–11 billion French francs at that time) and it caused French wine production to fall from 80 million to 25 million hectolitres between 1875 and 1890.

In Bessarabia, 20 June 1886 was the critical day. Inspectors had been travelling the Russian Empire since 1883, searching vineyards for signs of the root-sucking louse, but until then there had been no sign of it. And at that time, Bessarabia then accounted for around 20 per cent of the Russian Empire's wine production. On that day, a researcher called Afanasii Pogibko found 3 hectares of dead and dying vines about 25 kilometres north of Kishinev (as

Chişinău was then called). This wasn't its first appearance in the Russian Empire – Crimea and Georgia had already been infested, and it had been spotted in neighbouring Romania in 1884, so it came as no real surprise. The Russian authorities had plans in place since 1880 and these kicked into action – with infested vines uprooted and incinerated, and the soil fumigated. In fact, there had been a ban on importing plant material from Europe since 1873 but this had proved impossible to police – the Bessarabian outbreak was traced to vines imported in 1877 or 1878.

Unfortunately, the initial response failed, possibly due to high-density grapevine plantings in the region, and by 1892 phylloxera had infested 88,642 hectares in Bessarabia, roughly three-quarters of the total vineyard area. Three years later, 100,000 hectares were sick. The fact that most infections occurred in new vineyards, typically among Loire and Burgundy varietals such as Chasselas, Pinot Noir and Gamay, made the losses all the more painful. By then, 4.2 million ruble had been spent across the south-western fringe of the empire in an unsuccessful attempt to stem the spread of blight.

We need to go back a little to put what went wrong in Bessarabia into context. In France, in 1868 phylloxera was identified as the cause of the blight. The French offered significant sums of prize-money for a cure. A French museum director came up with the idea of the subsoil fumigation technique, using carbon disulphide to fight against phylloxera. This was part-funded by a French railway company who stood to profit from shipments of the chemical. By the early 1880s, use of soil fumigation in France had faded as not only was carbon disulphide toxic and unpleasant, it wasn't even a cure for the problem of phylloxera. However, by 1881 one technique was finally proving effective. North American vine species were resistant to the phylloxera pest that they carried. The problem was that their foxy flavour was not acceptable for wine directly but grafting French vines to rootstocks based on these American vines did work. Of course, this required shipment of enormous numbers of vines and expensive grafting, and was not a cure for the existing vines, which were doomed.

In the Russian Empire, a natural scientist called Kovalevski was appointed chairman of the Bessarabia phylloxera committee. He was friends with the French museum director who had come up with the idea of fumigation with carbon disulphide. For Kovalevski, the use of carbon disulphide represented the modern era. This was because it was made in a factory and injected by machine, making it a triumph of science over old-fashioned practical methods such as grafting. Kovalevski was a proponent of Darwin's ideas but with his own interpretation, seeing competition and selection as between species, rather than within a species. He saw the phylloxera problem as causing a Darwinian struggle between French vine species and American species. And the Americanization of the grapevine by grafting in this region was not politically popular either – it was perceived as something that was damaging the purity of the noble French vine. For these reasons, Bessarabia continued to recommend the use of quarantine, pesticides and fumigation for a decade after they had been discredited as a cure for phylloxera in France, and indeed they were still official policy as late as 1895. The state was deemed infallible, even though growers were aggrieved by seeing their vines ripped out for the common good. Apparently healthy vines were removed to create areas of quarantine, and growers were even forbidden from taking a final crop from vines that still looked healthy. In a talk in 1886, a speaker called Neruchev recognized that Bessarabian farmers were so poor that they couldn't afford to invest in modern farming practices. This meant that having to pay to replant with expensive grafted vines was prohibitive to many small farmers. By the time the blight began to wane in the early twentieth century, after grafting was finally accepted, 180,000 hectares of vines had died in Bessarabia, many of which were replantings. No wonder many growers then preferred the cheaper option of direct producer hybrids over grafted vines.

THE EARLY TWENTIETH CENTURY

In spite of phylloxera, Bessarabian wines were still regarded as high quality in the early twentieth century. A report by the jury for the Paris Exposition Universelle in 1900 notes the influence of foreign colonists in improving wines, and mentions exceptional wine made from the region's grapevines, notably Rară Neagră from Purcari and nearby villages. Between 1899 and 1900 the vineyards were producing an average of 1.53 million hectolitres, increasing to over 2.2 million hectolitres by 1910 when there were a reported 98,000 hectares of vines. Thirty per cent of wine production was for domestic consumption and the rest was exported.

Bessarabia briefly came under Romanian rule after the First World War in 1918, when the National Council of Bessarabia declared that the province was to be united with the Kingdom of Romania. Several large landowners in Bessarabia had thought that the Kingdom of Romania would be better for them than the leftist movement in Bessarabia at the time. However, one of the terms of the union was agrarian reform. Land was confiscated from large owners and 6-hectare plots were given to peasants (who made up 80 per cent of the population). This process dragged on until the 1930s. Revenues from wine, which had been a mainstay of the economy, were diminished in this period by the double blow of the loss of markets in Soviet Russia and preferential access for French wines in the Romanian market. In 1926 a trade war with Poland also disrupted one of the main export routes for Bessarabian wine. A series of droughts in 1921, 1924 and 1925 had also hit the struggling agriculture sector hard. Due to the wine oversupply, grapevines were only permitted to be planted on land not fit for cereals. There were also reforms on the naming of wines, decreasing hybrids and moves to reduce the production of fake wine. Despite these problems, wine quality was still praised. Writings from 1934 by Petru Ştefanuca describe the villages of Purcari, Răscăieţii and Olaneşti as renowned for their grapevines.

In 1940, Bessarabia was annexed by the Soviet Union under the Molotov–Ribbentrop pact, and then after another brief period of Romanian occupation, in 1944 it became the Moldovan Soviet Socialist Republic (MSSR). By this time, vineyards were usually small – less than 5 hectares. French varieties had come to dominate, along with large areas of hybrids planted by poor peasants who couldn't afford grafted vines. Certain local vine varieties (Plăvaie, Mustoasă, Rară Neagră and Busuioacă) that were more resistant to phylloxera also survived. Professor Savin (a leading Moldovan expert on viticulture) refers to a report of a 1945 census (written about by Dobrovolskii in 1947) which showed that 91 per cent of Bessarabia's grapes were hybrids and of the rest, 84 per cent were Western European varieties and only 16 per cent indigenous varieties.

THE SECOND WORLD WAR AND ITS AFTERMATH

The MSSR had to undergo collectivization and sovietization over a much shorter period compared to other republics which had joined the Soviet Union in the 1920s. The Second World War, which took a harsh toll on the Moldovan people, was followed by two drought years and widespread famine. Collectivization was largely completed by 1950, though this had been a period of poor productivity, and vineyard area in the whole Soviet Union (mainly Bessarabia, Ukraine and Georgia) had fallen from 425,000 hectares to 378,000 hectares by 1953. Collectivized farms were set up in two ways: *kolkhoz* which were collective farms where workers were paid by share of outputs, and *sovkhoz* which were state-owned farms where workers were paid wages.

Post-war policy was to develop western MSSR for agriculture while industry was located in the eastern part (today's Transnistria) and Slavs from Russia, Ukraine and Belarus were brought in to work in these factories. The post-war period was also difficult for many Moldovan families as there was a policy of 'russification' of the country aimed at reducing the power of the ethnic Moldovan population. Wealthier peasants with land (*kulaks*) and successful merchants, as well as settler populations were all targets. Many Moldovan families were deported to Siberia, often dying in the labour camps or gulags.

SAVED BY THE VINES

Ion Luca (Carpe Diem Winery) says: 'Grapevines saved my grandfather in 1949. He had survived the Second World War but what came after was worse for many families. Stalin had a policy of sending anyone with land and success to Siberia, and many Moldovans died in the gulags. Back then people often stayed away from home to work in their vineyard. Luckily for my grandfather he wasn't at home on that black night when the authorities came to take the rest of the family and sent them to forced-labour camps. In 1953, the ones who survived came back but there was no private property by then.'

In the 1950s, post-Stalin, there was a drive to increase wine production. Wine was seen as a prestige product that could put the achievements of the Soviet Union on display to the world and improve standards of living for Soviet citizens. In *Reassessing the Cold War*, Jeremy Smith quotes instructions issued by the Ministry of Economy of Food Products 'to liquidate the backwardness in the wine industry'. The plan was then to increase economic success by deploying innovative technology and investing in research. This meant mechanization, use of tractors and application of copious quantities of fertilizers and insecticides. The next few years also saw modernization of the grapevine assortment until 60 per cent of the vines were noble varieties. Viticulture switched to higher trellis training for increased yields. However, this also meant vines were more vulnerable to frost damage, so research was directed to development of cold resistant vines. Grapes like Viorica and Alb de Oniţcani were selected in this programme. The MSSR started to become one of the great agricultural centres in the Soviet Union, including production of 8.2 per cent of all its wine.

As part of the Soviet Union, the Moldovan economy was centrally planned. Under this system enterprises were 'labour collectives' (*kolkhozes* and *sovkhozes*) and the state controlled the supply of inputs, prices, production targets and the destination of the outputs. Because production targets and incentives were set by the state through annual and five-year plans, the success of an enterprise depended more on the political and bureaucratic connections of directors than customer satisfaction. This was a production-led, rather than market-led approach, and quality was not a priority, so it was often erratic. Results were even published in the news. In 1952 the Sovetskaya Moldaviya newspaper (from the CIA archives) was reporting that 'champagne' production was meeting 168 per cent of its target and grape wine was achieving 118 per cent of its target, whereas in 1950 wine had failed to meet its production targets.

WINE AND THE GORBACHEV EFFECT

There was a huge expansion of the industry of growing grapes until the mid-1980s. At its peak, the MSSR produced a quarter of the USSR's wine (approximately 9.6 million hectolitres by 1983, when the MSSR was the sixth biggest producer in the world). Data from Savin et al. indicate that peak vineyard area was reached in the decade 1971–1980, with an average of 224,000 hectares producing over 1.1 million tonnes. The following decade showed an average area of 202,000 hectares and a crop averaging more than 1.2 million tonnes. This decade included a steep decline after 1985, when Gorbachev introduced his anti-alcohol campaign. This led to grubbing up of around 75,000 hectares of vines in Moldova.

17

MODERNIZATION AND REFORM

THE NEW ERA OF LAND REFORM IN MOLDOVA

Land reform in Moldova was a far from smooth process. In 1991, when the newly independent Republic of Moldova was founded, the population was around 4.37 million people. Two-thirds were ethnic Moldovan, 13 per cent Ukrainian and Russian, 2 per cent Bulgarian and 3 per cent Gagauz (a Turkic Orthodox Christian people living in southern Moldova).

As part of the Soviet Union, MSSR had become an important net exporter of agricultural goods. In 1991, agriculture and food (including wine) were 43 per cent of the GDP and employed more than 50 per cent of the active labour force, according to *Politics of Agrarian Reform* (Gorton & White). Moldovan soil and its agricultural potential were the country's most strategic assets (it lacks significant mineral, oil and gas resources) and under communism, there had been 850 agricultural enterprises. This included 470 *sovkhozes*, typically holding 2,000 hectares; the rest were *kolkhozes* with an average of 3,000 hectares. The only private agriculture was in gardens around houses.

From 1991, the major reform debate was often bitter, with some arguing that existing structures should be retained, others saying there should be privatization, but with the same farm boundaries, and still others insisting there should be radical privatization by returning land to former owners or existing members of these collectives.

During the Soviet period, to become a state farm director, you had to be a party member, or be a loyal citizen and speak Russian, probably with a Russian wife too. These people were strongly opposed to the radical privatization model as they could foresee loss of their powerbase and status. Farm directors were effectively in charge of a whole rural institution, not just a farm. Social services like transport, health, schooling and food were provided by the collectives and this accounted for up to 30 per cent of the employees. This made collectivized farms appear inefficient in terms of productivity per person. And it seems there was also some pilfering of goods and agrochemicals to help people work their own gardens. Stalinism had destroyed rural villages, so it was important that state farms provided these services to fill the gap. There was also an ethnic split. Moldovans were more likely to support decollectivization, as collectivization was associated with the previous 'russification' of the country.

The first set of land reforms came about with the 1991 land code and 1992 law on peasant farms. These laws allowed members to leave collective farms, and workers and pensioners could receive a share of land. This included the 30 per cent of employees in community and social roles. No land sales were allowed for several years (2001 at first, though later rolled back to 1997). These reforms specifically ruled out return of property to previous owners (so this was different to the privatization procedures in Bulgaria and Romania). The aim was to support the rights of rural workers and not the pre-Soviet owners. Deportations of Germans and ethnic Moldovans in the post-war era had been used as a tool of fear to force people into the collectivized farms. All this land and assets were taken over by the state farms, so there were too many 'difficult questions' about pre-Soviet ownership for the new political system to address. A further step in land reform followed, allocating land to all workers, not just the members and retirees from the collective farms. This meant a recalculation and reduction in plot size which it took a long time to achieve. A national land plan finally saw the dismantling of collective ownership in 1998 in a process supported by USAID and the World Bank.

Moldova in the 1990s had significant financial issues, including debts to Russia's Gazprom, along with falling household incomes and loss of previous markets in the Soviet Union. The country had ended up with agriculture dependent on a shrinking export market and a very small domestic market, and it needed investment to reach international standards. As a prerequisite of access to International Monetary Fund (IMF) support, the IMF imposed a term that Moldova had to continue with privatization in agriculture (even though the rural population at the time seemed opposed to individual farming, as were political leaders). The American aid agency USAID was involved in developing the methodology for land reform in Moldova at the time and believed that private ownership would achieve free-market reform. The end result was, that by around 1999, approximately 1 million land beneficiaries were created, from a population of 4.43 million. These new owners ended up with an average holding of 1.4 hectares, typically in small divided parcels. Ion Luca (Carpe Diem Winery) explains: 'They divided everything equally, which seemed the right decision at the time. Each collective farm had a range of different crops, so everyone got a bit of each (forest, orchard, vines, arable land, etc.) but it wasn't necessarily suited to their skills or interests.'

Productivity declined heavily, and by 2000, was only one third of the level recorded in 1990 with output per person only reaching a quarter of 1990 levels. These land reforms had left Moldova with a problem of excess land fragmentation, small plots and poor, unprofessional farming. This meant irregular supplies to food processors along with a lack of quality control. Landowners, especially the retirees, were often old and didn't want to farm (or were unable to). But because there was an underdeveloped land market and few rental opportunities, it was difficult to sell the land. Poor agricultural productivity also meant low land prices so many did not want to sell for such small returns. Small landowners had little access to loans and credit, so purchase of agricultural inputs and equipment were unfeasible. Large areas of land, including vineyards, were lost.

Initially there was huge euphoria among Moldovans, who were happy to become owners of their own land. 'But this only lasted for five to six years, until people realized it was a huge problem. The country is still suffering because of this division,' says Ion Luca.

Wineries started to realize that they needed their own land, and entrepreneurs began to buy up plots. USAID had helped to create a land registry, so it was possible to identify new landowners, but wineries often had to deal with hundreds of small owners. Sometimes people were glad to sell if they could not do anything with the land, but others wanted to hold on to their inheritance, or ask astronomical prices, and some had died leaving no family to trace. Dan Prisacaru (Minos Terrios) illustrates this, 'There's a plot I want to buy, but the owners died, and their children are in prison in Russia. I've managed to get permission to use the land, but I can't buy it while the owners are in prison.'

WESTERN INVESTMENTS

Moldova's neighbours, especially Hungary and Romania, and to a lesser extent Bulgaria, have all benefited from Western investments into their wine industries. As Moldova was part of the Soviet Union, rather than just being in the communist bloc, it was harder for Western companies to make inroads. Pepsi's deal in the 1970s was an exception. In 1972, a *New York Times* article by Frank J. Prial reported on a Pepsi deal in Russia and its need to import Russian wines into the USA. Pepsi had done a considerable number of barter deals to get its cola into the communist bloc and had often taken wine in return. This article explained that the best Soviet wines came from Crimea and Moldova. Pepsi had bought a distributor called Monsieur Henri Wines to manage these trades because it was already an importer of Stolichnaya vodka and had a foothold in trading with the USSR.

FIRST FORAYS

One of the first Westerners in Moldova was winemaking consultant Angela Muir MW, who was there in 1992–1993:

I went on behalf of a wine merchant who had met a man in a pub, so it was a scary thing to do. I had a doctor and an architect as my drivers and they had to buy petrol in jerry cans in the back streets of Chișinău. I ended up at Mileștii Mici where I tasted through over 100 tanks. Most had 'cracked up' because of rust in the vats and too much air, but we did find a couple of tanks' worth of Cabernet Sauvignon. We also had a battle over price – they wouldn't believe how cheap French wines were, even though I showed them copies of La Journée Vinicole (a newspaper that published French bulk wine prices). They thought it was fake. We did find a customer for that wine – Sainsbury's bought it and sold it in about six weeks flat. But to make it work longer term, we would have needed a live-in winemaker to manage that metal problem and we would have had to pay them danger money. Grapes were being stolen by hungry people to eat so you couldn't guarantee there would be a crop. Logistics were tricky too – overland shipping via Poland was the shortest route but paying bribes was routine. It was pretty eye-opening and made working in Romania look like a cakewalk.

Around the same time, a Southcorp joint venture with flying winemaker Hugh Ryman at Hinceşti involved exchanging equipment and expertise to the value of €412,000 for wine. Con Simos was the Australian chief winemaker, 'It was hard, but I would do it all again in a heartbeat. There's a lot of potential here that hasn't gone away.' The wines were marketed as Hinceşti in the UK and Hickory Ridge in the US and three vintages (1993 to 1995) were successfully produced and sold in supermarkets such as Morrisons in the UK. Volumes reached around 150,000 cases (1.8 million bottles), though the first shipment had to leave under armed guard. In due course, issues of quality control, price pressure (consumer price inflation in Moldova reached 269 per cent in the first half of 1993) and the complexities of importing dry goods such as bottles and corks finally made the venture unappealing and by 1996 it had collapsed with unpaid bills. There was also a Dutch project with French winemaker Jacques Lurton in the early 1990s. In 1994, the European Bank of Reconstruction and Development approved a €24.7 million loan to Moldova over 10 years. That money was aimed at developing a glass plant (to help solve that problem of dry goods) and bottling and winery equipment. Grape production continued to decline during the 1990s, due to both fragmentation of vineyards and privatization of the wineries themselves by voucher distribution (during the period from 1995–1998). This left them without funds to pay for grape supplies or to make investments. The Moldovan wine industry was further hit hard by the economic crisis in Russia and devaluation of the ruble between 1998 and 1999.

TURNING TO THE EAST

By the turn of the century, wine was a growing trend again but with the focus on exporting wine to Russia and other former Soviet states. In 2001, vineyard area was 149,700 hectares and 200,000 tonnes of grapes were processed for wine (a precipitous fall compared to volumes in the 1980s). Not long after, in 2005, vineyard area had dropped a little to 139,000 hectares but grape harvest for wine had more than doubled to 420,000 tonnes. In 2003, wine had become Moldova's second biggest export earner (after foreign worker remittances) at around a quarter of gross merchandise exports. That year, semi-dry and semi-sweet wines accounted for 75 per cent of production, dry wines 10 per cent, sparkling wines 10 per cent and fortified 5 per cent. Moldova was exporting 93 per cent of production, bringing in US$195 million and Russia accounted for over 80 per cent of exports. In turn, Moldova was supplying 45 per cent of Russia's wine imports, though this was a fall from Moldova's 57 per cent share of Russian imports in 1999. Aid agencies such as USAID had already identified that this was a sector under pressure. Moldova was supplying cheap semi-sweet wines in ornate 'bling' bottles but with no branding or marketing – in effect just behaving as a bottling line for Russian distributors. Premium categories were taken by Georgia, France and Italy. At the cheaper, volume end of the market, Chile, Argentina, Italy, Spain and Bulgaria were gaining market share at Moldova's expense. Nonetheless, Moldova was increasing the value of its sales and by the end of 2005, wine revenues had gone up to €257 million. Of this €247 million-worth was going to CIS states and Russia was taking 85 per cent of that. Wine had reached 9 per cent of GDP in 2005, making Moldova almost certainly the most dependent country in the world on wine.

By 2005, USAID had set up its first CEED (Competitive Enhancement and Enterprise Development) project with the aim of enhancing Moldovan private sector enterprises in the global market. Its stated goal was stimulating sustainable economic growth and providing better paying jobs for Moldovan citizens. Unusually for a US government-sponsored project, which would normally avoid supporting alcohol production, wine was identified as a key economic sector. As one CEED report explained, 'Wine is of significant importance to the Moldovan economy because it is one of the only products exported with its full value chain completed in country, and high employability in rural areas.' I was one of a team of foreign experts that arrived in 2006 to work on identifying partners that could benefit from support.

THE TURNING POINT – 2006

In March 2006, Russia's Rospotrebnadzor agency imposed a total ban on Moldovan wine, based on claims of contamination by pesticides. It appears that no documentary evidence was ever produced, and in any case, many of Moldova's grape growers were too poor to pay for agrochemicals. The timing of the ban also happened to coincide with disputes with Russia over border controls with Transnistria and Ukraine. In July 2006 Valeriu Ostalep, Deputy Minister for Foreign Affairs and European Integration, said, 'It came immediately after we changed the system of monitoring border controls with Ukraine.' The ban was financially devastating, with immediate direct losses, from loss of market and destruction of stock, reaching €148 million (later rising to an estimated €247 million) in a country that was already Europe's poorest. Twenty-seven wineries were bankrupted, and most wineries laid off staff and struggled to find the money to buy grapes.

Personally, having seen (and unfortunately tasted) some of the wine that was typically being sold to Russia (complete with every fault in the winemaking book), it was clear that this was a problem waiting to happen. Much of the wine Moldova was selling to Russia was of inadequate quality, sold purely on price with the inevitable cutting of corners. The taste in this part of the world is for semi-sweet wines, often fortified and pasteurized, and much was made from hybrids like Isabella and Lidia with their strangely perfumed stickiness. However, tastes were changing, even in Russia, with increasing exposure to imports from South America, Spain and Australia. Moldova was inevitably going to have to deal with this at some point.

Unfortunately, this was not just a story of politicians flexing their muscles but was an economic catastrophe causing real misery to workers and growers. Most wineries sent staff home on unpaid leave. Rob Cameron, Cellarworld consultant winemaker working at AurVin winery near Vulcanesti in 2006 said, 'The winery is like ghost town.

I'm not sure how the winemakers lived on salaries of 250 dollars [just over €200] a month anyway and now they seem to be surviving on handouts from family abroad.' Most wineries had loans secured against sales to Russia and official figures at the time showed that 18 per cent of all bank credit went to wineries (with another quarter going to related industries and employees), based on guarantees against Russian wine sales revenue. Further credit to buy grapes was halted. Wineries were telling growers (and at this time two-thirds of grapes were coming from small growers) they would only take grapes on credit during the 2007 season with no future payment guarantee, so grape prices collapsed. One wine sector expert for USAID's project in Moldova said, 'The situation is desperate in the industry right now. People are starving in the countryside. Apparently, they (the government) don't seem to understand the seriousness.'

BY THE NUMBERS: THE IMPORTANCE OF THE WINE SECTOR TO MOLDOVA

Pre-ban

- Roughly 25 per cent of resident population connected to wine
- Wine made 9 per cent contribution to GDP (2005)
- Wine accounted for 28 per cent of exports (2005)
- 80 per cent of wine produced sold to Russia
- Grape growers had highest, most stable farmer incomes

Post-ban

- Wine production fell by 63 per cent in 2006 compared to 2005
- €148 million loss in wine sales March 2006–January 2007
- Wine only 16 per cent of exports (2006)
- Wine share of GDP fell to 4 per cent (2006)
- 4 per cent economic growth rate in 2006 (from 7.1 per cent in 2005), due to wine ban and increase in Russian gas import prices

Russia sent inspectors to Moldova to approve wineries for export in the early part of 2007 and 21 wineries had gained Russian approval by June that year. However, further delays were caused by Russian imposition of a single export window via one wine import agency, which was taking a commission on all sales. Onerous quality control certification was introduced by the Moldovans at Russia's insistence. This included a state trademark and a paper seal with a unique code and website so consumers could check the authenticity of their wine. Unfortunately, Moldova's single state-owned laboratory was under-equipped and struggled to meet demand. Nonetheless, after several false starts, shipments finally started moving back to Russia just before Christmas 2007. As Costia Stratan (then consultant winemaker at Dionysos-Mereni) said, 'Soviet mentality is this country's curse. The government is creating new bodies to control quality, but it is just bureaucracy. Ultimately Moldova needs Russia considerably more than Russia needs Moldova.'

However, as an industry source pointed out, 'Basically many Moldovan companies have been sending shipments to Russia without pre-payment. Many of those Russian importers are also dependent on bank loans – with the credit squeeze and ruble crisis they have not been able to make payments to Moldovan suppliers.' Another winery reported, 'The minimum interest on bank loans is now 27 per cent, but in practice loans are not available to us. Wine companies have no money to procure grapes or to finance any marketing support in their outlet markets.' Apart from issues and extra costs linked to certification of wineries, Russia then changed its tax regime in January 2008. All semi-sweet and semi-dry (sweetened with grape concentrate) wines were removed from the 'natural' wine category and became taxable at 15.8 ruble per 75 cl bottle, while natural wine paid a much lower rate of 2.2 ruble. One winery source in Moldova said that 'the new higher tax will basically just about finish off Moldova even when the market opens – Moldova used to export around 70 per cent of its wine to Russia as low-priced, semi-sweet and semi-dry.'

By the time the ban was lifted completely there was no empty niche for Moldovan wine to reclaim, though many wineries did return to Russia, a market they understood and were set up for. Both Bulgaria and so-called 'Russian' wine (finished in Russia from imported bulk), had gained market share at Moldova's expense. The other problem for Moldova is there is no other significant market in the world with a taste for the kind of semi-sweet wines that were being produced for Russia. Another industry spokesman said, 'The Russian market made producers lazy. They didn't have to care about quality or marketing, and they also didn't pay attention to the local market.'

Moldova's battles with Russia may have been less bloody and violent than those in Georgia, but still there's been a devastating war of economic attrition apparently aimed at keeping Moldova close at heel. Moldova's wine industry seems to have borne the brunt of these measures, probably because the industry is the most economically critical of any country in the world.

PERSONAL EXPERIENCE

When I arrived in Moldova for the first time it was quite a shock. I was naively expecting to see a mini Romania but what I found was a country deeply scarred by its Soviet years. I landed at a distinctly communist airport in the middle of the night, queued for my visa and hoped that the promised taxi would be there. I had to shake off being hassled by taxi drivers, face down the greatcoated policeman and venture out into the chill air, hoping that the man who had grasped my suitcase was legitimate. It was March 2006 and the coldest winter for decades, with roads still piled high with snow, and people even fishing through ice holes in the lake in the city's central park. USAID had set up a project (called CEED) to help bring Moldova's key industries up to Western standards. IT, clothing and wine had been identified as the strategic industries and I was there as the wine expert.

The first part of the project was to visit a number of wineries, audit their facilities and taste and review their wines to see what development potential there was and analyse their 'preparedness' to improve. By this time, I'd been to places like Bulgaria and Hungary just after the Iron Curtain had fallen, and spent many hours trawling round pretty basic southern French co-operatives to put together table wine blends, so I thought I'd seen some poor winemaking. But I was not prepared for Moldova.

This was some of the worst winemaking I've seen in my life – old Soviet-style reactor tanks, cellars reeking of stale wine, rusting painted vats, dirty pipes strewn anyhow across the floor and vile-smelling leaky barrels. Bottling lines were sloppy, even with walkways over open bottles of wine and relying on pasteurization, rather than actual hygiene to get bottles to the end consumer in acceptable shape (and this was a very long way from anything the West would have considered acceptable). These were often vast complexes with glass pipes everywhere ('but you can see what's in them,' said one winemaker, clearly never having heard of the phenomenon of light strike). Several wineries even had railway sidings in the winery to ship wine directly by the train-load to the Soviet Union. And as for tasting, that was a chore to say the least. Spittoons were rarely offered without asking, and the poorer the wine, the more offended the winery director was when you wanted to spit.

But what I did see was an industry that made a difference to people's lives and provided jobs and employment in a desperately poor country. There were some wineries that had potential, with the right people and mindsets to make a difference. While the Russian ban in 2006 was brutal and probably political in its motivation, it halted the broken Moldovan wine industry in its tracks and forced it to modernize. There's no doubt in my mind that the awful quality of wine at the time was a problem waiting to happen, and actually the ban gave the industry the kick-start it needed to make positive changes on a massive scale.

A NEW STRATEGY

In 2007, the CEED project continued on to its second step. Its plan was to encourage the state agency Moldova-Vin to consider updating its wine strategy. CEED cofinanced a team of international wine experts from the USA, the UK, France, Australia and Moldova to write a comprehensive wine sector analysis, published in November 2007. This included recommendations on short- and long-term actions that could be considered by Moldova-Vin and the Moldovan wine industry, if they were to take on the task of developing a modern-day wine sector. The government strategy at the time was based on outdated assumptions about sales to Russia and

CIS. However, it had recognized that much of the vineyard would need to be replaced over the next decade or so, as 79 per cent was already over 15 years old, and 16 per cent already over 25 years old. In addition, it acknowledged that much was planted with the wrong varieties, on the wrong rootstocks, or had been planted with high yields as the main objective.

During research for the CEED wine sector assessment, it emerged that wine was subject to enormous bureaucratic burdens, including an estimated 150,000 pages of regulations, many obsolete but still in place, or even conflicting. For instance, every single wine had to have its own 'technological instruction' taking time and expense (around 15,000 lei or approximately €900 for each application), and restricting freedom to react to the market. Just as an example, one element of the wine law required weekly statements during the harvest on grape varieties processed, by sugar level and by variety, with the full address and details of precisely which grower they had come from. There was also a requirement for twice yearly declarations of stocks by category and variety, and an obligation to declare future bottling plans and bulk wine.

RISE OF THE SMALL WINERIES

In other countries in Eastern Europe, it has often been the small producers that lead the way in quality improvements because the passion and flexibility of individuals can set new standards, and such individuals can take risks. Bureaucracy had made this almost impossible in Moldova, and there were only a very few souls who have braved the 150,000 pages of wine regulations to strike out on their own. Pioneers included both Costia Stratan (Equinox), with his own personal vineyard, and French-trained oenologist Gheorghe Arpentin (current head of ONVV, the National Office for Vine and Wine). USAID helped to establish the Small Wine Producers' Association in 2008 which lobbied hard, and eventually effectively, for a change in the law in 2011 which allowed the small producers to bottle their own wine. Even in 2010, the law insisted that wineries must own bottling lines and 500 square metres of warehouse (the few small wineries at this point had been operating semi-illegally under licences of other bigger wineries). Each winery had to pay a yearly licensing fee of 20,000 lei regardless of size (around €1,400 at a time when vineyard workers were earning well under €150 per month).

It was also important to distinguish these professional small producers from the home-made wine category, so the association proposed a definition of ownership of 1 to 50 hectares and a maximum production of 300,000 litres. Today the association has eight members and they are producing some of the best wines in the country. It is also really delightful to see them working together. Ilie Gogu (Gogu Winery) agrees, 'All the small wineries support each other, help each other and grow together. It's the only way to present Moldova abroad as people know nothing about our country.'

BENCHMARKING THE FUTURE

By 2011, there were several international aid projects supporting the wine industry in Moldova including a second CEED project which also worked closely with CBI (a Dutch government agency promoting exports in developing countries). Together they set up a benchmarking exercise where several international tasters and winery staff did a blind tasting of Moldovan wine against successful international brands in the same price category. Moldovans were still very much stuck in the 'we are proud of our wines and how much of our produce we export' mentality. This tasting highlighted that the whites were considerably better than the red wines, and Sauvignon Blanc appeared to be a local strength, but the rest of the world outperformed Moldova across the board. Moldovan wines were still showing signs of fundamental viticultural problems, resulting in under-ripe, hard reds and thin, neutral but fiercely acid whites. Winemaking was also still flaky, with wines suffering from bad oak use, oxidation and incomplete malolactic fermentation. A positive result of this exercise was a group of wineries who actually wanted to listen and were prepared to work together. Minister of Agriculture and Food at the time Vasile Bumacov was surprised himself by this new mood of cooperation. He admitted, 'I can't believe Moldova can have a cooperative discussion and I'm happy to see that we are not trying to invent the bicycle again.'

It's perfectly understandable that people who were forced to be collectivized in the past are reluctant to work together in the new era, but ironically Moldova, which was most scarred by its Soviet history, has a head start over both Bulgaria and Romania in producers working together. There's been a dramatic change since 2007 when one report by

CEED noted, 'There's a deep-seated aversion to any form of association that resembles the collectivization of the Soviet era and deep mistrust of each other.' Maybe it's been helped by the work of the aid agencies and the brutality of Russia's political bullying, but the changes haven't simply been imposed – the wineries have been the drivers and motivators. The fact that so many of the wineries (both big and small) who are working on a new approach are owned by families with a background in wine may help too. The lack of outside investment is both a blessing and a curse: while there is no external money to help in tough times, the owners have a real connection to the industry and motivation to improve things. Moldovan wineries of all sizes now go together to international shows such as Prowein in Germany and wine shows in Asia, and present a united front. It's probably not the same behind closed doors, but the outside world sees Moldova together and that is vital for a tiny country like this in a huge world of wine.

TOWARDS THE EU

A huge number of people have contributed to making changes in Moldova, not least the wine industry itself, and I played just a tiny part in all that. Still, it was good news to get this email in November 2012 from the chief of party of one of the aid projects: 'I just wanted to pass along some good news from Moldova. Yesterday Moldova's Parliament passed a new law containing far-reaching (and long-overdue) reforms to the Moldovan wine industry. It is the culmination of many years of work, in which you played a part. Now we move to helping implement the law, which will also be a challenge; but at least we will have the correct legal and regulatory structure in which to operate.'

By February 2013, the new wine law was in place and it represented a complete switch from state regulation to industry control. Ion Luca (head of the Small Wine Producers' Association) agreed, 'The biggest help to us was the change in the law in 2013. A fair wine law is undoubtedly the biggest help we got from USAID.' The law is overseen by the ONVV which was established to implement the government policies in the field of viticulture. The basic missions of the ONVV are to promote quality wines through the Wine of Moldova program; to manage the production of PGI and PDO wines; and to provide assistance and consultancy to the Moldovan wine industry. Its board includes members from both big and small wineries and at least part of the funding comes from an industry levy of 10 bani per litre on wine exports or sales to customers. Wine of Moldova is its public face, promoting wine through a wine country brand, launched in 2014, with the strapline 'Wine of Moldova – a legend alive'. Exports will remain the key priority, as most Moldovans are too poor to buy anything other than home-made wine. According to Moldova's statistics bureau, in 2016 the average monthly salary in agriculture was 3,321 lei or €163, while the overall average salary was 5,084 lei or €250.

In addition, the European Investment Bank (EIB) signed a €75-million financing deal to support the wine industry. This funding was aimed specifically at developing wines with Protected Geographical Indication (in line with EU legislation), together with investing in winemaking and viticultural improvements through the Filière du Vin project, and re-equipping quality control facilities. Four regions were identified and three PGIs for wine were put in place in time for the 2014 vintage. By 2017, there were 8,600 hectares of PGI vineyards used by 64 producers. There are plans to develop PDO wines too, though this is still in the initial stages.

DOMESTIC CONCERNS

In the domestic market, consumption of commercial bottled wine remains low, though Constia Stratan (of the Moldovan Small Wine Producers' Association and Equinox) reports that wine is becoming trendy. This is supporting the development of more premium wines and small wine estates, several of whom report that domestic sales are an important category for them. January 2012 brought the end of excise duties on wine in Moldova, removing a major administrative burden, even if it does not make a significant difference to wine selling prices. There is a programme to encourage wine drinking over spirits consumption, so duty on vodka has been increased (though it will still be cheaper than a bottle of wine). Moldovans are ranked second in the WHO league table of the heaviest drinking nations in the world at 16.8 litres of pure alcohol, and only around 5 per cent of this is wine. Recently sommelier wine education has been introduced in Moldova and several wine shops and wine bars have appeared in Chișinău. One source reckons the whole market for consumers of quality bottled wine in Moldova may only be 100,000 people.

THE BIG BEAR LOOMS AGAIN

'Wine shouldn't be about politics,' a Moldovan winemaker told me recently, but that seems an impossible dream in a country where wine has so often been used as a political football. In 2013, Russia imposed another ban on Moldovan wine, just before Moldova signed a free-trade agreement with the EU. A Moscow spokesman announced that 'Moldovan wine should be used to paint fences' and the Russian authorities claimed to have found plasticizers (dibutyl-phthalate and ethyl-hexylphthalate) in two batches of wine and one of brandy. However, these compounds were at levels below those permitted in mineral water, and below reliable gas chromatograph detection levels. In addition, there was no maximum limit in place for wine anyway. An industry spokesman said, 'Evidently this was not a problem with hygiene as claimed by Moscow. It appears to be a political question. The more we advance towards the European sector the more the pressure mounts from Russia.' Wines from Transnistria were excluded from this ban, and within a few months, the embargo was lifted for certain wineries in Russian-leaning Gagauzia. This ban did not shake the industry as badly as the 2006 one. It was estimated that the industry lost €25 million, though given the still precarious situation after the first ban, the prohibitive cost of bank loans and difficult trading conditions, it was still a huge problem for many wineries. Dimtri Munteanu (former Director of Wine of Moldova) said, 'Our exports dropped by 30 per cent, because Russia remained the key market for our wines even after the first embargo in 2006.' Some wineries have been hit harder than others, according to Ruxanda Lipcan of Fautor, 'For wineries who had laid hopes on the Russian market, things are grim, others who had ignored Russia are OK.' Victor Bostan (Purcari and Bostavan) says, 'We didn't go so massively back into Russia but we had gone back – Russia took 14 per cent of our exports, though this time we made sure our stock wasn't liquidated and our payments were mostly secured.' Graham Dixon (winemaking expert to Filière du Vin) points out, 'Some Moldovan wine exporters have reoriented successfully to Western markets since the first Russian embargo in 2006 and are offering wines at least as good as other exporters into Western Europe. However, most are still marooned, with business models and wine styles tuned to the traditional Russian market.' And by this he means, 'Inappropriate wine styles for priority markets, for example sweet reds, from grapes often picked under-ripe, that the Russians used to appreciate.' Arpentin adds that there is a considerable amount of stock of this unsaleable wine in Moldova: to the 1.8 million hectolitres of declared stock holding at end of August 2014 was added a further 1.1 million hectolitres, produced from 2014's harvest. Arpentin says, 'This should be distilled as it is often undrinkable and was made for bulk markets like Russia.'

TOUGH TIMES

Moldova continues to be battered by financial and political challenges, often beyond its control, and wine gets caught up in all this. Many Moldovans have left to make a living in better paid Western countries (around 1 million of the active population is working abroad). The country has a GDP of close to €6.6 billion, while exports are worth just €150 million. To add to its woes, in 2015 this troubled country was hit by massive bank losses. Unsecured loans to banks with links in Russia worth 10 per cent of GDP were transferred out of the country, forcing several banks into administration. Tracing the money has been fruitless so far with the trail allegedly ending at an offshore shell company registered in Edinburgh via Latvia and the Seychelles (according to the BBC's *File on Four* report from 6 October 2015). The money is believed to have ended up in Russia. Protestors took to the streets, quite rightly, to demand action to recover these funds and punish those responsible. This also left the country with reserves of less than €1.7 billion, making it incapable of acting to limit currency devaluation, and seeking possible bailout from the IMF.

On top of the financial troubles, come inevitable concerns about Moldova's neighbour Ukraine, previously an important export market for Moldova, but due to the war, 'There has been a decline of exports to this country of both bulk and bottled wines, about 70 per cent and 25 per cent respectively,' according to Munteanu. Standing in the vineyards at Purcari highlights quite how close this vineyard zone is to both the breakaway region of Transnistria and Ukraine, with the border just a few kilometres away. However, one winemaker with friends in Transnistria believes that Moldova is talking up these concerns to secure more support from Europe, 'We had our war in 1992 and no one wants to go through that again,' he says. The pro-Russian autonomous province of Gagauzia is another concern. Even developing new PGIs for Moldova gets political – it seems the key towns of Comrat and Vulcăneşti would prefer their own PGI rather than being part of Valul lui Traian, according to Arpentin. And there is some concern that Moldova's south-eastern Ştefan Vodă region could be cut off by these two regions turning east. On the other hand, neither Gagauzia nor Transnistria have any direct border access to Russia without going through Western-friendly countries. Several wineries in Gagauzia theoretically have the right to sell in Russia outside the embargo although in reality they don't, because the Russian market is too hard to get back into given the poor reputation of Moldovan wine there.

One of the things that these multiple bans made clear to the industry was the need for a complete vineyard register and *cadastre* to ensure full product traceability. Moldova has every reason to invest time, money and effort into getting wine right, and it can't afford to be left behind as the rest of the world is already tackling many similar issues effectively.

SUSTAINABILITY

One of the options that the wine industry is exploring is to develop an industry-wide programme of sustainability. This is something that several New World countries, including New Zealand and South Africa, have put a lot of effort into but as yet nothing of this sort exists in Europe.

In recent years, economic woes have meant that Moldovan farmers have had very little money to spend on agrochemicals, so observers regard the soil and air as very clean. Pesticide use in Moldova was very heavy during the Soviet period though, and in 2015 an EU-funded FAO project removed leftover stockpiles of obsolete pesticides for safe and environmentally responsible disposal in Poland. The FAO has started an education programme to help minimize pesticide use today.

In wine, there are several producers in the country particularly in the south who are already focusing on organic and more sustainable production. Certified organic vineyards include Equinox and Gitana winery, while Gheorghe Arpentin has been pursuing biodynamic production for several years but is not certified. Natural winemaking is often rather too close to home-made wine to be a strong trend (as in Moldova's neighbours). Equinox has produced the country's first orange wines under the 5 Elemente label and also produced a 'natural' Chardonnay.

TOURISM

Moldova is not on many tourist maps yet. It is the least visited country in Europe in terms of tourism, but direct flights from the UK and hubs like Vienna and Frankfurt now make it quite accessible. Chişinău itself is a cosmopolitan city of tree-lined boulevards and buzzing café culture, with churches and museums to explore, and the cave monastery and ancient village of Old Orhei are worth a trip. In Moldova, wine and tourism are totally intertwined. The country makes a headline feature of its record-breaking wine collections in huge underground wine cellars, possibly among the largest in the world, created during the communist era in the late 1950s and early 1960s at Cricova and Mileştii Mici. Wine routes, tastings and traditional food are all being developed to help tourism and wine culture together. Moldova's traditional carpets were added to UNESCO's list of Intangible Cultural Heritage of Humanity in 2016 and they add a colourful note to the scene.

LEGAL ISSUES

In 1994, Moldova agreed to cease using protected international geographical names for their wines. So, champagne was to become Spumant, cognac became Divin, cahor became Pastoral and sherry became Ialoveni or Shervin. This was not strictly observed until Moldova joined the World Trade Organization in 2001. Brandy and champagne had disappeared from the market but cahor and sherry continued to be used in CIS countries and local markets. Under the free-trade agreement with the European Union in 2013, Moldova agreed to a period of five years to use up reserves of the sweet red wine cahor (sometimes called kagor) and to rename it Pastoral (though a number of producers are unhappy about this loss of a traditional and well-recognized category).

THE WINE INDUSTRY TODAY

In 2018, wine is still an essential part of Moldova's economy. It's the most important sector in food and agriculture (16 per cent by value, compared to 40 per cent in 2005); it accounts for 12 per cent of external trade balance (compared to more than 25 per cent in 2005) and 3 per cent of GDP (10 per cent in 2005). Today wine employs around 10 per cent of the country's active resident workforce, which is about 150,000 people. There were 181 wineries in 2017 but only 106 processed grapes for that harvest.

The ONVV industry summary in 2018 declares that there are 81,000 hectares of *Vitis vinifera* vineyards, of which 78,000 hectares are yielding (this is commercial plantations and does not include back garden grapevines). This accounts for 7 per cent of all agricultural land and 3.8 per cent of the total land surface in Moldova. Overall Moldova is in sixteenth place worldwide for vineyard area. The last decade has seen a fifth of vineyards modernized, though the overall area under vine has decreased by 43 per cent in the last 25 years. In addition, table grapes account for 15,100 hectares and a further 9,600 hectares are planted with Isabella (see p. 284) giving a total area under vine of 105,700 hectares. This means Moldova has a considerably bigger area of *Vitis vinifera* than Bulgaria (and even Hungary) and is not far behind Romania. In 2017, the wine grape harvest reached 311,000 tonnes of grapes. Wine volume production was 1.8 million hectolitres, 29 per cent above the seven-year average.

The structural make-up of the industry has changed, with more wineries owning vineyards, though the aftermath of privatization is still having an impact. In 2017, 60 per cent of vineyards were owned by private individuals with holdings of under 1 hectare. Farming households (private enterprises mostly in Gagauzia similar to the former *sovkhoz* farms) with an average holding of 500 hectares account for 22 per cent of vineyards, while wineries own the remaining 18 per cent directly. A significant number of small wineries have appeared since the reform of regulations and in 2017 forty wineries processed under 500 tonnes, while just seven processed more than 10,000 tonnes of wine grapes.

EXPORT TRENDS

Moldova has gone from having all its eggs in one export basket to a healthier spread of customers, so all those production changes and efforts in communication appear to be paying some dividends at last. Exports will continue to be the main focus – the home market will be small for a long time, unless some economic miracle occurs. In 2017, Moldova exported 1.405 million hectolitres of wine (up 5.5 per cent on the previous year) at a value of €104.6 million (up 16 per cent) so it is encouraging to see growth in volumes and a bigger increase in value. Currently, bulk wine takes a 71 per cent share by volume and ONVV would like to see a shift to nearer half and half. By value, the picture looks better, with bulk taking only a 42 per cent value share, with an average price of €0.45 per litre. Leading bulk markets are Belarus, Georgia, Russia, Ukraine and Romania. But given 2017's poor harvest and the resulting price pressure in Western Europe, this may well be a strong opportunity for Moldova.

As for bottled sales, in 2017 there were 54.2 million bottles shipped (a 15 per cent increase over the previous year). Leading destinations and share by volume were: Poland 14 per cent, China 12 per cent, Romania 12 per cent, Russia 12 per cent, Czech Republic 11 per cent, Ukraine 7 per cent. By value share, China is the number one market, taking 17 per cent, then Romania 13 per cent, Poland 13 per cent, Russia 10 per cent and Czech Republic 10 per cent. Average bottle price paid is €1.09, an increase from €0.99 in 2015 – China pays €1.51 per bottle, compared to Russia's €0.90. This supports comments from wineries about Chinese buyers paying higher prices. However, it appears China is not always easy – a Romanian producer recently explained how happy he had been to sell a container to China at a very generous €8 per bottle. But it was never paid for, so he lost both wine and money. China is a market that has potential as it has no preconceptions about Moldovan wine, but nor does it have any loyalty. Moldova is still a long way from the easy money of selling to Russia before 2006, but appears to be a country moving onto a stronger footing.

PROBLEMS AND CHALLENGES

By no means are all of Moldova's problems solved, though considerable progress has been made, and there are now wines that definitely meet global standards. One issue that still needs to be tackled is that of ensuring that every time anyone picks up a bottle of Moldovan wine it is clean, pleasant and appropriately priced for the quality. Sadly, that is still sometimes not the case (some disheartingly bad wines appeared at the 2018 Black Sea region wine contest). Dirty, old, green or under-seasoned oak, oxidation, secondary fermentation and poor-quality bottling are to blame for some of these problems. It is a real surprise to hear winemakers who announce proudly that they achieve malolactic fermentation. This has long been standard practice for red wines in developed wine countries and is rather taken as the norm. However, it seems that this has often been difficult to achieve in Moldova due to a combination of cold temperatures in winter and high acidity wines (ironically these are exactly the wines that need to undergo malolactic fermentation but it's hard to get the malolactic bacteria to start the fermentation).

Education is vital at all levels – there are still too many winemakers who are really just process technicians and who don't seem to grasp the need for scrupulous hygiene. It's not hard to scrub barrels, vats and floors; hang up hoses and make sure tanks are repaired, especially given low labour costs. Producers also need to understand that there is no room for compromise in the quality of their cooperage and barrels. What is surprising is that Moldovans are still often wedded to expensive French barrels, whereas decent quality and less expensive alternatives are produced in Hungary and by the better coopers in Romania. Education is also vital for consumers, to encourage them to drink commercial wine rather than home-made stuff or vodka. The WHO estimates that at least 60 per cent of alcohol consumption in Moldova is unofficial and that 80 per cent of this is wine, so even converting a small part of that would help the wine industry.

In the vineyard, the country is still in the early stages of really understanding terroir – the detailed differences that specific plots of land and microclimates can give to wine. I was struck recently by one big producer who announced that 99 per cent of Moldova was suitable for grape growing, so he didn't mind where he bought vineyards as long as he avoided frost risk. Varietal make-up of the vineyards is still work in progress – especially for the local grape varieties that are of such interest. The reality is that four European varieties make up 55 per cent of vineyard area and two of these (Aligoté and Rkatsiteli) are not very good or appropriate for modern winemaking or global tastes. Producers thinking about clonal selection and rootstocks are still rare.

Despite these challenges, Moldova has come a huge way since it regained its independence and seems to be firmly on the right track to continue. Progress from there to here has been simply astonishing, and I'd happily recommend the best of today's wines to anyone. I am just a tiny little bit pleased if my small contributions have helped along the way in improving the lot of this tiny and heavily wine dependent country.

18

GRAPE VARIETIES IN MOLDOVA

There is considerable overlap between the varieties that are native to Moldova and Romania (see Chapter 13 for full details). There are a few varieties that are specific to Moldova and not found in Bulgaria or Romania so these will be covered here. While Moldova is in the process of building a vineyard register and *cadastre*, by December 2017 only just over 28,000 hectares had been registered, so no one will actually know exactly what is grown in Moldova or how much there is of it until this work is complete. There are limited production statistics too, though declarations of volume for leading varieties are available from ONVV for 2017.

These declarations show that production was led by Merlot at 299,000 hectolitres, Cabernet Sauvignon 298,000 hectolitres, Chardonnay 186,000 hectolitres, Sauvignon Blanc 161,000 hectolitres, Muscat group (95 per cent Ottonel) 108,000 hectolitres, Pinot Gris and Blanc 99,000 hectolitres, Aligoté 99,000 hectolitres, local grapes 47,000 hectolitres, Pinot Noir 39,000 hectolitres, Riesling 33,000 hectolitres and Saperavi 20,000 hectolitres. This is an industry still heavily reliant on well-known international grapes, though the question of using local grapes as flagships, and to create a point of difference for Moldovan wine is often talked about within the industry. A breakdown of volumes for leading local grapes in 2017 shows just 14,012 hectolitres of Rară Neagră, Fetească Neagră was next, with 13,560 hectolitres, Fetească Albă 9,040 hectolitres and Fetească Regală 8,588 hectolitres. While the grapes are undoubtedly good and even exciting in the right hands, this is not much volume to build an export strategy on.

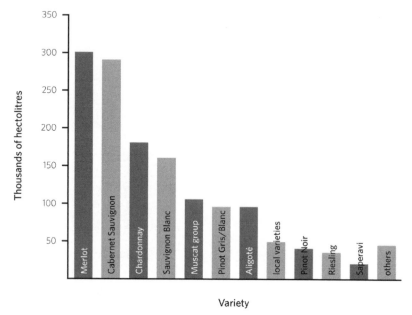

Moldova 2017 harvest, all varieties (data from ONVV)

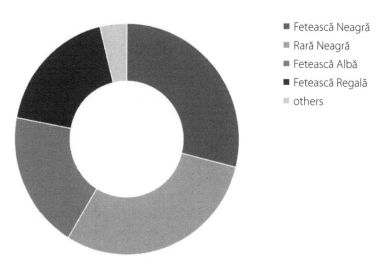

*Moldova local grapes 2017 harvest volume – total 47,000 hectolitres
(data from ONVV)*

In the 2017 catalogue of plant varieties of Moldova 29 white and
13 black wine grapes were listed as grown or available to grow in the
country. As far as published information at the time of writing goes,

around 73 per cent of the total *Vitis vinifera* vineyards are European varieties. Seventeen per cent are Caucasian varieties (such as Saperavi, Rkatsiteli) and some 10 per cent are local varieties (Fetească Albă, Fetească Regală, Rară Neagră, Fetească Neagră and Plăvaie). This is bound to change once the *cadastre* is completed.

LOCAL GRAPES

Alb de Onițcani

Alb De Onițcani or Onitskanskii Belyi is only vinified by Novak Winery in Moldova. It was produced in around 1970 by researchers from Chișinău working in the village of Onițcani. It is the offspring of crossing an obscure grape called Chil Gyulyabi with a mixture of pollen from Pierrelle (itself offspring of Villard Blanc) and Seyanets 244. The variety has medium-sized dense bunches, with light green, mid-sized and slightly oval berries with juicy pulp. The variety can withstand frost up to -28°C and has good resistance to fungal diseases like grey mould, oidium and mildew. The Novak winery has concluded that it is important to keep the trunk height to no more than 70 cm and keep yields to a maximum of 7 tonnes per hectare (this means dropping as much as 30 per cent of the crop through green harvesting). By doing this, maturity is brought forward a week (useful in this very late ripening variety) and acidity falls to a more balanced level (5.8 to 6.5 grammes per litre compared to 9 grammes per litre with traditional high trellising). The winery's owner, Andrey Novak, believes that Alb de Onițcani has recently shown real promise in the southern part of Moldova.

Producers worth trying: Novak Winery.

Bastardo

This is also called Bastardo de Magarach as the grape was produced at the Magarach research Institute in Ukraine. It was originally believed to be a crossing of Bastardo with Saperavi, but genetic analysis has shown that it is in fact a cross of Trousseau and Saperavi. It was produced in 1949 and is planted in small quantities in Moldova as well as being imported by Purcari for its Freedom Blend.

Producers worth trying: Purcari (Freedom blend), Vinuri de Comrat Plai (Saperavi/Bastardo blend).

Fetească Albă

Until the vineyard register is complete no one will know how much of this variety is grown. Estimates range from 200 to 4,000 hectares, but given the 2017 harvest volume was only 9,040 hectolitres, the lower end of this range seems more realistic – 316 hectares had been registered by December 2017. In Moldova, it produces delicate, restrained wines with good acidity.

Producers worth trying: Asconi, Atú, Carpe Diem, Castel Mimi, Radacini.

Fetească Neagră

An ancient variety, believed to originate in the area of the historic principality of Moldavia, it had virtually disappeared in Moldova itself by the mid 2000s. Today there is increasing interest in replanting because of its local connection and possibly inspired by exciting results in Romania. It is gaining attention as a regional flagship. In 2017, 13,560 hectolitres were produced.

Producers worth trying: Et Cetera, Fautor (Negre blend), Radacini, Vinăria Nobilă, Vinaria Din Vale.

Fetească Regală

This grape had almost disappeared in Moldova but is enjoying renewed attention as a traditional variety of the region, even though it is known to originate from Transylvania. As in Romania, it produces wines with more texture and structure than its parent Fetească Albă. There were 8,588 hectolitres produced in 2017

Producers worth trying: Carpe Diem, Château Vartely, Gitana Winery.

Rară Neagră

This is the Moldovan name for Romania's Băbească Neagră. In Romania it gets only moderate respect at best and many producers still regard it as tricky to grow well; however, in Moldova, it only grows in the south-east around Purcari, and seems to have the potential to achieve much higher levels of colour, flavour and substance than is normal for Romania. Producers in Moldova reckon their clones are different from the Romanian ones. Costia Stratan was the first to bottle this as a single varietal wine under the Carlevana label. When he first planted his personal vineyard, he had to take cuttings from old vines in the Purcari region because no vines were available commercially. The grape is also an important ingredient in the famous Negru de Purcari blend. At Purcari, Victor Bostan explains: 'We selected our own plants because it was almost extinct in Moldova. We originally planted it just for Negru but when we saw how well-accepted it was by consumers, we decided to plant more. One clone goes into the Negru de Purcari blend but proved interesting enough to produce a varietal version too. The other is paler in colour and is better for rosé.' Data on plantings of Rară Neagră in Moldova are hard to obtain but vineyard area is almost certainly still small, as just 14,012 hectolitres were declared in 2017. There is increasing interest in adding this to blends and there are a few bottlings as a single variety.

Producers worth trying: Purcari, Timbrus, Cricova. In blends: Bostavan, Carpe Diem, Château Vartely, Equinox, Fautor, Minos Terrios, Purcari, Timbrus.

Viorica

A local grape developed at the Chișinău research Institute in 1969, it is officially a crossing of Seibel 13666 x Aleatico. It was developed in a research programme looking for grape varieties that could make good wine but were also resistant to Moldova's very cold continental winters. Ion Luca, who works with it, says it is prone to very high yields and sugar rises 'by the minute' near harvest time. Initially used for distillation because it keeps elevated levels of acidity, now that summer temperatures are warmer, it is starting to prove interesting as a wine grape in its own right. Several wineries are now producing this as a dry wine and even as a sweet version as it has appealing light, floral, Muscat-like aromas, though it is best drunk young.

Producers worth trying: Carpe Diem, Cricova, Kvint, Sălcuța, Suvorov-Vin, Timbrus.

INTERNATIONAL RED GRAPES

Cabernet Sauvignon

A grape with a long tradition in Moldova, this is especially important in some of the country's more famous blends such as Codru and Negru de Purcari. In 2017, there were 298,000 hectolitres, just behind Merlot. In

Moldovan conditions, it can produce firm, long-lived wines but is also prone to green, austere tannins if overcropped.

Producers worth trying: Bostavan, Castel Mimi, Château Vartely, Equinox, Fautor, Gitana, Purcari, Suvurov-Vin, Vinaria Din Vale.

Merlot

This is the top grape by volume share in Moldova in 2017 with a production of 299,000 hectolitres. Several producers believe that this is actually Moldova's top red grape as it gets ripe enough, but also keeps good acidity and avoids the green tannins that Cabernet Sauvignon is prone to here.

Producers worth trying: Asconi, Bostavan, Castel Mimi, Château Vartely, Doina-Vin Artitude, Equinox, Et Cetera, Gitana, Minos Terrios, Purcari.

Pinot Noir

In theory, Pinot Noir should suit Moldova's growing conditions, but in fact it is proving tricky to grow well. 39,000 hectolitres were produced in 2017. The south of the country is arguably too warm, while the centre of the country is regarded as too cool and damp. It seems to be at its best in sparkling wines and rosés.

Producers worth trying: Cricova (sparkling), Purcari (sparkling and red), Château Vartely, Carpe Diem 19/11 blend.

Saperavi

Originally a Georgian grape, this is now widely planted across the former Soviet Union. In Moldova there were 20,000 hectolitres in 2017. It is producing some very exciting results here, though no one seems to know whether that is down to the clonal selection planted in Moldova or the grape's response to the climate. At its best, it gives deep-coloured wines, with bright acidity and intense, spicy, dark cherry flavours, and appears well worth more attention. It also plays a useful role in blends, famously Negru de Purcari.

Producers worth trying: Bostavan (Dor blend), Carpe Diem (Bad Boys blend), Gitana Winery, Gogu, Novak Winery, Timbrus.

INTERNATIONAL WHITE GRAPES

Chardonnay

In 2017, Chardonnay was the leading white grape in Moldova at 186,000 hectolitres. Most commonly it is vinified in a fresh, crisp style, with no malolactic fermentation, or notably oak-fermented and aged. It also appears in sparkling wines and a few very good sweet ice wines.

Producers worth trying: Agrici, Albastrele, Asconi, Bostavan, Château Vartely, Equinox, Et Cetera, Fautor, Gitana.

Pinot Gris

Often labelled Pinot Grigio, this is a grape that appears to do well in Moldovan growing conditions. Styles vary from clean commercial Italian-lookalikes (some shipped in bulk recently to the UK and other Western markets) to richer and fuller-flavoured versions. Pinot Blanc is also included in the 2017 production volume of 99,000 hectolitres.

Producers worth trying: Albastrele, Asconi, Castel Mimi, Fautor, Purcari, Podgoria-Vin, Sălcuţa.

Riesling

This is the true German Riesling, which has been in Moldova since the early nineteenth century, linked to the arrival of German and Swiss settlers. It produces successful dry wines and also some fine, sweet ice wines. In 2017 33,000 hectolitres were produced.

Producers worth trying: Château Vartely, Fautor, Gitana, Gogu, Sălcuţa.

Rkatsiteli

This is another Georgian grape that became widespread across the Soviet Union, due to its suitability for high trellis volume viticulture. It is a neutral grape that retains notable acidity, so much of production in Moldova is for distillation into Divin brandy. Harvest volume for wine was insignificant in 2017 though historical industry data suggest it is one of Moldova's most planted wine grape varieties, which should be confirmed once the register is complete. It is also the grape used for one of Moldova's sweet fortified wines, Grătieşti.

Producer worth trying: Agrici.

Sauvignon Blanc

Sauvignon Blanc seems to suit Moldova's climate. Production in 2017 was less than that of Chardonnay, at 161,000 hectolitres. Crisp acidity and varying degrees of aromatic expression typify Sauvignon Blanc here but the best wines show great varietal expression and mouth-watering freshness. There are even successful barrel-fermented versions appearing.

Producers worth trying: Asconi, Château Vartely, Et Cetera, Fautor, Gogu, Mezalimpe, Minos Terrios, Purcari, Radacini (Albastrele, Chi).

THE REST

Other international grapes planted include Albarino (Fautor), Aligoté (hugely important in terms of area but a lot goes for distillation, with 99,000 hectolitres of wine produced in 2017), Malbec (Castel Mimi, Purcari Vinohora red, Roşu de Purcari), Muscat group 108,000 hectolitres (Muscat Ottonel Atú, Moscato Agrici), Tempranillo (Fautor), Traminer (Atú, Château Vartely for dry styles, Fautor Ice Wine, also historically Traminer was famous for a sweet fortified wine called Auriu, still to be found in some archive cellars), Shiraz, Montepulciano, Carmenere and almost certainly more, but until the vineyard register is complete the full picture will not be clear.

HYBRIDS

The ONVV estimates that there are still 9,600 hectares of hybrids, especially Isabella (a *vinifera* x *labrusca* hybrid of unknown parentage). Because Moldova is outside the EU, Isabella can still be bottled for commercial sale, often as a semi-sweet red. Other hybrid varieties available for sale from grapevine nurseries in Moldova include Cuderca, Noah, Isabella, Lidia and Zaibar; all typically planted for back garden production.

THE BLEND STORY

Negru de Purcari is Moldova's best-known wine, possibly dating back to the nineteenth century and famously enjoyed by Queen Victoria and Queen Elizabeth II. As such, it has inspired many other producers to produce blends, at least for their more premium offerings. It's a blend of Cabernet Sauvignon with Saperavi (about 25 per cent) and Rară Neagră (around 5 per cent) and is now a registered trademark belonging to Vinaria Purcari. Other producers have also been inspired by the idea of using the tricky Rară Neagră to add a sense of local place to their blends, or alternatively Fetească Neagră or even Saperavi. The traditional blend from the centre of the country is Codru, based on Cabernet Sauvignon plus Merlot to give it some flesh. A few serious white blends have also appeared more recently.

Other notable red blends

Carpe Diem Bad Boys, Castel Mimi Roșu de Bulboaca, Château Vartely Individo, Equinox 5 Elemente, Equinox Echinoctius, Et Cetera Cuvée Rouge, Et Cetera Serendipity, Fautor IIlustro, Gitana Lupi, Gogu Metafora, Minos Terrios Roșu Împărat, Purcari Freedom Blend and Purcari Roșu de Purcari.

Notable white blends

Equinox 5 Elemente Alb, Gitana La Petite Sophie, Et Cetera Cuvée Blanc, Fautor Illustro Alb, Purcari Alb de Purcari.

SWEET LIFE

Another style that is looking exciting in Moldova is ice wine. This was a wine traditionally made in Moldova before Soviet times, but forgotten in the switch to volume production. Costia Stratan made the modern era Riesling ice wine called Brumariu (meaning hoar frost) from the 2003 vintage at Dionysos-Mereni, which was released to instant acclaim. Ice wines have become a regular feature at several wineries, as Stratan says, 'Unlike Germany, Moldova gets -15°C frosts every winter!' Arcadie

Foșnea at Château Vartely has put his German training to effective use, also releasing stunning Riesling ice wine from the 2005 vintage onwards. Chardonnay, Traminer and Muscat can also make appealing, rich sweet wines in Moldova, indeed Fautor produces a lovely ice wine from a blend of Traminer and Muscat.

More unusual and perhaps unique is Moldova's tradition of sweet reds. Traditionally called cagor, kagor or even cahor, it should now be called Pastoral. This style originated from the tradition of the Russian Orthodox Church which shipped wine from Cahors in France and sweetened it with honey, especially for christenings. During the Napoleonic wars, French wine couldn't be imported, so a similar style of sweet red was developed locally. The wine is usually made by thermo-vinification, heating the must to around 70°C, then fortifying once the fermentation has reached just a few per cent alcohol. It usually has 16 per cent alcohol and 160 grammes per litre of residual sugar. It's a product that Moldovans are very proud of, though really only of local curiosity.

MOLDOVAN FOOD

When it comes to food, there are a lot of shared influences between Moldova and Romania, though Moldova has also been influenced by its Russian history. Meals always start with a salad with whatever is in season – cabbage and carrots in the winter or leaves, cucumbers and tasty tomatoes with white-brined cheese called *brânza*. Soup (*ciorbă* or *borș*, from the fermented bran sometimes used as the souring ingredient) is usually next and chicken *zeamă* is particularly popular – a hot and sour chicken noodle soup. *Borscht* and other vegetable soups are also served. Main courses tend to be meaty – pork, lamb and beef based – such as grilled meatballs called *parjoale* and *chiftele*, while the most famous dish is a pork stew called *tochitură* or *tocăniță* served with an egg and *mămăligă* (see below). *Sarmale* are stuffed leaves, usually cabbage, filled with rice, vegetables and sometimes meat, served with sour cream. Despite the good range of vegetables grown (peppers, aubergines, courgettes and beans), vegetarians get short shrift apart from during Lent when a lot of people still observe a fasting menu without meat (so beans, aubergines and mushrooms appear). Fish is relatively rare – and due to Moldova's lack of coastline is usually river or lake fish when it's on offer. The main staple is *mămăligă* (a cornmeal mush like polenta) often served with grated brânza cheese, sour cream and garlic sauce. It has a special status in Moldovan culture because it wasn't a tribute crop in the Ottoman era, so people survived on it. *Mămăligă* is typically cut with a thread and always in a cross first. *Plăcintă* is a kind of national dish, served to accompany wine tastings or early on in a meal. A thin, layered dough like filo (not too far from Bulgaria's *banitsa* in style, though not usually rolled up here), is stuffed with local cheese, potatoes, pumpkin or with walnuts and sour cherries. Pudding may include smoked plums stuffed with walnuts, or for a special occasion a cake called *Baba Neagră* which takes about six hours to cook slowly in the oven.

Breakfast is typically bread and cheese with cold meats, or eggs. Tomatoes and cucumber will be on offer too. Walnuts and honey are a regular feature – many of Moldova's roads are lined with walnut trees and these provide essential nutrients (especially iodine) that are missing from the diet of this landlocked country with its hard water. Fruit like apricots, plums and sour cherries are popular – fresh or dried.

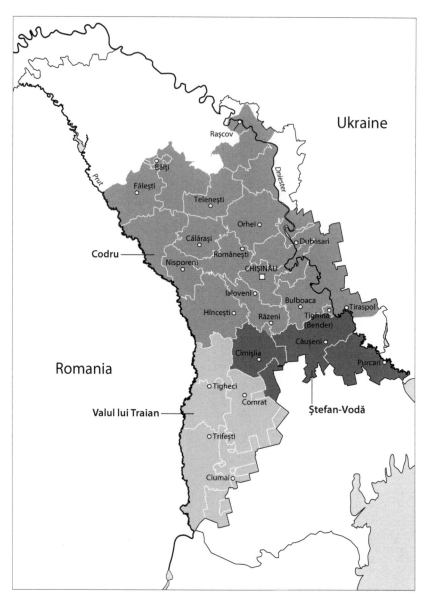

The PGIs of Moldova (information courtesy of ONVV)

19

MOLDOVAN REGIONS

Moldovans like to describe their country as roughly the shape of a bunch of grapes dropped into the map (possibly after sampling some of their local brew). It lies between latitudes 46 and 48°N, on the same latitude as Bordeaux, although it is climatically closer to Burgundy as it is much more continental. It's a landlocked nation with Romania to the west, with the two countries separated by the River Prut along the whole boundary. Ukraine borders the country to the north, east and south. The Dniester runs along part of this border and between Moldova and the self-declared breakaway Republic of Transnistria. There is a small 'coastline' of a few dozen metres where the country's southern tip meets the Danube to give it access to the Black Sea. The total area of the country is 33,670 square kilometres. It is a landscape of gentle rolling hills, with its highest point reaching only 430 metres and an average altitude of 147 metres.

Annual sunshine hours range from 2,100 to 2,500 and annual rainfall is from 350 to 600 millimetres per year, most of which falls during the summer months. Some years, particularly in the south, there is apparently insufficient rainfall for successful grape growing but in spite of lack of irrigation, producers report that the grape harvest does not usually suffer (perhaps due to deep-rooting). The period above freezing ranges from 260 days in the north to 290 days in the south. The sum of active temperatures above 10°C ranges from 3,000 to 3,450°C. Peak summer temperatures may reach over 40°C while lowest winter temperatures can fall to -30°C. This puts Moldova in a frost risk area, mainly during the winter, though there is also a chance of early autumn and late spring frosts.

Moldova has a very high proportion of rich chernozem topsoils (a type of fertile black soil containing a high proportion of humus and carbonates) – perhaps not the first choice for high-quality viticulture, but fortunately the relatively dry climate forces the vines to root down into the limestone bedrock, enabling vines to survive drought where other crops would fail, and improving quality potential. As Jon Worontschak (an international winemaking consultant who has worked in Moldova) says, 'The soils are excellent, with some of the best natural potential I've come across.' Most of the vineyards are on gently sloping sites, and forested hilltops give protection from high winds. Dionisio Vizzon (former Italian viticulture consultant to Albastrele) points out that, 'This is one of the best places in the world to grow grapes – sun and temperature are sufficient, the soils are deep, and they store water well.'

Moldova has three PGIs for wine, accepted by the EU in 2013. The area registered for PGI wine production has increased significantly since then and by the end of 2017 accounted for 8,600 hectares with 64 grape producers and winemakers that had produced PGI wines. Plans are being developed for PDO wines in due course.

CENTRAL (CODRU) REGION

This is the central region of Moldova, bordered by Leova, Cimişlia and Tighina and was extended in 2016 to include the area around Bălți and vineyards in Transnistria. It is the area believed to have the largest overall vineyard area and 2,258 hectares had been declared for PGI wines by 2017. The climate is eastern continental with 2,100–2,200 sunshine hours per annum. Annual rainfall is 450–550 millimetres and winters are long, but not usually extreme, while summers and autumns are warm. Altitude above sea level is 100–150 metres, 79 per cent of the zone is on slopes and soils are typically grey forest soils and chernozems. There are lots of forested hills that provide favourable microclimates and protection from frost for vine-growing. The region is noted for white grapes, but red varieties can also be grown in warmer microclimates.

SOUTHEASTERN (ȘTEFAN VODĂ) REGION

This region in the south-east of the country is bordered by the Dniester. There were 1,107 hectares declared for PGI wines by the end of 2017. The climate is moderate continental, influenced by the Black Sea, and enjoys 2,200–2,300 sunshine hours per annum. Annual rainfall is 450–550 millimetres and average altitude is 120 metres, and the zone has 73 per cent slopes. Typical soils are podzolized and carbonated chernozems with clay in some areas. The region is particularly noted for red grapes.

SOUTHERN (VALUL LUI TRAIAN) REGION

This southern part of Moldova is the warmest and driest region with 3,070 hectares producing PGI wines by the end of 2017. The climate here is Mediterranean, with warm, dry summers, short, mild winters and 2,500 sunshine hours per year. Annual rainfall is 350–500 millimetres and altitude ranges from 5–310 metres and averages 110 metres. Vineyards are on the slopes of the Dniester and Prut river valleys. Soils are leached and carbonated chernozems, with some areas of sandy and clay soils. The region is noted for red grapes, full-bodied whites and sweet red wines.

HARVEST TIME

In the Orthodox Church that most Moldovans recognize, the transfiguration of Christ is celebrated on 19 August. Grapes are brought to church for blessing and for permission to pick and eat them. The belief is that anyone who eats grapes before this time 'curses their guts'.

20

MOLDOVAN PRODUCER PROFILES

There were 181 registered wine producers in 2017 though only 106 declared a harvest, suggesting that many are not operating commercially, and some are in the business of bulk wine only. It continues to be a Moldovan mystery how wineries that are technically bankrupt keep operating, no one can explain it. But it is a dynamic scene with the appearance of several new wineries, especially since the change in the wine law in 2013. At the same time some of the former state dinosaurs are learning to do better, in some cases helped by the involvement of a second generation. This is a personal selection of wineries who have an international presence for bottled wines, or who have impressed for quality with at least part of their portfolio, or might be a significant tourist destination, given that wine and tourism are so closely interlinked in this country.

STATE-OWNED COMPANIES

Cricova

Strada Petru Ungureanu 1, Cricova 2084, Moldova
Tel.: +373 22 604 035
www.cricova.md

One of Moldova's famous grand-scale cellars, just 15 kilometres from the capital, this is a hugely popular tourist destination. This underground maze was first dug out in the fifteenth century when limestone was mined to build Chişinău. It was turned into a wine-ageing cellar in 1952 and today there are around 120 kilometres of accessible tunnels (and still growing). It is still state-owned and has been designated by law to be a site of national cultural heritage. Famously Hermann Goering's wine collection ended up here. The story is that Soviet soldiers who found his collection of art and wine (which included several famous châteaux) divided it into three parts and sent them to Moscow, Georgia and Moldova. A number of world leaders and famous figures have wine collections here including Vladimir Putin (who celebrated his fiftieth birthday at Cricova) and Angela Merkel.

Part of the Cricova wine collection

Cosmonaut Yuri Gagarin famously spent two days lost in the cellars in 1966, which earlier were also used to hide Jews during the Second World War. Cricova's so-called 'underground wine city' has streets named after grapes and wines. It is about 100 metres deep and stays at a cool 14–16°C so is perfect for ageing sparkling wines, first made here in 1957. It produces up to 10 million bottles per year 60 per cent of which is sparkling wine. This includes half a million bottles of 'traditional method' wine, all hand-riddled by a team of six women who pass on their roles through the family. At one time, every third bottle of bubbly sold in the USSR came from Moldova and much of that would have come from Cricova. Tank-fermented Crisecco is light, fresh and easy to drink – clearly going after consumers who enjoy a certain famous Italian product. Pinot Noir Extra Brut Blanc de Noirs and Grand Vintage have impressed and dry wines such as the legendary Codru have improved recently while the Oraşul Subteran range features local grapes. Cricova has over 600 hectares of its own vineyards and over the last decade has planted around 300 hectares of young virus-free vines including local grape varieties.

Mileştii Mici Combinatul de Vinuri de Calitate

Mileştii Mici, Ialoveni, Republica Moldova, MD-6819
Tel.: +373 22 382 336
www.milestii-mici.md

Mileştii Mici was founded 1969, in a former limestone mine just 10 kilometres from Chişinău. Of the roughly 200 kilometres of tunnels, 55 are used for wine ageing. It's naturally cool as the cellars are around 30–85 metres deep, and like Cricova the tunnels are named after grapes and wines. Lining the tunnels are hundreds of huge barrels, which were assembled here in the 1970s and 1980s with wood from Russia and Ukraine, and are still used for ageing wine. In 2007, Mileştii Mici was recognized by Guinness World Records for the largest wine collection in the world, with over 1.5 million bottles. Best are the sweet collection wines, as some are amazingly long-lived.

LARGE AND MID-SIZED PRODUCERS

Asconi Winery

Ştefan cel Mare 1, Puhoi village
Tel.: +373 79 988 133
www.asconi.md

This has been a family-owned project since 1994. As with all the state wineries, it was sold without vineyards, so the family realized they needed to do something about this. Beginning in 2005 it took around six years to put together the first 350 hectares, and today they have increased this to 550 hectares, all no further than 10 kilometres from the winery. To begin with, their focus was on making good examples of international varieties, but recently local grape varieties such as Saperavi, Fetească Neagră and Fetească Albă have been added to the range. Asconi was the first winery in Moldova to use harvesting machines at night, particularly for Sauvignon Blanc, to make sure that the grapes are as fresh as possible (during the day it can be over 30°C at harvest time but drops to 16–18°C overnight). They have also invested €7 million on a state-of-the-art winery and have built a traditional restaurant complex and some small guesthouses.

Andrei Sîrbu (whose family owns the winery) explains that these have been constructed with local materials by their own carpenter. He adds, 'My father was a poor boy from the village and he made good during privatization. He used to sell bulk wine to Russia, and the state was keen to sell assets for pennies just to get rid of them.' Business had been very good in Russia until the embargo in 2006, which prompted Asconi to switch direction to better quality and higher-priced wines. They took the brave step of abandoning the Russian market completely after 2006. Today export is 99 per cent of their 3 million bottles a year business. Around one third goes to the USA, China and Japan, another third to the EU and they also have good business in Africa where there's still a real sweet tooth for dessert wines. The Exceptional range whites are fresh and crisp, while the premium Sol Negru (literally black soil) line offers a bit more complexity, often with generous oak flavours.

Castel Mimi

Bulboaca village, Anenii Noi
Tel.: +373 26 547 248
www.castelmimi.md

It's impossible not to be impressed by the huge undertaking of renovating the mansion and winery at Bulboaca. It was originally founded in 1893 by the last governor of Bessarabia, Constantin Mimi. He spent two years in Montpellier, France, learning winemaking and brought back revolutionary ideas such as gravity flow and reinforced concrete as well as grapes like Pinot Gris, Pinot Noir, Riesling, Traminer and most famously Aligoté. Castel Mimi was also one of the first to make blends. During the Soviet era, this site became Agrovin Bulboaca and at its peak was the biggest wine factory in the whole of the USSR. Its grand courtyard was filled with ranks of horizontal tanks (1964 picture below), producing 2 million bottles every month and the same volume again in bulk wine. Today Castel Mimi is a stunning place offering wine tours, a tasting room and a stylish restaurant serving modern interpretations of traditional Moldovan food. Wines, overseen by Oleg Boboc (also of Vinăria Nobilă), include good fresh whites and rosé, and a stylish red blend called Roşu de Bulboaca made from Cabernet Sauvignon, Merlot and Malbec.

In 1964 Agrovin Bulboaca was the largest winery in the whole Soviet Union

RESTORATION OF AN ICON

General manager Cristina Frolov has a deep-rooted family connection at Castel Mimi. Her family comes from the village of Bulboaca and her grandparents worked as agricultural labourers for the winery. She explains: 'My grandma, she was one of the best workers as she always produced the maximum yield per day. The second day after she gave birth to my father, by then aged 44, she wrapped him in a cloth sling, and took him to "the hills" to do field work.' Her father also started here as a porter when he was still at school, working his way round most of the jobs at the winery, before leaving to study law. 'He was 33 when, after a brilliant career in law, he came back to his village to buy the winery from the old owners. That was in 1998. I was 11 years old.' Cristina explains that they began the restoration project in 2010, using photos from the 1930s to guide them, 'It was one afternoon, when my father asked for my advice (what advice can you ask from a 24-year-old new graduate with just 1 year of experience?) about whether we should take the old Soviet plaster off the castle. So we did and from that moment on we had no way back.'

Cristina has no regrets, though admits the project was very demanding and tough on the whole family: 'Now when I look back I am not sure I could go through that process again.' She explains her view that projects like this would normally be undertaken by the state, or a huge corporation, not just a Moldovan family from an average village. 'We came here not really prepared for the burden and it was a huge war that we, for a few times, almost lost.' But the final result is something truly stunning and a must-see for anyone visiting the country.

Château Vartely

170/B Eliberarii str., Orhei
Tel.: +373 22 829 891
www.vartely.md

Château Vartely is just 50 kilometres to the north of the capital Chișinău. It was one of the first of the new wave of smaller private wineries, pioneering high-quality dry wines in 2004, the year of their first proper harvest. The winery had been bought and renovated by Nicolai Ciornii, previously vice president of Lukoil and owner of a Chișinău football club as well. Vineyards came soon after and the winery now owns 260 hectares in both Codru in the centre of the country and Valul lui Traian to the south-west. The long-standing winemaker Arcadie Foșnea trained in Germany, which shows in the refreshing crispness of his white wines. The historic site of Old Orhei ('place of the fortress' or *vár hel* in Hungarian) is nearby, so it was logical to open a restaurant and hotel complex, not least to help educate Moldovans about food and wine culture.

Today more than 8 per cent of their sales are in Moldova, and their focus is on fresher, younger wine styles, not heavily oaked, with local grapes always a strong feature. Fetească Regală and Cabernet Sauvignon are reliable, Individo is a recent range of intriguing blends and Chardonnay is well done in the serious barrel-fermented Taraboste and as a luscious sweet botrytis version. Lovely ice wines from Riesling and Muscat Ottonel are also produced, as winters are reliably chilly enough to freeze the grapes most years.

Doina Vin

s. Razeni, r-ul Ialoveni
Tel.: +373 22 228 133
www.doinavin.md

The history of this cellar goes back to 1875 when a Polish *boyar* first made wine here. His family left when the Soviets came, and everything was burnt down, though the original brick cellar survived. Back in 2006, it was a disheartening place to visit, but today this is a winery undergoing transformation. By 2002, when the Bors family took over, the winery had been left to decay for a decade. Feodosie Bors had studied oenology and worked for the national wine institute in the previous era but in 1993 he founded his first winery (though on a different site). Back then property had been cheap to buy, and he says it was possible to make a 20–30 per cent profit margin on volume wines for Russia. He named his winery after his daughter Doina. Luckily the 2006 ban did not hurt them as much as some, because they were only sending 60 per cent of their wine to Russia, while the rest went to Germany.

Today the winery is reinventing itself with the help of support from USAID, and by the return of the dynamic Doina Bors herself, who has come back to work in the family firm after 12 years studying and working in Germany and Austria. One of her ideas has been to create a range especially for young people, with easy-to-understand wine styles and bright, colourful labels in a range called 6N. There is also a more serious Merlot called Artitude, with a different local painting on the label each year. The winery's top wine is named Black Pearl for its rarity and needs tucking away for a few years. The winery also has a collection of fascinating Auriu sweet wines made from Traminer, which date back to 1963.

Fautor

s. Tigheci, r-ul Leova
Tel.: +373 22 233 393
www.fautor.wine

Fautor is growing in self-confidence and in quality every year. In 1997, the Diaconu-Croitoru family bought the winery, which had been a small collective farm in the Soviet era. Executive Director Tatiana Croitoru was previously a winemaker in the state system and keen to do her own wine. The family started investing in vineyards in 2003, gradually increasing to today's 350 hectares, close to the winery. Their first market release was only in 2010 but how they have continued to improve since. Ruxanda Lipcan (Tatiana's daughter) who runs the sales and marketing team says, 'Our ambition is simple, we want to be one of the best wineries in Moldova.' Mother and daughter clearly make a wonderful team, though they are both quiet and understated, and let their wine speak for themselves. A modern winery that is beautifully clean allows the fruit from the Tigheci hills to shine. The vineyards here are high for Moldova, at 310 metres, and here they have identified the best parcels of land for their top wines. They have a clever deal with the local prison, where they provide work opportunities for day-release prisoners – and get a reliable source of labour too. Their most unusual wine is a very good Albarino. 'My husband went on holiday to Spain and liked it, so we decide to experiment,' Ruxanda explained. There's also a layered and complex barrel-fermented Sauvignon Blanc called Fumé Blanc and attractive Chardonnay and Pinot Gris. The 310* range is all blends, the name referring to the altitude of their vineyards, and the Negre red is excellent, a blend of Fetească Neagră with 40 per cent Rară Neagră.

Gitana Winery

Vinăria Țiganca SRL, rn. Cantemir s.Plopi
Tel.: +373 022 243 012
www.gitana.md

In 1999, Svetlana and Petru Dulgher bought the Țiganca wine factory, where Svetlana had worked as winemaker. It was in a deplorable state, but Svetlana knew it had one huge asset – its underground cellars with constant temperatures in both summer and winter. Petru had been in commerce, trading wine from the winery where his wife worked. He was doing good business in Russia which enabled the couple to take out bank loans to buy the winery, making this the first fully private winery in Moldova. Vineyards came later, between 2001 and 2005, and gathering 360 hectares in small parcels was very difficult, though Petru was always careful to choose plots that were not too vigorous. Today, the couple's two daughters Lilia and Iuliana are also closely involved in the business. Iuliana is multi-talented, having studied viticulture, oenology and marketing in France, Spain and Italy. 'Colleagues asked to taste our wine, but it was impossible as it was all sold in bulk, so it was my challenge to start to bottle,' she says. Their Italian consultant Nicola Ricci first came in 2013. He says, 'I was astonished by the potential quality and tasted some incredible wines but only here and there. I saw soils like those in France and Italy just after the Second World War with ploughed-in grass, animal manure and no synthetic fertilisers.'

This is an area where the climate is dry but doesn't get too hot, there's no rain in summer but the soil holds enough water, so there is little disease pressure and minimal spraying. There's is a good day–night temperature difference as the altitude is around 360–380 metres, which is really high for Moldova. There's very little need to treat the vineyards for disease. Fermentation is all done in open wooden vats with hand punching-down. Some of the winery's wooden casks date back to 1953 and Nicola admits that it took two years to clean them up properly, 'I thought for 18 months it will be better to chop them all up, but I wanted to see what they would do.'

Petru still works in the business and Iuliana explains that his main job is to manage the vineyards and the workers, though she says, 'He gets up angry from August to November calling 200 people, who may or may not turn up, and managing their payments. We thought about a harvesting machine, but we feel that we have a moral duty because there is such high unemployment in the region. Also, if we use hand labour we can focus on specific plots.' Each wine in the excellent Autograf range is signed by a member of the family. There's also a very good Riesling, food friendly Surori (sisters) rosé and super-concentrated rich Lupi red. La Petite Sophie is a lovely white blend, while spicy Saperavi, fermented in clay amphorae, is an exciting revelation and highlights the potential of this grape in Moldova.

KVINT (Tiraspol Winery & Distillery)

38 Lenin Street, Tiraspol, MD-3300, Pridnestrovie,
Tel.: +373 53 396 170
www.kvint.md

This is the only significant wine producer to the east of the River Dniester. The name KVINT comes from the Russian words for 'Divins, wines and beverages of Tiraspol'. It dates back to 1897, when the first distillery was built here, originally making vodka from grapes, but in 1938 it started to age these grape spirits to make brandy. It has 2,000 hectares, 30 grape varieties and 11 million litres of grape spirit in the cellars, ranging in age from 1 to 60 years. Wines have recently been gaining more attention and are improving as a result. The Cabernet Sauvignon–Merlot red looks promising as does intriguing Viorica ice wine.

Purcari Wine Group

Purcari village, Ștefan Vodă
Tel.: +373 22 294 696
www.purcari.md

There are four producers in the Purcari wine group (which listed on the Romanian stock exchange in January 2018) including Bostavan, Vinaria Purcari and Crama Ceptura in Romania as well as spirits producer Bardar. Winemaker Victor Bostan heads the group and is also a shareholder. The Purcari winery is the crown jewel of the group with its nineteenth-century château in the Ștefan Vodă region. It dates to 1827, when it received a special decree from Tsar Nicholas I as the first specialist winery in Bessarabia. Its wines were shipped all over the world and the winery is particularly proud that Queen Victoria was one of its customers. The royal connection continued in the 1980s when Negru de Purcari was the only wine with an English language label exported from the Soviet Union for Queen Elizabeth II.

Historic Purcari labels, including the English label for the British royal family

There's not too much information about what was grown in the nineteenth century as Bostan explains, 'There are no archives in Moldova, they all got taken to Odessa or Moscow in Soviet times, but folk knowledge says that Cabernet and Merlot were grown here.' Production of the famous Negru and Roşu de Purcari was restarted in the 1950s on Soviet orders, when Malbec was also introduced. In the new era, there was a thirteen-year gap in production, until in 2003 the winery had a fresh start under its current owners. They have worked hard to improve their quality and 260 hectares of vines have been replanted. It's gone from using second-hand barrels and slightly old-fashioned winemaking to one of the most state-of-the-art wineries in the country and is supported by Italian consultancy company Giotto. The latest launch is a new bottle-fermented sparkling range while Negru de Purcari (with its iconic blend of Cabernet Sauvignon, Saperavi and Rară Neagră) continues to be a flagship for the country. A very good white sister blend called Alb de Purcari was launched in 2010. The year 2011 saw the first vintage of 'bottled politics' in their Freedom Blend – to celebrate 20 years of freedom from the Soviet Union, and to symbolize three countries that have all had fights with Russia. It includes Saperavi, a Georgian grape, Bastardo from Ukraine and Rară Neagră from Moldova. Varietal wines, Vinohora blends with local grapes (especially Rară Neagră/Malbec) and rosé are also very good.

Sister company Bostavan is a 20,000-tonne winery totally rebuilt in 2002, when it was bought by Victor Bostan. It has around 800 hectares in production with 500 hectares of Cabernet, Merlot, Pinot Noir and Saperavi in Etulia in the south and a smaller vineyard at Oneşti in the centre of the country. The brand portfolio now includes Dor for well-made, commercial, dual-variety blends and Dor Reserve for single varieties, especially Merlot.

Radacini winery (Cimislia, Albastrele, Chi)

3, Burebista Str, MD 4101, Cimislia
Tel.: +373 24 122 184
www.radacini.md

This is a group of wineries under a holding company, with vineyards in several Moldovan regions. It sells wines under a number of brands including Chi, Radacini and Albastrele. Well-made and good varietal expression is the hallmark with excellent bottle-fermented sparkling Cuvée Aleksandr and very good Pinot Grigio and Sauvignon Blanc under the Albastrele, Taking Root and Chi labels. There's also good Fiori Fetească Neagră from Radacini. Albastrele in particular has a long-standing partnership with the UK's Direct Wines/Laithwaites.

ADVENTURES IN MOLDOVA

Tony Laithwaite, whose company started importing Moldovan wines in the early 2000s, tells the story of one of his early trips to Moldova:

I rented us a plane to get to Moldova … not something I've done before, but then you try getting to Moldova avoiding airlines that fly converted bombers and like to crash. Most people don't even know where Moldova is … squashed between Romania and Ukraine, it's on the western edge of the Russian Steppes and just about the poorest country in Europe. Its entire industrial economy seems to have collapsed, ruined factories are strewn everywhere. As we circle to land at Chişinău, the capital, it looks like the bomb has fallen here.

Mind you the air is crystal clear, there is no pollution. The roads are empty too, but there is lots of lovely dark, black, rich-looking soil and agriculture seems to be doing well … in a pre-war sort of way. Geese flock everywhere, and the horse seems to be the main rural form of transport. Moldova is a northerly wine region … like Burgundy, Alsace, Germany and the Tokaj region of Hungary; it has the potential, and indeed the tradition, of making wine of the very highest and most refined flavour. All it needed was a brand-new, well-designed, well-run winery and some top winemaking talent. All of which it now has. Jean Marc [Laithwaites' own winemaker] spent two days combing through hundreds of vats and cherry-picking the best. My role was to distract Moldovan attention from this and attend banquets and press conferences, make speeches and drink toasts.

Sălcuța Winery

r-ul Causeni, s. Sălcuța, str. Basarabia, 1
Tel.: +373 22 245 252
www.salcutawine.md

Sălcuța village has a long connection with wine, first mentioned in 1706 as being in the heart of a valley known for wine. This winery site was originally developed in 1950, then modernized in 1970. In 1995 the current owners, the Pislaru family, got involved in a joint Belgian–Moldovan project. Eugen Pislaru graduated in agriculture in 1974 and growing things is at the root of what he does. Sălcuța was one of the first, certainly among the large wineries, to understand the need for their own vines and control over the full production cycle, even down to setting up their own nursery. Now they own 500 hectares, but also buy grapes under contract. There's no doubt this is a huge scale winery and twelve years ago, it was not exactly paying much attention to winemaking quality, because it didn't have to. Today everything has been renovated and modernized with substantial investments in winemaking, and wines are very much improved as a result. Bulk wine is still important and accounts for 95 per cent of the business. The latest wines are clean, correct and commercial, based on tank samples tasted in 2018.

Vinaria din Vale

Basarabia street 8, Cantemir city,
Tel.: + 373 68 464 647
www.vinaria.md

Co-owner Elena Davidescu says:

> Everything started with Bucur, my great-grandfather, who owned around 18 hectares of vines in 1920 in Chioselia Mare in south Moldova. Then my grandfather, Ilie, kept a few vines in his courtyard, though everything was nationalized during his lifetime. After the collapse of the Soviet Union, Ilie and my father Vladimir thought about working the vineyards. They started small at first, buying tractors and some small parcels in their own village, then many local people were willing to make cooperation agreements, so they would rent the land and grow grapes. In the early 2000s,

they acquired their first winery. It was an extremely old and rusty one from the USSR. And it wasn't easy to start. Like so many wineries they were selling to eastern markets and had to rebuild and invest in modern equipment.

Today, the company is still very much a family business with four members already involved and hoping their younger siblings will join too. It owns over 1,000 hectares so bulk and volume products remain important. But since 2010, and after Elena and her brother Andrian spent time studying in London, they realized that bottled wines needed to become more of a focus, so in recent years have been working on selecting fruit from the best locations and bottling them, with a stork on the label. This is inspired by the legend of the storks who saved soldiers trapped in the Slobozia Fortress during battles between Ştefan Cel Mare and the Ottoman Turks. Local grapes especially Fetească Neagră will continue to be a focus and they want to explore organic production, 'Moldova is a country where there is an average 250–300 millimetres rain per year in the south and low disease pressure. This makes us think that our terroir can be very beneficial for organic wines.' They also hope to help put their region on the tourist map as their Slobozia Mare site is close to Romania and is famous for Lake Beleu, with its rich birdlife and the largest populations of pelicans and storks in the country.

Vinuri de Comrat (Plai)

R. Moldova, or. Comrat, srt. Vinzavodscaia 1
Tel.: +373 29 822 344
www.vinuridecomrat.md

Comrat is the de facto capital of the Gagauzia region in south-west Moldova. The town name apparently means 'black horse' in the Gagauz language – after the favourite horse of a Turkish pasha who loved riding here. There was a factory here as early as 1897, destroyed in a peasants' revolt in 1917, though the cellar survived, and in 1920 a school of winemaking was set up in the courtyard. By the 1950s this had become a major industrial wine processing plant, and in 1995 its new private era began. It's still equipped with 'Soviet reactor' tanks for red winemaking though some modern equipment has been acquired. Its signature Plai label is better than expected – lower yields from selected plots result in straightforward, fruity red wines, best drunk young.

SMALL PRODUCERS

Atú

bd. Dacia 58, Chișinău,
Tel.: +373 69 222 237
www.atu.wine

Proudly proclaimed as Moldova's first urban winery, its location on the outskirts of the capital should be useful for attracting visitors when it is finished. From the outside, it is still a concrete communist warehouse, though the owners have plans for landscaping and a terrace. The winery itself was started in 2016 by a young couple, Victor and Vlada Vutcarau. Victor explains, 'Our main family business is the biggest grapevine nursery in Moldova, producing around three million plants a year. My idea was to close the cycle.' He now has 20 hectares of vines of his own and the winery processes just 50 tonnes of grapes. Costia Stratan (of Equinox) helps with the winemaking, and bottling is done at Et Cetera (it's encouraging to see several of the small wineries helping each other out). There's a clean, crisp Sauvignon Blanc–Chardonnay blend, promising young versions of Fetească Albă and Chardonnay and an exotic, scented dry Muscat Ottonel, as well as a very good red blend of Cabernet Sauvignon and Merlot called Kara Gani.

Carpe Diem

136, Columna Street, MD2004, Chișinău
Tel.: +373 79 578 818
www.carpediem.md

'Carpe Diem is my personal motto,' explains Ion Luca. 'There are four generations of my family involved in wine, including my father and brother, who work at Cricova. When I started, if you wanted to do wine you had to choose a state company, so I studied economics instead. My dream was always to do wine, but differently, to create my own wines and bring my family into these dreams.' For Ion 4 January 2018 is a significant date as that's when he finally got permission for construction to begin on his own winery in his home village of Cricova, where his recently retired father will also be able to help out. So far, he has been renting winery space for his own tanks and equipment at Nisporeni (where he also worked on the Crescendo wine project, which is now finished). It was clear to Ion from the start that he wanted to work with native grape varieties and he has planted five of them. He explains that, 'One of the problems for the small guys is that it's easy to buy equipment and use immediately, but vineyards take years for a crop to be produced, never mind reaching profitability.' Ion also works with some farmers and has found this a very successful cooperation for him and a workable solution for them. For certain grapes like Rară Neagră, he pays double the market price, but imposes strict demands such as cutting off 50 per cent of the crop to concentrate the fruit. Ion has also opened his own wine shop and wine bar in Chișinău. For him, the local market is important, now taking around 30 per cent of his volume. He says, 'You have to be strong in your own country. I am also happy to represent the other small producers too and help educate the local market.' Exports remain essential though, because the domestic market is small. Carpe Diem's eye-catching labels all have photos of people on them and Ion's idea is to show people screaming with joy, so it's important to him that the faces are happy. There are fine attractive versions of Fetească Albă and Fetească Regală, and in 2016 he was inspired to blend the two in his top-selling Femme Fatale. There's also a light, grapey Viorica and an intriguing blend of Pinot Noir and Rară Neagră, named 19/11 for his twins' birthday. His latest Bad Boys blend of Fetească Neagră and Saperavi is a cracking wine with beautiful fruit, polished oak and lovely personality.

Equinox

r-l Ştefan Vodă, s. Olanești
Tel.: +373 69 500 505
www.equinox.md

Constantin Stratan, or Costia, is much admired in Moldova as one of the pioneers of the new era. Ion Luca (head of the small winemakers' association) says, 'He was the bravest in making that first step to be a small producer. He's been a mentor and an example for all of us.' After studying oenology in Chișinău, Costia joined the team at the Hugh Ryman–Southcorp wine project in Moldova in 1994, which also gave him the chance to travel to Spain and France. Vintages in California and New Zealand followed and when he came back to Moldova, he took a role at Dionysos-Mereni. Here he pioneered premium dry wines with the Carlevana range, including the first varietal Rară Neagră, the first Shiraz, then the first ice wine and first botrytis wines in Moldova. One night in 2002, he and his friend Oleg (of Vinăria Nobilă) were having a drink (or perhaps several, according to Oleg) and pondering the idea of making their own wine. The next day Costia and Oleg jumped into a car and headed off in search of vineyards. Costia started with 2 hectares in 2002, located close to Olaneşti village, on the hills overlooking the Dniester river valley, and has gradually increased to 5 hectares. He's been certified organic since 2013 and in his own words, 'The grapes are grown organically, because we strongly believe this method allows us to make wines that showcase the terroir.' He goes on, 'Back in 2002, the first parcel was planted with Cabernet Sauvignon. The next year we planted Shiraz, Malbec and Merlot. It was difficult to buy the indigenous varieties, so we had to take our own cuttings of Rară Neagră from old vineyards nearby and we planted this in 2005. Our first Equinox wines came out in 2006.' The lovely 5 Elemente red which is Costia's best-known wine came about by accident in 2010. The harvest was so bad there weren't enough grapes to do anything separately, so everything was blended. He says, 'There were only 4 barrels, but what a result, so I kept the concept.' White and orange versions of 5 Elemente followed. He also makes a 'natural' Chardonnay and Echinoctious is the winery's long-lived and impressive flagship.

Et Cetera
s. Crocmaz, Ştefan Vodă
Tel.: +373 79 445 010
www.etcetera.md

Et Cetera is the brainchild of two brothers, Alexandru and Igor Luchianov, who went to work in the USA in the 1990s in the casino business. One day they took some Moldovan wines to show to British friends and were shocked to be told, politely, that the wines weren't good. After that, they travelled and tasted as much as they could to learn about wine, 'We loved drinking wine, especially good wine in the USA and couldn't find anything drinkable in Moldova.' Alexandru wanted to study winemaking in the USA to add to his maths degree but circumstances meant he had to return home. After this adventurous life spent travelling (learning to scuba-dive and skydive along the way), he swapped one thrilling life for another adrenaline ride – the rollercoaster of starting a winery.

Et Cetera was registered in 2003 and Alexandru started buying land near their home village. This wasn't easy as he had to deal with 90 people and do many land swaps to end up with a vineyard in one place. 'We were naive when we started and planted a lot of Cabernet Sauvignon, though I think this is a mistake in Moldova,' Alexandru says, while admitting he prefers Merlot. His no-compromise attitude means he has just pulled out around 4 hectares of Cabernet, leaving them today with around 40 hectares of vines planted to 18 varieties. The first official vintage of the winery under its own name was 2009, and the winery is unusual in Moldova in pioneering the idea of building the cellar within the vineyards. The two brothers are very different; the quiet and studious Alexandru is happiest in the winery and vineyards, a self-taught winemaker good enough to consult on projects in Georgia and in the south of France. Igor is the outgoing, chatty one who deals with sales and customers. The rest of the family have been persuaded to join too, their mother and both wives help with the small family restaurant. At vintage time they also bring in friends to help. Igor explains, 'We do a Facebook announcement for the harvest and get hundreds of people, who bring tents with them. This way they feel part of the wine even if they only pick for a couple of hours.'

The brothers are big believers in blends and are particularly famous for their signature Cuvée Rouge, which includes Rară Neagră, Saperavi, Cabernet Sauvignon and Merlot. Recently there's been success with their excellent Serendipity blend of Fetească Neagră and Cabernet Sauvignon, and there is also a very classy Merlot. The Et Cetera philosophy is one of no half measures, and Alexandru says, 'My main objective is not to spoil what nature gives us. Clean, nice and fair priced is my aim, if I'm not happy it goes back to the tank for bag-in-box.'

Gogu
87 Pacii str., Causeni, MD4301
Tel.: +373 79 825 409

Ilie Gogu owns just 3 hectares of wine grapes, though he is planting more – little by little, every year. He comes from an agricultural family and his father was keen that he studied wine. His first job was working in one of the big wine companies. His decision to start making his own wine came after the Russian embargo in 2006. 'Basically, I didn't have a job – thank you Mr Putin,' he says. 'This started a new era and we [the small winemakers] are all results of this embargo.' So Ilie started to produce home-made wine, which he did until 2011 when small wineries could start to bottle and sell wine. USAID support allowed him to start investing in his own winery in 2014, in the south-east in the Ștefan Vodă region. And like many small owners, he has another part-time job, in his case distributing bottled water and soft drinks to help pay the bills. Ilie makes a bright, citrusy, green apple Riesling; an appealing grassy, crisp Sauvignon Blanc and a fresh, summery rosé. The best wine to date is Metafora, a blend of Cabernet Sauvignon, Merlot and Saperavi (from 30-year-old vines), with lovely fruit intensity and refinement. 'I think I'm growing up in the same sun as my grapes,' he says.

Mezalimpe

Răscăieţii Noi, MD4231, Ştefan Vodă raion
Tel.: +373 69 144 378

Owner Anatoly Yurko lived in Russia for 30 years as a qualified naval navigator. One day he persuaded his Russian wife to come back to Moldova because he wanted to set up a family business to leave to his children and couldn't do that in Russia. At first, all went well and in 2004, he invested all his savings into buying 10 hectares in the Purcari zone. He added a small winery two years later. But then came the disaster of the Russian ban; in 2007 he had to sell all his grapes because there was no market. Along the way, he praises Costia Stratan for helping him learn about winemaking. Since 2011, he has moved away from oak and added some whites to his selection. He also hopes to switch to organic production, though he admits this is hard when his neighbours use herbicides, though he has persuaded them not to spray if the wind is blowing towards his vineyard. Firm Cabernet Sauvignon and fresh Sauvignon Blanc best represent his style.

Minis Terrios

18 Calea Basarabiei str., Chişinău, MD2023
Tel.: +373 79 584 163
www.ministerrios.com

Dan Prisacaru is a first-generation winemaker who never expected to be making wines. A small sketch on the back of a napkin was transformed into a micro-winery in Chişinău in just four months in 2013. Dan had studied business administration in Lithuania and when he met his wife, Diana, they discovered a shared passion for wine. This took them both to Dijon in Burgundy to study for masters degrees in the wine business. Diana was offered an internship in Champagne but then they had a change of heart and decided to come back to Moldova.

Dan and Diana couldn't find a winemaker they trusted, so they decided to make the wine themselves. 'I want to concentrate on local varieties; my motto is I love to do things that seem impossible,' he explains. Dan admits he's found it difficult to find the right people to work with as, 'The old attitude about quantity is still common, it's hard to convince them to do green harvesting and I really have to pay.' Therefore, Dan planted 5 hectares of his own vines in 2015. The wines have been improving every year and the latest red blend Roşu Împărat (Red Emperor) is impressive. It's a blend of Fetească Neagră, Rară Neagră and a little bit of Cabernet Sauvignon. It came about by accident because the Rară Neagră in 2015 was fruity but had no colour or body, so Dan decided to make his first ever blend.

Vinăria Nobilă
Sociteni MD6827, Ialoveni raion
Tel.: +373 69 352 734

Oleg Boboc tells the story of his 'road-to-Damascus' evening. Over a few drinks with his friend Costia (of Equinox) after they had just returned from a winemaking trip to California, they hatched a plan to make their own Moldovan wine. Next day they set off by car to the south and after two weeks, Oleg managed to find 2 hectares of land to buy and plant. He started with international grapes and rents some tanks in a winery nearby. He believes in ageing his reds in oak, and his Fetească Neagră Reserva is remarkably classy and complex. He is also the winemaking consultant at Castel Mimi.

Pelican Negru
str. A. Mateevici, 76 Chişinău
Tel.: + 373 69 712 122
www.pelicannegruwines.com

The personal project of Gheorghe Arpentin (former MP and now head of ONVV), started in 1998. He was attracted to the region of Ştefan Vodă and the village of Olaneşti for its long history with wine, having come under the influence of the Swiss winemaking colony close by at Chabag, later Shabo. Seven hectares were planted in 2000 at a high density (for Moldova) of 5,000 vines per hectare. Land management is by organic and biodynamic methods, though not certified. The winery just produces three red blends (Soft Red, Velvet Red and Silk Red), using very natural approaches to winemaking and no oak – for Gheorghe this is not a Moldovan tradition.

NEW NAMES AND NEW APPROACHES

Wineries listed here are either very new to the market so haven't had time to establish a track record or larger ones who are making positive changes but are still inconsistent or in the early stages of a new phase.

Agrici

Vinaria "Mileștii Mici" SRL, MD-6819, v. Mileștii Mici, Ialoveni
Tel.: +373 26 868 535
www.agrici.md

This is the winemaking part of the large former state factory Mileștii Mici. The wine-ageing cellars remained under state control, while the production site was privatized in 1997. It's a family business run by Efim Agrici, helped by his wife, with daughter Ala as commercial director. Efim has worked here since finishing his studies in 1977 and had risen to head winemaker. The core business still produces around 3.5 million litres of wine a year, but in 2000 the family started planting their own vines nearby and now have 76 hectares. With support from USAID they have invested in modern, smaller-scale equipment and launched their family brand Agrici in 2017, only for hand-crafted wines from their own immaculately kept vines. There's an attractive Moscato and refreshing Cabernet Sauvignon Rosé and a decent red blend so far.

Migdal P (Château Cojusna)

1, Mecanizatorilor,str., Straseni, Cojusna
Tel.: +373 22 221 630
www.migdal.md

Rather prouder of its spirits and its dusty 'collection' bottles than its latest wines, this is a greenfield winery, one of only two in Moldova, founded in 1995 and with 220 hectares of its own vines nearby. Nonetheless, technical help from aid projects means it now makes competent modern, varietal wines under the Umbrella label. It also makes decent Pastoral.

Novak Winery

or. Comrat, str. Suvorov 58/1
Tel.: +373 68 888 814

A bright new face in Moldovan wine, Andrey Novak is an economist by training with a passion for wine. His father began with vineyards, and then found he had to buy a winery because he had grapes and needed somewhere to process them. Bulk wine is still important business and bottled wine didn't appear until August 2016 after some €4 million had been spent on renovating the winery and vineyards. Andrey's vision is to have a separate boutique winery, but for now he has a separate tank hall filled with small tanks in all shapes and sizes, to allow him to explore what he grows.

One variety that has put Novak on the map is the local Alb de Oniţcani – which was a bit of an accident. He explains, 'I ordered Sauvignon and Aligoté from France but didn't receive enough vines, so I went looking for something else to plant. I found this variety that was not very popular, so there were some vines available to buy.' At first Andrey admits he didn't know what to do with the grape so he did various trials. 'It ripens very late, even into November and it keeps high acidity,' he says. It has pretty aromas, with floral notes, and refreshing citrus and grapefruit flavours but a version made in oak did not work so well, 'possibly due to the very bad Moldovan barrels,' he reckons. There's also an exciting-looking Saperavi from 40-year-old-vines, though frustratingly, 'The vines belong to my father's friend, but the guy won't sell his plot.' More local grapes are on the plan for the future, and possibly a joint project with his sister, pairing Moldovan food and wine, as she runs a hotel in nearby Comrat.

Timbrus

Bravo Wine SRL, MD 4229, 134 Grigore Vieru Str, Purcari Village Ştefan Vodă
Tel.: +373 22 234 244
www.timbrus.com

Timbrus is an international project that aims to do things differently. It's based in the village of Purcari with 150 hectares planted from scratch to European standards in 2009, but no winery as yet. They own all the right equipment, currently in a rented corner at Sălcuţa winery. The idea here is only premium bottled wines and all with PGI status. The winemaker and co-owner Manuel Ortiz is Spanish and has selected his own strain of yeast in the vineyards. The project only launched its wines last year but already there is promising Chardonnay, Traminer, Viorica, Rară Neagră and Saperavi and some interesting red blends called Polifonia.

21

FINAL THOUGHTS

The last quarter of a century and more has taken me on a fascinating journey to explore the wines of Eastern Europe. There's been so much change since my first visits at the beginning of the new era. I feel privileged as I look back, though sometimes it didn't seem quite that way at the time. If I had chosen to write about anywhere more established I might have seen a little evolution, not the complete revolution I've seen in these three countries. And perhaps the most exciting of all are the personal stories of people with a real passion for both wine and their countries.

These are three very different but equally fascinating countries. All share an experience of communism, collectivization and a break in the link between understanding wine quality and connection with the land. And each is rediscovering wine in its own way. All three countries need to educate, build a culture for drinking proper wine and persuade people to switch from beer or spirits, or home-made wine. The three countries all need to work on creating a country image and reinventing themselves away from the legacy of the past. But I firmly believe all three countries really do have something exciting and genuine to offer. These are not upstarts but are rebuilding their wine histories for a new audience.

I hope I have, at least in part, answered the question of what happened to Bulgaria, and its fellow Eastern European countries. This is my outside perspective, as someone who's been tasting and travelling in Eastern Europe for nearly three decades now. In that time I've tasted amazing (and some horrible, though less of those now) things, have met wonderful people and continue to find it an endlessly fascinating place to keep exploring, to keep learning about and to keep sharing the stories that I have come across. It's been a fascinating rollercoaster of a career so far, but I suspect there is plenty more to discover and to keep me busy for years to come.

Caroline Gilby MW

APPENDIX I: BULGARIAN WINE LAWS AND STATISTICS

Controlled Origin (Controliran) wines 1978 act

Gamza from Suhindol

Gamza from Pavlikeni

Rosé of the South Coast

Misket of Sungurlare

Mavrud from Asenovgrad

Rose Valley Misket

Gamza from Novo Selo

Merlot from Sakar

The Treasure of Kralevo

Chardonnay of Novi Pazar

Cabernet Sauvignon from Svishtov

Brestnik Wine

Old red from Oryahovitsa

Cabernet Sauvignon from Lozitsa

Melnik wine from Harsovo

Chardonnay from Varna

Khan Krum Traminer

Merlot from Stambolovo

Aligoté of Lyaskovets

White wine from Rousse Beach

Cabernet Sauvignon from the Yantra Valley

Chardonnay from the South Coast

Bulgaria's PDOs

Sakar	Lom	Septemvri
Asenovgrad	Lyubimets	Slavyantsi
Bolyarovo	Lyaskovets	Sliven
Brestnik	Melnik	Stambolovo
Varna	Montana	Stara Zagora
Veliki Preslav	Nova Zagora	Sungurlare
Vidin	Novi Pazar	Suhindol
Vratsa	Novo Selo	Thracian Lowlands
Varbitsa	Oryahovitsa	Targovishte
Struma Valley	Pavlikeni	Khan Krum
Dragoevo	Pazardjik	Haskovo
Danube Plain	Perushtitsa	Hisarya
Evksinograd	Pleven	Harsovo
Ivaylovgrad	Plovdiv	Northern Black Sea
Karlovo	Pomorie	Shivachevo
Karnobat	Ruse	Shumen
Lovech	Sandanski	Southern Black Sea Coast
Lozitsa	Svishtov	Yambol

Vineyards in Bulgaria 2007–16

Year	Area planted with vines (hectares)	Vineyards outside agricultural holdings (hectares)	Total vineyard area (hectares)
2007	97,387	22,954	120,341
2008	88,570	22,246	110,816
2009	74,018	27,416	101,434
2010	56,968	25,707	82,675
2011	52,567	25,901	78,468
2012	62,701	14,640	77,341
2013	58,236	4,900	63,136
2014	52,587	10,298	62,885
2015	50,705	12,086	62,791
2016	50,892	12,024	62,916

Source: MAFF, Agro Statistics Department (Agrarian Report 2017)

Quantity of wine and grape must produced by commercial producers, vintage 2016

		Volume produced (hectolitres)
Wine with PDO	White	2,212
	Red and rosé	7,299
Wine with PGI	White	135,344
	Red and rosé	225,640
Other wines (inc. table wines)	White	470,729
	Red and rosé	366,562
	Must	37,207
Total wines	White	608,285
	Red and rosé	599,500

Source: Executive Agency on Vine and Wine in Agrarian Report 2017

Vineyards harvested by administrative region in 2016

Regions	Total area (hectares)	Vineyards harvested (hectares)	Percentage harvested (%)	Average yield (tonnes/ hectare)	Wine grapes harvested (tonnes)
North-west	4,827	3,196	66	4.79	15,037
North central	3,254	1,647	51	4.79	7,475
North-east	4,229	2,704	64	5.92	15,245
South-east	18,110	13,206	73	5.99	75,838
South-west	3,889	3,492	90	5.80	19,534
South central	16,583	12,306	74	5.91	66,418
Total	**50,892**	**36,551**	**72**	**5.77**	**199,547**

Source: MAFF, Agro Statistics Department (Agrarian Report 2017)

Bulgarian wine grape varieties by area

Executive Agency of Vine and Wine, EU returns from 2013.

Variety	Hectares	Share of plantings (%)
Merlot	10,550	17
Cabernet Sauvignon	10,191	17
Pamid	6,029	10
Rkatsiteli	5,409	9
Red Misket	4,388	7
Muscat Ottonel	4,136	7
Chardonnay	3,416	6
Dimiat	2,869	5
Mavrud	1,362	2
Syrah	966	2
Shiroka Melnishka Loza	957	2
Sauvignon Blanc	954	2
Gamza	855	1
Traminer	822	1
Ugni Blanc	699	1
Other red	3,901	6
Other white	2,795	5
Total	**60,299**	**100**

Bulgaria bottled wine

Leading export markets (MAFF Agrarian Report 2017)

	2015 (litres)	2016 (litres)
EU Total	**22,918,372**	**17,563,103**
Poland	14,878,353	11,730,809
United Kingdom	2,238,415	1,519,672
Czech Republic	1,231,745	1,053,519
Romania	1,321,540	760,338
Germany	524,956	476,360
Belgium	439,600	413,312
Slovakia	402,594	397,899
Lithuania	435,693	363,745
Sweden	222,805	322,558
Latvia	186,345	322,558

cont.	2015 (litres)	2016 (litres)
Other countries	**5,043,990**	**2,453,412**
Russia	3,606,984	1,045,311
China	315,715	450,068
USA	237,183	296,912
Japan	219,471	189,426
Belarus	149,805	58,302

Bulgaria bulk wine
Leading export markets (MAFF Agrarian Report 2017)

	2015 (litres)	2016 (litres)
EU Total	**9,791,352**	**8,050,284**
Poland	3,439,653	4,811,021
Sweden	2,180,859	2,181,048
Germany	476,590	340,422
Belgium	150,920	175,739
Third countries	**445,238**	**611,101**
Russia	299,397	369,538
Japan	96,000	122,000

APPENDIX II: ROMANIAN WINE LAWS AND STATISTICS

Wine production by category, 2017 Harvest (MADR)

Total production: 4,264,100 hectolitres
Noble varieties: 2,798,006 hectolitres
Interspecific hybrids: 1,465,500 hectolitres

Production by colour for noble varieties, 2017

Wine region	Total (hectolitres)	White wine (hectolitres)	Rosé wine (hectolitres)	Red wine (hectolitres)
Transylvanian Plateau	311,649	295,649	7,053	8,947
Moldovan Hills	1,230,967	968,834	24,384	237,749
Muntenia and Oltenia Hills	712,075	335,976	122,051	254,047
Banat Hills	259,168	127,163	32,096	99,908
Crişana and Maramureş Hills	109,908	66,257	2,219	41,432
The hills of Dobrogea	166,068	8,318	17,006	65,882
Danube Terraces	4,430	3,533	393	503
Sands and other favourable land in the south	4,311	2,574	274	1,462
TOTAL	**2,798,579**	**1,883,169**	**205,477**	**709,933**

Data source: Operational data MADR 2017

Wine production trends 2007–2017

Specification	2007	2008	2009	2010	2011	2012	2013	2014	2015	2016	2017
Total area cultivated with vines for wine (hectares)	180,400	181,540	181,790	181,560	181,000	183,160	181,310	179,930	178,290	178,570	177,150
Average purchase price grapes for wine (lei/kg)	0.89	1.28	1.08	1.54	1.36	1.94	1.07	1.64	1.35	1.35	1.40
Total wine production (hectolitres)	5,289,000	5,369,200	4,957,400	3,287,200	4,058,200	3,310,600	5,113,300	3,750,000	3,627,600	3,267,000	4,264,100
Total area subject to restructuring and replanting (hectares)	4,861.00	4,834.20	5,339.50	5,124.00	4,058.70	4,455.40	7,406.50	5,959.00	2,900.00	1,730.00	1,200.00

Wine production of noble varieties by quality category and wine-growing regions in 2017

Wine region	Total (hecto-litres)	Wines with DOC	Wines with PGI	Varietal wines	Table wines
Transylvanian Plateau	311,649	79,588	0	695	106,062
Moldovan Hills	1,230,967	272,086	118,225	45,742	794,913
Muntenia and Oltenia Hills	712,075	168,929	16,556	11,278	515,310
Banat Hills	259,168	89,015	495	95,745	73,913
Crişana and Maramureş Hills	109,908	44,730	35,364	2,528	27,286
The hills of Dobrogea	166,068	64,446	63,927	2,954	35,176
Danube Terraces	4,430	0	3,711	0	719
Sands and other favourable land in the south	4,311	0	0	0	4,311
TOTAL	**2,798,579**	**819,510**	**262,869**	**158,943**	**1,557,692**

Data source: Operational data MADR

Grape varieties planted by area July 2017 (source ONVPV)

Name	Area (hectares)	Name	Area (hectares)
Fetească Regală	12,661.3	Codană	26.5
Fetească Albă	12,383.0	Ezerfurtu	26.4
Merlot	11,367.7	Creaţă	24.5
Other noble grapes	8,754.4	Alb Aromat	24.4
Riesling Italico	7,519.8	Sémillon	23.9
Sauvignon	5,614.4	Viognier	23.4
Aligoté	5,545.0	Sauvignon Petit	22.6
Cabernet Sauvignon	5,406.0	Crâmpoşie Selecţionată	20.0
Muscat Ottonel	4,898.0	Alicante Bouschet	19.7
Fetească Neagră	2,949.8	Negru de Drăgăşani	18.8
Roşioară	2,661.2	Columna	18.2
Băbească Neagră	2,614.9	Furmint	18.1
Pinot Noir	2,023.5	Moldova	10.8
Chardonnay	2,004.8	Ardeleancă	10.5
Tămâioasă Românească	1,668.0	Touriga Nacional	10.4
Pinot Gris	1,589.0	Blasius	10.2

Grape varieties planted by area July 2017 (source ONVPV) *cont.*

Name	Area (hectares)	Name	Area (hectares)
Burgund Mare	697.8	Marcelan	10.1
Grasă de Cotnari	562.3	Majarcă Albă	7.8
Traminer Roz	515.1	Malbec	7.5
Syrah	502.6	Moirița	7.0
Crâmpoşie	451.3	Saint Emilion	6.7
Busuioacă de Bohotin	448.1	Moscato Bianco	4.8
Rkatsiteli	423.7	Silvania	4.5
Galbenă de Odobeşti	406.8	Mourvedre	4.4
Frâncuşă	352.7	Muscadelle	4.2
Riesling de Rhin	330.5	Touriga Franca	4.0
Iordană	303.9	Raluca	4.0
Băbească Gri	295.5	Ugni Blanc	3.7
Şarbă	282.7	Primitivo	3.6
Mustoasă de Măderat	281.7	Roz de Miniş	3.4
Oporto	250.1	Sauvignon Gros	2.7
Plăvaie	154.4	Bătută Neagră	2.6
Chasselas	127.7	Cetatuia	2.6
Sangiovese	87.6	Kerner	2.5
Cabernet Franc	85.5	Amurg	2.2
Cadarcă	80.1	Negru	2.1
Zweigelt	80.0	Splendid	1.8
Neuburger	75.5	Select	1.7
Novac	73.9	Dornfelder	1.7
Tempranillo	64.8	Alutus	1.6
Zghihară de Huşi	63.5	Negru Aromat	1.5
Traminer Aromat	61.9	Interspecific hybrids	83,204.4
Aromat de Iaşi	57.0	Other varieties	1,937.0
Traminer Alb Aromat	37.8		
		TOTAL	**182,363.4**

Vine varieties as per specifications with the designations of origin permitted for use in Romania

No.	DOC	Permitted vine varieties for production of still wines according to specifications
1.	Banat	Whites: Muscat Ottonel, Sauvignon Blanc, Pinot Gris, Fetească Regală, Fetească Albă, Riesling Italian, Riesling de Rhin, Majarcă, Chardonnay Reds: Cabernet Sauvignon, Merlot, Pinot Noir, Fetească Neagră, Burgund Mare, Cadarcă, Syrah, Novac
2.	Recaş	Whites: Muscat Ottonel, Sauvignon Blanc, Pinot Gris, Fetească Regală, Fetească Albă, Mustoasă de Măderat, Riesling Italian, Riesling de Rhin, Chardonnay, Tămâioasă Românească, Traminer Roz, Viognier Reds: Cabernet Sauvignon, Merlot, Pinot Noir, Fetească Neagră, Cabernet Franc, Negru de Drăgăşani, Alicante Bouschet, Burgund Mare, Cadarcă, Syrah, Novac
3.	Babadag	Whites: Muscat Ottonel, Chardonnay, Sauvignon Blanc, Pinot Gris, Fetească Albă, Columna, Fetească Regală, Riesling Italian, Aligoté Reds: Cabernet Sauvignon, Merlot, Pinot Noir, Fetească Neagră, Băbească Neagră
4.	Murfatlar	Whites: Chardonnay, Pinot Gris, Muscat Ottonel, Sauvignon Blanc, Riesling varietal (Riesling Italian, Riesling de Rhin), Fetească Regală, Fetească Albă, Tămâioasă Românească, Crâmposie, Columna Reds: Cabernet Sauvignon, Merlot, Pinot Noir, Fetească Neagră, Syrah, Burgund Mare
5.	Sarica Niculiţel	Whites: Muscat Ottonel, Fetească Albă, Sauvignon Blanc, Aligoté, Riesling Italian, Riesling de Rhin, Fetească Regală, Chardonnay, Rkatsiteli, Pinot Gris Reds: Merlot, Cabernet Sauvignon, Cabernet Franc, Pinot Noir, Fetească Neagră, Burgund Mare, Băbească Neagră, Syrah
6.	Crişana	Whites: Muscat Ottonel, Sauvignon Blanc, Traminer Roz, Pinot Gris, Fetească Regală, Fetească Albă, Riesling Italian, Riesling de Rhin, Chardonnay, Mustoasă de Măderat Reds: Cabernet Sauvignon, Merlot, Pinot Noir, Fetească Neagră, Burgund Mare, Syrah
7.	Miniş	Whites: Muscat Ottonel, Traminer Roz, Sauvignon Blanc, Pinot Gris, Furmint, Fetească Regală, Riesling Italian, Riesling de Rhin, Mustoasă de Măderat, Chardonnay, Tămâioasă Românească, Pinot Blanc, Viognier Reds: Cabernet Sauvignon, Merlot, Pinot Noir, Fetească Neagră, Cabernet Franc, Cadarcă, Burgund Mare, Syrah, Novac, Negru de Drăgăşani
8.	Bohotin	Whites: Muscat Ottonel, Sauvignon Blanc, Pinot Gris, Fetească Regală, Fetească Albă, Riesling Italian, Chardonnay, Aligoté Reds/Rosé: Cabernet Sauvignon, Merlot, Pinot Noir, Fetească Neagră, Băbească Neagră, Busuioacă de Bohotin
9.	Cotnari	Whites: Grasă de Cotnari, Frâncuşă, Fetească Albă, Chardonnay, Sauvignon Blanc, Pinot Gris, Traminer Roz, Tămâioasă Românească, Muscat Ottonel Reds/Rosé: Fetească Neagră, Busuioacă de Bohotin
10.	Huşi	Whites: Muscat Ottonel, Sauvignon Blanc, Pinot Gris, Fetească Regală, Fetească Albă, Riesling Italian, Chardonnay, Tămâioasă Românească, Zghihară de Huşi, Aligoté, Aromat de Iaşi, Băbească Gris, Crâmposie Selecţionată, Donaris, Frâncuşă, Plăvaie, Traminer Roz, Şarbă Reds/Rosé: Cabernet Sauvignon, Merlot, Pinot Noir, Fetească Neagră, Băbească Neagră, Busuioacă de Bohotin, Negru Aromat, Portugais Bleu, Codană

11.	Iasi	Whites: Muscat Ottonel, Sauvignon Blanc, Pinot Gris, Chardonnay, Traminer Roz, Riesling Italian, Riesling de Rhin, Fetească Albă, Fetească Regală, Aligoté, Golia, Tămâioasă Românească, Şarbă Reds/Rosé: Cabernet Sauvignon, Merlot, Pinot Noir, Fetească Neagră, Băbească Neagră, Busuioacă de Bohotin, Arcas
12.	Iana	Whites: Aligoté, Fetească Regală, Riesling Italian, Fetească Albă, Sauvignon Blanc, Muscat Ottonel Reds/Rosé: Cabernet Sauvignon, Merlot, Pinot Noir, Fetească Neagră, Băbească Neagră, Busuioacă de Bohotin
13.	Dealu Bujorului	Whites: Fetească Albă, Sauvignon Blanc, Muscat Ottonel, Riesling Italian, Fetească Regală, Aligoté, Băbească Gri Reds: Cabernet Sauvignon, Merlot, Fetească Neagră, Burgund Mare, Băbească Neagră
14.	Nicoreşti	Whites: Sauvignon Blanc, Fetească Regală, Fetească Albă, Riesling Italian, Muscat Ottonel Reds: Cabernet Sauvignon, Merlot, Fetească Neagră, Băbească Neagră
15.	Panciu	Whites: Aligoté, Băbească Gri, Chardonnay, Crâmpoşie, Crâmpoşie Selecţionată, Fetească Albă, Fetească Regală, Frâncuşă, Mustoasă de Măderat, Pinot Gris, Riesling de Rhin, Riesling Italian, Sauvignon Blanc, Galbenă de Odobeşti, Plăvaie, Traminer Aromat, Traminer Roz, Furmint, Şarbă, Muscat Ottonel, Tămâioasă Românească Reds: Fetească Neagră, Cabernet Sauvignon, Merlot, Pinot Noir, Băbească Neagră, Burgund Mare, Codană, Cadarcă, Negru Aromat, Portugais Bleu, Arcaş
16.	Coteşti	Whites: Aligoté, Băbească Gri, Chardonnay, Crâmpoşie Selecţionată, Fetească Albă, Fetească Regală, Frâncuşă, Mustoasă de Măderat, Pinot Gris, Riesling de Rhin, Riesling Italian, Sauvignon Blanc, Galbenă de Odobeşti, Plăvaie, Traminer Roz, Traminer Aromat, Furmint, Şarba, Muscat Ottonel, Tămâioasă Românească Reds/Rosé: Fetească Neagră, Cabernet Sauvignon, Merlot, Pinot Noir, Băbească Neagră, Burgund Mare, Cadarcă, Busuioacă de Bohotin, Negru Aromat
17.	Odobeşti	Whites: Aligoté, Fetească Albă, Fetească Regală, Galbenă de Odobeşti, Pinot Gris, Riesling Italian, Riesling de Rhin, Sauvignon Blanc, Plăvaie, Traminer Roz, Chardonnay, Furmint, Băbească Gri, Crâmpoşie Selecţionată, Crâmpoşie, Donaris, Mustoasă de Măderat, Frâncuşă, Şarba, Muscat Ottonel, Tămâioasă Românească, Traminer Aromat, Reds/Rosé: Fetească Neagră, Cabernet Sauvignon, Merlot, Pinot Noir, Băbească Neagră, Codană
18.	Pietroasa	Whites: Fetească Regală, Fetească Albă, Riesling Italian, Sauvignon Blanc, Chardonnay, Pinot Gris, Grasă de Cotnari, Tămâioasă Românească Reds: Burgund Mare, Fetească Neagră, Băbească Neagră, Pinot Noir, Merlot, Cabernet Sauvignon, Busuioacă de Bohotin
19.	Dealu Mare	Whites: Chardonnay, Pinot Gris, Pinot Blanc, Riesling de Rhin, Riesling Italian, Sauvignon Blanc, Fetească Albă, Fetească Regală, Muscat Ottonel, Tămâioasă Românească, Viognier, Aligoté, Traminer Roz, Grasă de Cotnari, Crâmpoşie Selecţionată, Trebbiano Reds/Rosé: Busuioacă de Bohotin, Cabernet Sauvignon, Cabernet Franc, Pinot Noir, Fetească Neagră, Merlot, Burgund Mare, Syrah, Novac, Negru de Drăgăşani, Negru Aromat, Sangiovese, Grenache, Mourvedre, Petit Verdot, Nebbiolo, Barbera, Băbească Neagră
20.	Drăgăşani	Whites: Crâmpoşie Selecţionată, Chardonnay, Fetească Regală, Riesling Italian, Sauvignon Blanc, Pinot Gris, Tămâioasă Românească, Muscat Ottonel

20.	Drăgăşani (cont.)	Reds: Cabernet Sauvignon, Merlot, Pinot Noir, Syrah, Fetească Neagră, Novac, Negru de Drăgăşani, Burgund Mare
21.	Sâmbur-eşti	Whites: Chardonnay, Fetească Albă, Fetească Regală, Riesling Italian, Sauvignon Blanc, Pinot Gris Reds: Cabernet Sauvignon, Merlot, Pinot Noir, Syrah, Fetească Neagră, Novac, Negru de Drăgăşani
22.	Ştefăneşti	Whites: Chardonnay, Fetească Albă, Fetească Regală, Riesling Italian, Sauvignon Blanc, Pinot Gris, Muscat Ottonel, Tămâioasă Românească Reds: Cabernet Sauvignon, Merlot, Pinot Noir, Fetească Neagră, Burgund Mare
23.	Banu Mărăcine	Whites: Tămâioasă Românească, Muscat Ottonel, Sauvignon Blanc, Pinot Gris, Chardonnay, Fetească Regală, Fetească Albă, Riesling Italian Reds: Cabernet Sauvignon, Cabernet Franc, Merlot, Pinot Noir, Fetească Neagră, Syrah, Novac, Negru de Drăgăşani
24.	Segarcea	Whites: Tămâioasă Românească, Tămâioasă Roză, Sauvignon Blanc, Pinot Gris, Chardonnay, Fetească Albă, Riesling Italian, Riesling de Rhin, Viognier Reds: Cabernet Sauvignon, Cabernet Franc, Merlot, Pinot Noir, Fetească Neagră, Marselan, Syrah, Negru de Drăgăşani
25.	Mehedinţi	Whites: Tămâioasă Românească, Muscat Ottonel, Sauvignon Blanc, Pinot Gris, Chardonnay, Fetească Regală, Fetească Albă, Riesling Italian, Viognier Reds: Cabernet Sauvignon, Cabernet Franc, Merlot, Pinot Noir, Fetească Neagră, Marselan, Syrah, Novac, Negru de Drăgăşani
26.	Aiud	Whites: Traminer Roz, Pinot Gris, Muscat Ottonel, Sauvignon Blanc, Chardonnay, Neuburger, Riesling Italian, Riesling de Rhin, Fetească Regală, Fetească Albă, Furmint, Iordană Reds: Cabernet Sauvignon, Pinot Noir, Fetească Neagră, Syrah, Merlot
27.	Alba Iulia	Whites: Traminer Roz, Pinot Gris, Muscat Ottonel, Sauvignon Blanc, Neuburger, Riesling Italian, Fetească Regală, Fetească Albă, Furmint
28.	Sebeş-Apold	Whites: Traminer Roz, Pinot Gris, Muscat Ottonel, Sauvignon Blanc, Chardonnay, Neuburger, Riesling de Rhin, Riesling Italian, Fetească Regală, Fetească Albă, Furmint, Iordană Reds: Cabernet Sauvignon, Pinot Noir, Fetească Neagră, Syrah, Merlot
29.	Lechinţa	Whites: Traminer Roz, Pinot Gris, Muscat Ottonel, Sauvignon Blanc, Neuburger, Riesling Italian, Fetească Regală, Fetească Albă, Chardonnay Reds: Cabernet Sauvignon, Fetească Neagră, Pinot Noir, Merlot
30.	Târnave	Whites: Traminer Aromat (Gewürztraminer), Chardonnay, Pinot Gris, Muscat Ottonel, Sauvignon Blanc, Neuburger, Riesling Italian, Riesling de Rhin, Fetească Regală, Fetească Albă, Furmint, Selena, Blasius, Kerner, Radames Reds: Cabernet Sauvignon, Pinot Noir, Fetească Neagră, Syrah, Merlot, Zweigelt
31.	Oltina	Whites: Fetească Albă, Chardonnay, Sauvignon Blanc, Pinot Gris, Muscat Ottonel, Fetească Regală, Riesling Italian, Crâmpoşie Reds: Cabernet Sauvignon, Pinot Noir, Merlot, Fetească Neagră, Syrah, Burgund Mare
32.	Adamclisi	Whites: Chardonnay, Sauvignon Blanc Reds: Fetească Neagră, Cabernet Sauvignon, Pinot Noir, Syrah
33.	Însurăţei	Whites: Chardonnay, Pinot Gris, Riesling Italian, Riesling de Rhin, Fetească Regală, Fetească Albă, Aligoté, Băbească Gri Reds: Cabernet Sauvignon, Fetească Neagră, Syrah, Băbească Neagră

Source: ONVPV, the National Office of Vine and Wine Sector Products

DOC: Controlled Denomination of Origin

Vine varieties as per specifications with the designations of origin permitted for use in Romania (*cont.*)

No.	DOC	Permitted varieties for production of premium sparkling wines according to specifications
1.	Târnave	Whites: Chardonnay, Pinot Gris, Muscat Ottonel, Sauvignon Blanc, Riesling Italian, Riesling de Rhin, Fetească Regală, Fetească Albă, Iordană Reds: Pinot Noir
2.	Sebeş-Apold	Whites: Chardonnay, Pinot Gris, Muscat Ottonel, Sauvignon Blanc, Riesling Italian, Riesling de Rhin, Fetească Regală, Fetească Albă, Iordană, Traminer Roz, Furmint Reds: Pinot Noir, Fetească Neagră, Cabernet Sauvignon, Merlot, Syrah
3.	Recaş	Whites: Chardonnay, Fetească Regală, Mustoasă de Măderat Reds: Fetească Neagră, Pinot Noir, Burgund Mare, Cadarcă, Syrah
4.	Dealu Mare	Whites: Chardonnay, Pinot Gris, Pinot Blanc, Sauvignon Blanc, Riesling Italian, Riesling de Rhin, Fetească Regală, Fetească Albă, Traminer Roz, Viognier Reds/Rosé: Pinot Noir, Merlot, Burgund Mare
5.	Panciu	Whites: Aligoté, Chardonnay, Fetească Albă, Fetească Regală, Riesling Italian, Sauvignon Blanc, Galbenă de Odobeşti, Muscat Ottonel, Şarba Reds/Rosé: Cabernet Sauvignon, Merlot, Pinot Noir, Băbească Neagră
6.	Crişana	Whites: Chardonnay, Fetească Albă, Fetească Regală, Iordană, Muscat Ottonel, Pinot Gris, Pinot Blanc, Riesling Italian, Riesling de Rhin, Sauvignon Blanc. Reds: Pinot Noir, Pinot Meunier

No.	DOC	Permitted vine varieties for production of quality sparkling wines of the aromatic type according to specifications
1.	Dealu Mare	Whites: Muscat Ottonel, Moscato Bianco, Tămâioasă Românească şi Busuioacă de Bohotin Rosé: Busuioacă de Bohotin
2.	Panciu	Whites: Muscat Ottonel, Tămâioasă Românească, Şarba

No.	DOC	Permitted vine varieties for production of sparkling wines according to specifications
1.	Dealu Mare	Whites: Fetească Regală, Fetească Albă, Riesling Italian, Riesling de Rhin, Chardonnay, Sauvignon Blanc, Muscat Ottonel, Tămâioasă Românească, Viognier, Pinot Gris Reds: Fetească Neagră, Merlot, Pinot Noir, Burgund Mare

No.	DOC	Permitted vine varieties for production of liqueur wines according to specifications
1.	Murfatlar	Whites: Muscat Ottonel, Pinot Gris, Chardonnay, Sauvignon Blanc, Tămâioasă Românească Reds/Rosé: Pinot Noir, Fetească Neagră, Merlot, Cabernet Sauvignon

Source: Courtesy of Violeta Stoicescu, ONVPV, the National Office of Vine and Wine Sector Products

Romania's PGIs

Colinele Dobrogei

Dealurile Crișanei

Dealurile Moldovei

Dealurile Munteniei

Dealurile Olteniei

Dealurile Sătmarului

Dealurile Transilvaniei

Dealurile Vrancei

Dealurile Zarandului

Terasele Dunării

Viile Carașului

Viile Timișului

Registered growers by size of holding Romania, 2017 (ONVPV)

Size of vineyard holding (hectares)	Number of registered growers
< 0.1	518,050
0.1–0.5	297,532
0.5–1	20,488
1–2	6,049
2–5	2,223
5–10	586
10–20	312
20–50	242
50–100	106
>100	104
Total	845,692

Romania exports by volume (MADR)

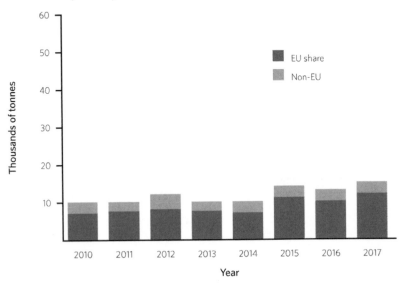

Romania imports by volume (MADR)

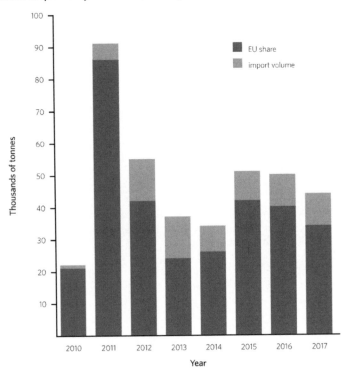

Romania wine import prices, 2016

Country	Litres	Price (€)	Litre price (€)
Spain	27,889,248	12,184,639	0.44
Italy	4,768,149	10,227,170	2.14
France	1,302,893	8,724,789	6.70
Republic of Moldova	10,068,535	8,004,308	0.79
Hungary	3,035,162	3,665,069	1.21
Germany	1,227,608	3,289,012	2.68
Bulgaria	688,036	598,755	0.87
Portugal	153,632	548,291	3.57
Netherlands	48,104	451,280	9.38
Total	**50,202,002**	**49,868,816**	**0.99**

EU data on number of vineyard holdings and average size, 2015

	Area (hectares)	Number of vineyard holdings	Average area per holding (hectares)
EU	3,230,241	2,484,963	1.30
Austria	45,574	14,133	3.22
Bulgaria	59,991	45,179	1.33
Croatia	20,393	46,068	0.44
Cyprus	7,781	14,202	0.55
Czech Republic	17,689	18,216	0.97
France	802,896	76,453	10.50
Germany	102,581	43,389	2.36
Greece	103,298	188,896	0.55
Italy	650,690	381,141	1.71
Hungary	65,049	35,741	1.82
Luxembourg	1,295	326	3.97
Portugal	198,586	212,128	0.94
Romania	183,717	854,766	0.21
Slovakia	12,054	5,933	2.03
Slovenia	15,806	30,224	0.52
Spain	941,154	517,615	1.82
United Kingdom	1,687	553	3.05

Note: figures for the following countries are zero: Belgium, Denmark, Estonia, Ireland, Latvia, Lithuania, Malta, Netherlands, Poland, Finland, Sweden
Source: http://ec.europa.eu/eurostat/statistics-explained

Regional varietal distribution (ONVPV, March 2016)

	Top 4 noble wine grapes	
Region	**Variety name**	**Area (hectares)**
Transylvanian Plateau	1. Fetească Regală	1,630
	2. Riesling	670
	3. Sauvignon Blanc	600
	4. Fetească Alba	440
	other varieties	3,619
	Total	**6,959**
Moldovan Hills	1. Fetească Alba	7,591
	2. Fetească Regală	6,982
	3. Aligoté	4,812
	4. Merlot	3,194
	other varieties	46,964
	Total	**69,543**
Hills of Muntenia and Oltenia	1. Merlot	5,122
	2. Fetească Alba	3,512
	3. Rosioară	2,822
	4. Feteasca Regală	,909
	other varieties	40,055
	Total	**52,420**
Banat Hills	1. Merlot	421
	2. Cabernet Sauvignon	342
	3. Fetească Regală	312
	4. Sauvignon Blanc	241
	other varieties	1,648
	Total	**2,964**
Crişana and Maramureş	1. Fetească Regală	750
	2. Pinot Noir	321
	3. Riesling	452
	4. Cabernet Sauvignon	422
	other varieties	7,675
	Total	**9,620**

Region	Variety name	Area (hectares)
Hills of Dobrogea	1. Merlot	2,485
	2. Cabernet Sauvignon	1,722
	3. Sauvignon Blanc	1,321
	4. Riesling	1,241
	other varieties	10,238
	Total	**17,007**
Danube Terraces	1. Cabernet Sauvignon	112
	2. Merlot	50
	3. Sauvignon Blanc	51
	4. Crâmposie	22
	other varieties	11,101
	Total	**11,336**
Sands and other favourable land in the south	1. Cabernet Sauvignon	192
	2. Băbească Neagră	122
	3. Riesling	114
	4. Merlot	70
	other varieties	12,415
	Total	**12,913**

APPENDIX III: MOLDOVAN WINE LAWS AND STATISTICS

2017 Harvest declarations for wine

Variety	Volume (hectolitres)
Merlot	299,000
Cabernet Sauvignon	298,000
Chardonnay	186,000
Sauvignon Blanc	161,000
Muscat group	108,000
Pinot Gris/Blanc	99,000
Aligoté	99,000
local varieties	47,000
Pinot Noir	39,000
Riesling	33,000
Saperavi	20,000
others	41,000
Total	**1,800,000**

Source: ONVV

Moldova 2017 harvest

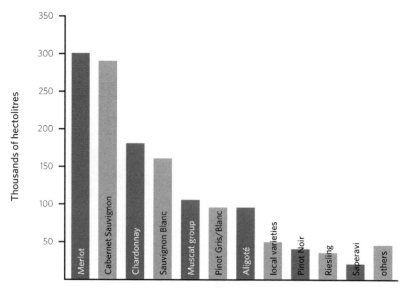

Source: ONVV

Winery size by crush volume

Volume of grapes crushed /tonnes	2013	2014	2015	2016	2017
>10000	7	3	2	4	7
5-10000	15	11	11	11	15
1-5000	50	35	35	28	34
501-1000	8	9	19	9	10
51-500	27	29	26	26	28
< 50	10	12	13	19	12

Source: ONVV

Moldova changes in vineyard area 2001 to 2017

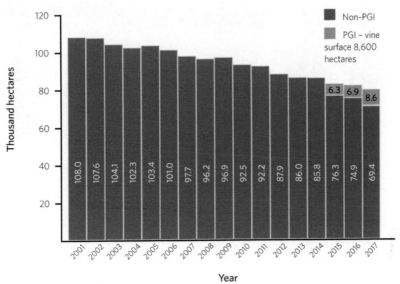

Source: ONVV

Top 5 bulk export markets by value (US$ millions)

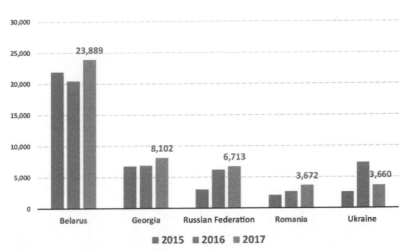

Source: ONVV

Exports in bulk trends

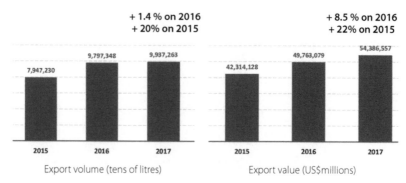

Source: ONVV

Exports in bottle trends

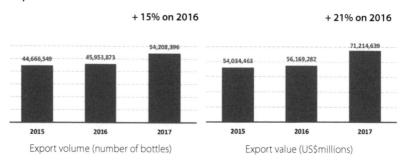

Source: ONVV

Moldova bottled wine export market trends (US$ millions)

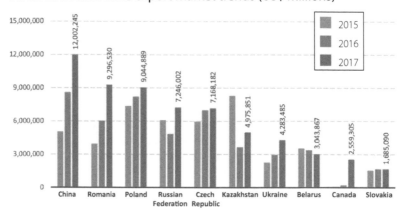

Source: ONVV

Moldova bottled wine export trends by volume (number of bottles)

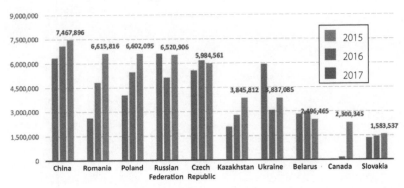

Source: ONVV

GLOSSARY

Active heat summation. A measure of total temperature above 10°C over the growing season.

Ampelography. The study of the visual features of grapevines for identification and classification.

Anthocyanins. A group of compounds responsible for the red, blue and purple colours in wine.

Aszú. Hungarian word for shrivelled and noble rot infected grapes, used to make Tokaji.

Biodynamic. Following the guidance of Rudolf Steiner from the 1920s. Similar to organic farming, but also considering the farm as a self-contained whole with astral forces, phases of the moon and homoeopathic-like treatments. Must be certified.

Brettanomyces or 'brett'. A species of yeast that can live and grow in bottled wine, especially high pH, high alcohol wines. Its metabolites give aromas often described as farmyard or medicinal. A wine fault.

Chernozem. A black soil, rich in humus and carbonates, in cool or temperate, semi-arid regions, such as the steppes and grasslands of Russia.

CIS. Commonwealth of Independent States, a union of former Soviet republics.

Comecon. An association of communist nations founded in 1949, to facilitate and coordinate their economic development.

Crama. Romanian word for wine cellar.

Cramele. Romanian word for wine cellars, often larger wineries.

Cultivar. Cultivated variety of plant. In grapevines this usually refers to *Vitis vinifera*, Chardonnay for instance is a cultivar.

Guyot. A form of vine training with a permanent trunk, a single or double cane and a spur, used in many high-quality wine regions; requires a trellising system.

Gobelet. French term for bush-trained vines without trellising.

Hectolitres. Unit of volume equal to 100 litres.

Hybrid. A cross between two different grapevine species (not cultivars) such as *Vitis vinifera* (the European grapevine) crossed with *Vitis labrusca, Vitis berlandieri, Vitis riparia* and other species, typically of American origin. Hybrids are commonly used as rootstocks and sometimes as direct producers of fruit.

Ice wine. Sweet wine made from grapes that are pressed while still frozen.

Kolkhoz (plural kolkhozes). A form of collective farm in the Soviet Union, owned by its members but under state control, organized in a similar way to a cooperative, but not voluntary. In theory members were paid by a share of profits.

Leu Moldova (MDL). Moldovan currency; 1 leu (plural lei) is made up of 100 bani, €1 was approximately 20 lei in March 2018.

Leu Romania (RON). Romanian currency; 1 leu (plural lei) is made up of 100 bani; €1 was approximately 4.65 lei in March 2018.

Lev (BGN). Bulgarian currency; 1 lev (plural leva) is made up of 100 stotinki. Exchange rate is pegged to the euro at 1.95583 leva to €1.

MADR. Ministry of Agriculture and Rural Development in Romania.

MAFF. Ministry of Agriculture, Food and Forestry in Bulgaria.

Malolactic fermentation. A bacterial fermentation typically brought about by lactic acid bacteria such as *Oenococcus oenos*. It breaks down sharp tasting malic acid and produces softer tasting lactic acid, along with secondary effects such as creamy or buttery flavours.

Microsatellite markers. Microsatellites or Single Sequence Repeats (SSRs) are extensively employed in plant genetics studies. Microsatellites are also used in population genetics to measure levels of relatedness between subspecies, groups and individuals.

Natural wine. A category of wines made with minimal intervention, no yeast or additives, and usually no sulphites either. Not legally defined.

Noble rot. Infection caused by *Botrytis cinerea* fungus. It may cause noble or grey rot depending on weather. In certain grapes with the right weather conditions, it causes shrivelling and a complex but positive change in flavour profile. Involved in many of the world's top sweet wines.

NVWC. Bulgaria's National Vine and Wine Chamber. A non-governmental association of professionals engaged in vine-growing and winemaking, it has a role of guaranteeing quality, origin and authenticity of wines.

PDO – Protected Denomination of Origin, includes traditional terms such as appellation d'origine protegée and DOC.

PGI. Protected Geographical Indication.

Phenolics. A large and complex group of grape compounds that give structure and mouthfeel to wine.

Phylloxera. More correctly called *Daktulosphaira vitifoliae,* but known as *Phylloxera vastatrix* in the past. A tiny aphid relative in the order *Hemiptera* that feeds on grape vine roots. It originated in America, where native grape vine species have evolved some resistance or tolerance to its damage. *Vitis vinifera* has very low resistance and typically dies within six years once infested. There is no cure.

ONVPV. Oficiul Naţional al Viei şi Produselor Vitivinicole. Romania's national office for vine and wine products, a subsidiary of MADR

ONVV. In Moldova, Oficiul Naţional al Viei şi Vinului or National Office for Vine and Wine. State institution based on a public–private partnership with responsibility for the wine sector.

Orange wine. Wine made from white grapes in a similar manner to red wines with extended skin contact.

Organic. A term regulated by EU and other national regulations so wines must be certified to make this claim. Wines so labelled must comply with defined standards on what inputs are allowed, including lower sulphite levels.

Rakia. Bulgarian spirit usually distilled from grape skins or *marc* left over from winemaking, making it closer to grappa than brandy.

Restitution. Return of property obtained through an improper means to the person from whom the property was taken. Used to describe return of land in former communist countries.

Rootstock. The underground part of the vine that forms its root system, specifically where this is a different species to the upper, fruiting part of the vine.

Russification. A form of cultural assimilation during which non-Russian communities, voluntarily or not, give up their culture and language in favour of the Russian one.

SAPARD. Special Accession Programme for Agricultural and Rural Development. This was a key financial instrument to support the beneficiary countries of Central and Eastern Europe in dealing with the structural adjustment in their agricultural sectors and rural areas to bring them closer to EU standards.

Scion. The above ground part of the vine, where it is different to the vine that forms its root system.

Sovkhoz (plural sovkhozes). A state farm in the communist era, where workers were paid a salary.

Standard case. One standard case of wine contains 12 x 75 cl bottles or 9 litres.

TCA. The compound most commonly associated with cork taint – 2,4,6-Trichloroanisole – though similar taints can come from other sources.

USAID. The United States Agency for International Development; an independent agency of the United States federal government that is primarily responsible for administering civilian foreign aid and development assistance.

SOURCES AND FURTHER READING

GENERAL

Anderson, K., Nelgen, S. & Pinilla, V. (2017) *Global Wine Markets, 1860 to 2016: A Statistical Compendium*, University of Adelaide

Consumer Expenditure (2016), www.nsi.bg

Eurostat Statistics *Vineyards in the EU* http://ec.europa.eu/eurostat/statistics-explained/index.php?title=Wine-growing_statistics&oldid=332951 retrieved Jan. 2018

Gale, G. (2011) *Dying on the Vine: How Phylloxera Transformed Wine*, University of California Press

Lacombe et al. (2012) 'Large-scale parentage analysis in an extended set of grapevine cultivars (*Vitis vinifera L.*)', *Theor. Appl. Genet.*, **126** (2):401–14

Panzone, L. (2011) 'The Lost Scent Of Eastern European Wines In Western Europe: A Hedonic Model Applied To The UK Market', *British Food Journal*, **113** (8):1060–78

Robinson, J., Harding, J., Vouillamoz, J. (2013) *Wine Grapes: A complete guide to 1368 vine varieties, including their origins and flavours*, Penguin UK

www.vivc.de (Vitis International Variety Catalogue VIVC)

BULGARIA

The Atlantic Religion (2014) *Sabazios – the 'other' Thracian god*, atlanticreligion.com

Borislavov, Y. (2004) *Bulgarian Wine Book: History, Culture, Cellars, Wines*, Sofia: Trud

Delev, V. (2000) *Bulgarian Wine Industry*, i-Links The Business Connection

Dimitrov, B. (2002) *Bulgaria Illustrated History*, Borina Publishing House

Gilby, C. (2007) *Bulgaria*, Harpers supplement

Gilby, C. (2013) *Whatever happened to Bulgarian wine?*, www.wine-pages.com

Hvarleva, T. et al. (2004) 'Genotyping of Bulgarian Vitis vinifera L. cultivars by microsatellite analysis', *Vitis* **43** (1), 27–34

Iontcheva, K. and Tanovska, T. 2017 *Catalogue of Bulgarian Wine*, Ka&Ta Ltd

Jung, Y. (2016) 'Re-creating economic and cultural values in Bulgaria's wine industry: From an economy of quantity to an economy of quality?' *Economic Anthropology* **3**: 280–92

Jung, Y. (2014) 'Tasting and judging the unknown terroir of Bulgarian wine: the political economy of sensory experience, food and foodways', *Explorations in the History and Culture of Human Nourishment*, **22** (1–2): 24–47

Jung, Y. (2013) 'Cultural Patrimony and the Bureaucratization of Wine: The Bulgarian Case' in *Wine and Culture*, eds Black and Ulin, Bloomsbury Academic

Jung, Y. (2011) 'Parting The Wine Lake', *Anthropological Journal of European Cultures*, **20** (1): 10–28

Kodzhivanova, A. (2017) *Sharp Competition in the Wine Market*, www.capital.bg 3 Nov 2017 (accessed 2018)

Kramer, M. (2017) In need of recognition: wine zones that crave – and deserve – it, *Wine Spectator*, www.winespectator.com

Mazarov, I. (2000) *Thracians and Wine*, Dunav Press

Ministry of Agriculture, Food and Forestry (2017) *Annual Report on the Situation and Development of Agriculture*, Bulgaria

National Vine &Wine Chamber (2012, 2009) *Who is Who: Wine & Spirits in Bulgaria*

Neuburger, M. C. (2013) *Balkan Smoke: Tobacco and the Making of Modern Bulgaria*, Ithaca: Cornell University Press.

Nivelin N. (2006) 'The Bulgarian Wine Sector: Policy Issues and Implications after 15 Years of Transition', *Journal of Wine Research*, **17**(2): 73–93

Nivelin, N. (2006) 'The Bulgarian Wine Sector: Policy Issues and Implications after 15 Years of Transition' *Journal of Wine Research*, **17**(2): 73–93

Nivelin, N. (2005) 'Wine Quality and Regional Reputation: Hedonic Analysis of the Bulgarian Wine Market', *Eastern European Economics*, **43**(6): 5–30

Novinite (2015) 'Bulgarian archaeologists discover 11th century *rakia* distillation vessel', www.novinite.com

Ovcharov, D. (2003) *Fifteen Treasures from Bulgarian Lands*, Bulgarian Bestseller, National Museum of Bulgarian Books and Polygraphy

Roychev, V. (2012) *Ampelography*, Academic Publishing House of the Agricultural University: Plovdiv

Schmitz, A. et al. (2012) *Privatization of Agriculture in New Market Economies: Lessons from Bulgaria*, Springer Science & Business Media

Simeonov, I. (2016) 'Concise economic description of the basic local grapevine varieties for the Republic of Bulgaria' *Phytol. Balcan.*, **22**(2)

State Gazette (1999) Wine and Spirit Drinks Act No. 86/1.10.1999

Tsakov, D. 2010 *Creation, Confirmation And Manufacture Of Wines With Controlled Designation Of Origin*, Sofia

Useful web sites

www.archaeologyinbulgaria.com
www.divino.bg

ROMANIA

Antoce A.O. et al. (2013) 'Some Considerations Regarding The Grapevine Variety Assortment and Wine Categories In Romania In Recent Years', *Bulletin de l'OIV*, **86**:27

Antoce A.O., Calugaru, L.L. (2017) 'Evolution of grapevine surfaces in Romania after accession to European Union – period 2007–2016', 40th World Congress of Vine and Wine, *BIO Web Conf.* **9**

APEV (2014, 2015, 2016) *Romanian wine industry report*

Ardelean, M. V. (2016) *The Wine Book of Romania*

Boc R. D., Dobrei A. (2015) 'Study on wine grape varieties worldwide and in Romania: a Review', *Journal of Horticulture, Forestry and Biotechnology*, **19**(2), 190–6

Brosure Soiuri de Vita de Vie Roditoare (2005) Bucuresti

Bucur, G.M., Dejeu, L. (2016) 'Climate Change Trends In Some Romanian Viticultural Centers', *Agrolife Scientific Journal*, **5**(2)

Constantinescu G. (1970) *Ampelografia Republicii Socialiste Romania*

Cotea, V.D., et al. (2005) *Vineyards and Wines of Romania*

Cotea, V.V., Andreescu F. (2008) *Romania The Land of Wine*

Dejeu, L. et al. (2013), '120 Years Of Research, Education And Vitivinicultural Production At Pietroasa', *AgroLife Scientific Journal*, **2**(1)

Euromonitor (2017) *Wine in Romania*

Hârța, M., Pamfil, D. (2013) 'Molecular Characterisation of Romanian Grapevine Cultivars Using Nuclear Microsatellite Markers', *Bulletin UASVM Horticulture*, **70**(1):131–6

Hârța, M., Pamfil, D. (2014) 'The Current State of Characterization of Romanian Vitis vinifera L. Germplasm by Molecular Markers' *Bulletin UASVM Horticulture*, **71**(2)

Irimia,L., Patriche, C.V., Quénol, H. (2013) 'Viticultural Zoning: A Comparative Study Regarding The Accuracy Of Different Approaches In Vineyards Climate Suitability Assessment', *Cercetări Agronomice în Moldova*, **XLVI**(3):155

Irimia, L. et al. (2017) 'Modifications in climate suitability for wine production of Romanian wine regions as a result of climate change,' *BIO Web of Conferences*, **9**, 01026

Itcaina, X., Roger, A., Smith, A. (2016) V*arietals of Capitalism: A Political Economy of the Changing Wine Industry*, Cornell University Press

MADR (2017) *Viticultura/Vinificatie*, www.madr.ro/horticultura/viticultura-vinificatie.html, retrieved 2018

MADR (2016) *Catalogul oficial al soiurilor de plante de cultură din România pentru anul 2016*

Maghradze, D. et al. (2012) *Caucasus and Northern Black Sea Region Ampelography*

Maul, E. et al. (2015) 'The prolific grape variety (*Vitis vinifera L.*) "Heunisch Weiss" (= "Gouais Blanc"): bud mutants, "colored" homonyms and further offspring', *Vitis*, **54**:79–86

Myles, S. et al. (2011) 'Genetic structure and domestication history of the grape', *Proc Natl Acad Sci USA*, **108**(9): 3530–5

National Rural Development Network (2015) *Rural Romania*, **33**

Nielsen (2017) *FMCG Pulse Romanian Wine Overview*

Nivelin N. (2007) 'Land, Wine and Trade: The Transition of the Romanian Wine Sector', *Eastern European Economics*, **45**(3):76–114

OECD (2000) *Review of Agricultural Policies: Romania*, OECD Publishing

Paul, H. W. (2002) *Science, Vine and Wine in Modern France*, Cambridge University Press

Popa, A. et al. (2006) 'Romania's Viticultural Identity While Joining The European Union', *Buletin Usamv-Cn*, **63**

Popescu, C. F., Dejeu L.C., Bejan C. (2015) 'Ampelographic characterization – preliminary results of the nine most appreciated autochthonous *Vitis vinifera L.* varieties from Romania', *Vitis*, **54** (Special Issue): 159–62

Popescu, C.F. et al. (2017) 'Identification and characterization of Romanian grapevine genetic resources', Vitis, **56**: 173–80

This, P., Lacombe, T., Thomas, M.R. (2006) 'Historical origins and genetic diversity of wine grapes', *Trends in Genetics*, **22**(9)

USDA (1971) *Report on Agricultural Economy and Trade of Romania*, usda.mannlib.cornell.edu

WEPA (2002) *Wine Industry Strategy Report*

Useful web sites

www.onvpv.ro
www.romaniatourism.com
www.agerpres.ro
www.crameromania.ro
www.premiumwinesofromania.com
www.revino.ro

MOLDOVA

Bittner, S. V. (2015) 'American Roots, French Varietals, Russian Science: A Transnational History of the Great Wine Blight in Late-Tsarist Bessarabia', *Past & Present*, **227**(1): 151–77.

Bratco, D. H. (2015) 'Din istoria vitiviniculturii Moldovei (de la origini până în secolul al XVIII-lea)', *Akademos*, **4**

Burkett, W. H. (2016) *The German Settlements in Bessarabia*, TIPS Technical Publishing, Carrboro, North Carolina

Cornea, V. & Savin, G. (2015) 'Exploration and revaluation of old autochthonous varieties in Republic of Moldova', *Vitis*, **54** (Special Issue): 115–19

Gander-Wolf, H. (2014) 'Once a Swiss Winegrower Colony CHABAG in Russia', *Swiss American Historical Society Review*, June/July edition

Gilby, C. (2015) 'Moldova's wine war', *Meininger's Wine Business International*, **2**(15)

Gilby, C. (2013) 'Russia's ban on Moldovan wine "unfounded"', www. decanter.com

Gilby, C. (2013) 'Noroc for Moldova's wine revolution', www.wine-pages.com

Gilby, C. (2008) 'Moldova's trials continue', *Meininger's Wine Business International*

Gilby, C. (2008) *Moldova*, Harpers Supplement

Gilby, C. (2007) 'Moldova now stymied by Russian tax regime', www. decanter.com

Gorton, M. and White, J. (2003) 'The Politics of Agrarian Collapse: Decollectivisation in Moldova', *East European Politics and Societies*, **17**(2):305–31

Joseph, R. (2007) 'Tackling the Big Bear', *Meininger's Wine Business International*, **4**

King, C. (2013) *The Moldovans: Romania, Russia, and the Politics of Culture*, Hoover Press

Monah, F. (2016) in *The origins and spread of domestic plants in southwest Asia and Europe*, eds Sue Colledge and James Conolly, pp.111–23

Novitchi Antohi, L. & Turtoi, M. (2013) 'Evolution of viticulture and winemaking in Republic of Moldova', *Papers of Sibiu Alma Mater Conference*, 28–30 March 2013

ONVV (2018) *The wine industry in Moldova current state and analysis of trends.*

Taran N., Antohi M. (2016) 'Starea Actuală ŞI Perspectivele DezvoltăRii Ramurii Vitivinicole În Republica Moldova', *The Scientific Bulletin of the State University* "Bogdan Petriceicu Hasdeu" from Cahul, **1**(15)

Savin, Gh., Cornea, V., Baca I., Botnarenco A. (2016) 'Grapevine Assortment – Component Of Food Security And Safety', *Lucrări Ştiinţlfice Seria Horticultură,* **59**(1)

Smith, J. (2011) 'Modernization of Soviet Winemaking', in *Reassessing Cold War Europe,* eds Sari Autio-Sarasmo and Katalin Miklóssy, p. 83

Sovetskaya Moldavya (1951) 'Moldavian SSR Tops third-quarter 1951 plan by 20 percent', www.cia.gov

Winestock, G. (1994) 'Moldova to use new loan to develop wine industry', www.joc.com

Useful web sites

www.wine-and-spirits.md
www.finewine.md

INDEX